SPIRAL GUIDE

FRANCE

AA
Publishing

Contents

the magazine 5

+ Regional Snapshots
+ Of Cabbages and Kings...
+ Hooked on Cartoons
+ C'est Chic + Celebrating Life
+ Wine: the French have a Word for it...
+ The "Grand Projet"
+ Famous in France
+ Gardens Galore + The Best of...

Finding Your Feet 25

+ First Two Hours
+ Getting Around
+ Accommodation
+ Food and Drink
+ Shopping
+ Entertainment

Paris and the Île de France 37

Getting Your Bearings + In Three Days
Don't Miss + Île de la Cité + Quartier Latin + Musée
d'Orsay + Tour Eiffel + Champs Élysées and Arc du
Triomphe + Musée du Louvre + Centre Georges Pompidou
At Your Leisure + 11 more places to explore **Walk +**
Montmartre and Sacré-Cœur **Further Afield +** 5 more
places to explore **Where to...+** Stay + Eat and Drink +
Shop + Be Entertained

Northwest France 73

Getting Your Bearings + In Three Days
Don't Miss + Rouen + Bayeux + Mont St-Michel
+ St-Malo + Rennes
At Your Leisure + 8 more places to explore
Drive + Cap Fréhel and the Côtes d'Émeraude
Where to...+ Stay + Eat and Drink + Shop
+ Be Entertained

Northeast France 95

Getting Your Bearings ✦ In Five Days
Don't Miss ✦ Lille ✦ Reims
✦ Strasbourg ✦ Dijon ✦ Beaune
At Your Leisure ✦ 10 more places to explore
Drive ✦ Through the Vosges on the Route des Crêtes
Where to...✦ Stay ✦ Eat and Drink
✦ Shop ✦ Be Entertained

The Loire 121

Getting Your Bearings ✦ In Five Days
Don't Miss ✦ Château de Chambord
✦ Château Royale de Blois
✦ Château de Chenonceau
✦ Château d'Azay-le-Rideau
At Your Leisure ✦ 12 more places to explore
Where to... ✦ Stay ✦ Eat and Drink
✦ Shop ✦ Be Entertained

Southeast France 139

Getting Your Bearings ✦ In Six Days
Don't Miss ✦ Carcassonne
✦ Nîmes and the Pont du Gard ✦ Arles and the
Camargue ✦ Avignon ✦ Gorges du Verdon✦ Nice
At Your Leisure ✦ 16 more places to explore
Drive ✦ Exploring Inland from the Côte d'Azur
Where to... ✦ Stay ✦ Eat and Drink
✦ Shop ✦ Be Entertained

Southwest France 173

Getting Your Bearings ✦ In Six Days
Don't Miss ✦ Bordeaux ✦ Toulouse
✦ Albi ✦ Lascaux
At Your Leisure ✦ 10 more places to explore
Walk ✦ Rocamadour
Where to... ✦ Stay ✦ Eat and Drink
✦ Shop ✦ Be Entertained

Practicalities 193

✦ Before You Go ✦ When to Go
✦ When You Are There
✦ Useful Words and Phrases

Atlas 201

Index 227

Written and compiled by Ann F Stonehouse
Contributors: Laurence Phillips (Magazine), Teresa Fisher (Magazine,
Paris), Lindsay Bennett, Colin Follett, Kathryn Glendenning, David &
June Halford, Cathy Hatley, Isla Love, Michael Nation, Lyn Parry, Alwyn
Sambrook, Andrew Sanger, The Content Works
Copy edited by Karen Kemp
Verified by Janet Beart-Albrecht

Published by AA Publishing, a trading name of Automobile Association
Developments Limited, whose registered office is Fanum House, Basing
View, Basingstoke, Hampshire RG21 4EA. Registered number
1878835.

ISBN-10: 0-7495-4537-2
ISBN-13: 978-0-7495-4537-6

A CIP catalogue record for this book is available from the British Library.

© Automobile Association Developments Limited 2005
Maps © Automobile Association Developments Limited 2005
Reprinted Dec 2006

Cover design and binding style by permission of AA Publishing
Colour separation by Leo Reprographics
Printed and bound in China by Leo Paper Products

Find out more about AA Publishing and the wide range of travel
publications and services the AA provides by visiting our website at
www.theAA.com/travel

A03274

the magazine

REGIONAL SNAPSHOTS

France has a strong regional identity. When a Frenchman talks of "*mon pays*" (my country), he is more likely to be referring to the area in which he grew up than to the nation as a whole. So Normandy remains resolutely Norman, Brittany defiantly Breton and the villages of the south decidedly contrary.

And because of this local sense of being, the baker from another region beyond the hills will be regarded as much of a foreigner as the welcome visitor from overseas, clutching a guidebook. And regional pride guarantees that shopkeepers, restaurateurs and even the old man playing *pétanque* on a dusty village square will upgrade the

Top: Oyster-eating in Cancale
Right: The landscape strengthens regional identity
Below: Breton costume, worn at summer festivals

Every town has its local hero, be it a literary or military figure, duly honoured with a museum; and a local craft or tradition, duly honoured with a museum – or at the very least a local eccentric, duly honoured with a museum.

welcome to any stranger if only to prove that their region is the only true France.

You'll soon discover that, as much as the landscape, it is the local food that defines each region of France. Chance encounters are sometimes the best – coming across a strawberry fair in the north, or an olive market in the south; happening upon monks tending their vines in a walled *clos*; filling cupped palms and any spare bottles with mineral water in a spa-resort; or watching the morning catch spill onto a harbour quayside.

Vive la différence!

Tables dot the allées Paul Riquet, Béziers' grand tree-lined promenade. Waiters dodge traffic to bring hot food and chilled wine from cafés to laid-back lunchers, who eye the talent parading in the shade. Flower stalls here on Fridays are dwarfed by the centuries-old plane trees. Cascades of jasmine, irises, willowy lilies and billowing baskets of trailing plants share groundspace with cages of exotic birds, crates of ducklings and trays of baby rabbits.

This leafy, lazy loitering reflects summer in Languedoc. Just as wintry wooden chalets selling mulled wine, gingerbread and hand-carved gifts outside the cathedral at Strasbourg is the epitome of Christmas time in Alsace.

And nothing highlights the happy contrast between French regions as clearly as market day. In Provence, for example, the aroma of olives and dried herbs begins

streets away from the big open market of Aix, and sunlight deflects from countless bright yellow ceramic bowls. Meanwhile Lyon's stalls are draped with curtains of hanging sausages and game, while Drôme's famous truffle markets are almost invisible – so valuable

are the cherished fungi that wares remain hidden under unseasonal coats, and money changes hands during surreptitious encounters at café tables.

On any given Sunday in Lille, you can follow the crowds to Wazemmes market. You'll pass antiques and bric-a-brac, puppies and kittens, new shoes and old jackets and piles of plump yellow chicory, to reach the ultimate reminder that every region loves its lunch: rotisseries turning corn-fed free-range chickens, dripping juices on to sliced potatoes and onions beneath.

The markets of the coastal ports reflect regional variations, too. The slight salt-pinch of St-Malo's morning air belongs to baskets of oysters and mussels, while Brittany's market bears the aroma of sweet and savoury *crêpes* prepared at the roadside. In Nice, minirainbows hover above the sheen of fresh fish, fragranced by mimosa and lavender on Cours Salleya.

Top: The catch of the day

Above: Local food reflects regional identities

Bellow: On the pétanque pitch

Popular history may claim that France became a republic after the Revolution of 1789 and the Terror that followed, but when Louis XVI and his queen, Marie-Antoinette, knelt to lose their heads in 1793, the French royal family still had at least another three reigns to go. Indeed, it takes more than a guillotine to get rid of a monarchy.

Of Cabbages and Kings...

It is true that this literal severing of the major line of château-hopping, empire-building, style-inspiring royals marked a turning point in France's history. But perhaps surprisingly, it paved the way for an even more imperial chapter: that of Napoléon Bonaparte and his grand ideas for France, Europe and immortality.

No sooner was Napoléon forced to downsize his ambitions at the Battle of Waterloo (1815) than the Bourbon family was already stepping back on the French throne. Louis XVIII (way down the line of succession but irrefutably alive) worked out a new constitution and reigned from 1814, just 21 years since the declaration of "the end of the monarchy".

Ten years later, Louis' successor Charles X was over-confident enough to try to bring back the grand old ways of his predecessors. The citizens of Paris did not appreciate a latter day Sun King and revolted, forcing him to abdicate and nudging the monarchy further away from its roots with the introduction in

1830 of the regal compromise: "Citizen-King" Louis Philippe. This "monarch of the people" rode a tightrope of public opinion in a newly media-savvy age until the February Revolution of 1848 finally brought Republicanism back to stay.

Left: Richelieu
Right: Emperor Napoléon III

France's natural instinct for continuity and its need to cling on to the past meant that in rejecting a king, the nation promptly elected to replace their head of state with another emperor, Napoléon III (1808–73). His charismatic blend of glamour and corruption kept political tempers on the boil just as effectively as any previous monarchy. In fact, it would be until 1870, the best part of a century since the original Revolution, that France finally shrugged off the tradition of being ruled by one man.

Divided Opinions

It is said that wherever you find two Frenchmen, you will find three opinions, so it is not surprising that, come the Revolution, France did not exactly rise up with one voice. Paris may have risen against the *ancien régime* in 1789, but the reaction around the country was as varied as the landscape itself.

In Vendée, for instance, the staunchly royalist community signaled its counter-revolutionary tactics with semaphore like turns of windmills. Provence, angered that Cardinal Richelieu had overridden the local parliament in Aix in order to grab local taxes, took any opportunity to join the popular mob. Marseille was comfortable with revolution, having already revolted against the king's great-great-grandfather, Louis XIV.

What's in a Name?

In a republic, everybody is equal – well, everyone who has not got an aristocratic "*de*" in his surname, at any rate. One of the great ironies of off-loading a monarchy is that snobbery loses its most obvious yardstick, and post-revolutionary France is riddled with local snobberies and anxiety over status. Noble families still receive overdue deference in local political arenas and when booking a table in restaurants. A former feudal lord is likely to hold at least one, if not several civic titles, whether mayor, councillor or even deputy.

Most telling of all, Sunday tabloid newspapers are filled with stories of every other royal family in Europe, most notably that of Monaco, France's surrogate modern-day monarchy – if only for gossip.

Noblesse oblige – the concept that nobility entails responsibility – still exists, most notably in the line of the Comte de Paris, the leading pretender to the French throne. Prince Jean de France, the Duc de Vendôme and the modern Dauphin (heir apparent), has a resumé that includes studying philosophy at the Sorbonne, gaining an MBA in California and doing military service in the republican army.

The young Louis XVII, whose fate remains a mystery

What's in a Number?

You don't have to be a mathematical genius to realize that French history is missing a king. Louis XIV, Louis XV, Louis XVI then Louis XVIII. So whatever happened to number 17?

The official story is that the heir to the throne, the 8-year-old Dauphin, was snatched from Marie Antoinette's arms as she was taken to her execution in 1793. The prince was allegedly locked up in a tower, where he died two years later, apparently of tuberculosis. Whatever the truth of the tale, monarchists and conspiracy theorists declare that on the execution of Louis XVI, the young Dauphin automatically became Louis XVII, even without the affirmation of a coronation.

Half of France (and, incidentally, most of Britain) was later convinced that the a substitute body was placed in the tower to enable the boy-king to escape and start a new life abroad. Two favourite stories have him seeing out his days as a German clockmaker, or that he was adopted by a Native American tribe and became a church minister. The real story will probably never be known.

Meanwhile, when the French monarchy was restored in 1814 the Dauphin's youngest brother took on the title Louis XVIII in recognition of the invisible reign of Louis XVII. In counting French regnal numbers, the 17 is not so much silent…as whispered.

Louis XVIII, who skipped past his missing brother to become king

Hooked on Cartoons

Cartoons for adults to enjoy are a peculiarly French phenomenon. Witness the international plaudits for Sylvain Chomet's 2003 animated movie *Belleville Rendezvous* (released as *The Triplets of Belleville* in the US), an 80-minute tale of a kidnapped Tour de France cyclist and his rescue by his indomitable grandmother, Madame Souza.

Comic strips (*bandes dessinées*) play a surprisingly big role in French adult life. In 2004 the St-Germain-des-Prés Métro station recognised this with a major exhibition, **Comics All Over Paris**. It was a celebration of the comic book and the strip cartoon, a French art form as admired and hotly debated by its followers as Impressionism, Cubism and Existentialism were in days gone by. The exhibition, spread over several other stations, lasted for three months and was promoted by the **Angoulême International Comics Festival**, an annual event held in the southwest every January.

Throughout France you'll see that comic books are accorded the same high profile in book shops as the ever-popular detective yarns or romantic fiction – a dedicated section on the grown-ups' shelves rather than a brightly coloured pile of paperbacks relegated to the kids' corner.

Once a year Angoulême is taken over by Félix the Cat and Blake & Mortimer. From the start, leading cartoon artists from around the world, including Hergé (Belgian creator of Tintin) and America's Will Eisner, have attended. Angoulême's cartoon festival has been going strong since 1974, and is the highlight of a calendar of events held all around France.

Above and below: Scenes and characters from the cycling fantasy, *Belleville Rendezvous*

C'est Chic:
(Behind the Scenes on the Paris Catwalk)

No matter what each year's fashion fad is, whether frivolous or enduring, it always contains one vital ingredient – the distinctive "*je ne sais quoi*" of French chic.

In the inimitable words of Coco Chanel, "fashions pass away; style lives on". It is always the household names – the Diors, the Yves Saint Laurents and the Jean-Paul Gaultiers of the fashion world, with their lavish *haute couture* creations, who receive the praise. Yet their success depends exclusively on *les petits mains* – the devoted team of seamstresses, button- and bead-makers, lace-makers, embroiderers and countless other rarely acknowledged artisans who create the vital accessories.

Their names are known only to a privileged few. **François Lesage** is one such example, with his Paris workshop of pearls and beads in rue Grange-Batelière, founded by his father in 1924. He claimed, "I was born on a pile of pearls and started making small designs when I was just three years old". The painstakingly detailed work of his embroidery school today graces the designs of Dior, Balmain, Lacroix and Gaultier.

Another great name is **André Lemarié**, whose firm in Faubourg St-Denis specialises in feathers and silk flowers for the likes of Chanel, Mugler, Nina Ricci, Valentino and Dior. It was founded in the days of Charles Frédéric Worth (see right) and has played a major role in *haute couture* ever since.

Gérard Lognon's family business – the art of pleating – operates in an apartment in rue Danielle-Casanova; **Patrice Wolfer** at the renowned Michel in rue Ste-Anne, an ancient street of milliners, is the principal supplier

Window shopping outside one of the great names in Paris

Fashion *pour l'homme* is just as important in France

of *haute couture* hats; while **Raymond Massaro** (2 rue de la Paix) is the most celebrated shoemaker in Paris. Creator of the famous Chanel-style shoe, he prides himself on the fine craftsmanship of his work.

Perhaps the most extraordinary aspect of *haute couture* is that all these designers cater for a clientele of no more than 2,000 women. In fact, *haute couture* constitutes only 6 per cent of a fashion house's turnover. An average outfit requires at least 100 hours' work with three or four fittings and costs around €8,000, while an evening dress would cost four times as much!

These extravagant and prestigious creations, the result of months of work, are presented, together with the less exclusive ranges, at the fashion shows staged at the **Carrousel du Louvre** every January and July, before 2,000 journalists and celebrities and 800 buyers. The atmosphere is electric, and tickets virtually impossible to obtain. Some of the seats are reserved for *les petites mains* – who can watch their handiwork come alive in movement as the world's top models step out on to the catwalk to rapturous applause, in a pivoting swirl of silk, chiffon, brocade, organza and *moiré*.

Below: Shopping for top style

The Inventor of Haute Couture

Ironically, it was an Englishman, **Charles Frederick Worth**, who founded French *haute couture*. Having moved to Paris from London in 1845, aged 20, he worked in a draper's shop until he could afford a shop of his own, 13 years later, at 7 rue de la Paix. Specialising in well-cut clothes, he not only radically changed the female silhouette but also introduced the rhythm of the seasons to fashion by preparing his collections in advance. Another of his innovations was the use of live models for fashion shows.

Above: Posing for a Paris fashion shoot

Left: Making a statement on the catwalk

Celebrating

LIFE

The French have a weakness for Life, with a capital L, ideally served with a bottle of something special. Mealtimes are unrestrained by the clock, and lunch can stretch from midday until it segues into a *p'tit apéro* before dinner.

Happily, the concept of summer is granted the same elasticity, and it comes with its own musical sound track thanks to the wealth and diversity of local festivals. The festival season may officially begin on 14 July and continue until the *rentrée* (the last weekend before back to school in September), but in truth, it seems that there are as many excuses for a festival as there are for a drink, and no mater how small or how powerful the town, village or city, France is ever ready to declare a party.

**Medieval revels at Moncontour
Below: Equestrian fun at Chinon**

Festival Time

In fact, festival season really kicks off at apple blossom time in April, with **Jazz sous les Pommiers** – music around the Normandy orchards at Coutances, providing an excuse to sip farmhouse cider and tap your feet late into the night. It lasts until **Burgundy's final wine festivals** of late autumn, when the local people drink the new Nuits St-Georges and toast a job well done.

The grand set pieces of Provence are big-budget blowouts, with **pageant-scale operas** staged in the Roman theatre at Orange and at Aix-en-Provence. The **Avignon International Festival** is a major world-class arts event to rival Edinburgh. Nice and Juan-Les-Pins host the big names of **international jazz** and blues for the wealthy Riviera set, and international cabaret and jazz singer Diana Krall sets up her piano in provincial parks and gardens, such as Montauban.

The **Perigord Noir** festival in the sleepy, rural Dordogne region fills village churches with renowned classical musicians, who play from moonrise till the small hours. The **Pierre Boulez Festival** at St-Étienne is likely to produce incongruities such as the London Symphony Orchestra in a suburban sports hall.

Across France the weekend nearest 21 June brings **National Music Day**, when from the smallest village to the most cosmopolitan of cities, the entire nation celebrates. Free staged concerts merge with café entertainers and impromptu sessions until barrels and throats become dry – well past everybody's bedtime. Around sites associated with composer Frédéric Chopin (such as George Sand's home at **Nohant**) summer is the excuse for wonderful piano recitals. And the late Yehudi Menuhin created the **Flâneries d'Été** in Rheims – a summer season of around 90 free concerts.

Above: Grand opera performed at Orange

Costumes add to the spectacle of an outdoor production

KEEPING IT LOCAL

The lure for artists as much as audiences is the infectious native pride of each region. Since festivals generally celebrate the local produce and skills as much as the talent of honoured guests, a wine-growing village will pull its corks long after the final encore, a fishing port may serve a communal banquet, and even a town with no agricultural USP of its own will remember a family recipe to be dished out well into the night.

During the fifty or so late autumn festivals to launch the **Vin Primeur** in Herault, the line between produce, tradition and the arts becomes as blurred as the genial *bonhomie*-impaired vision. A solemn unveiling of a new wine in a little-known wine cooperative may dissolve from pompous speechifying, through a chestnut- and olive-tasting session and into hardcore headbanging as a local band takes the stage. And the triennial **Marionnette festival** in the Ardennes town of Charleville-Mézières begins the days with worthy workshops and ends with the puppet equivalent of jam sessions in bars and on the streets.

History also plays its part in the festival scene. *Son et lumière* (sound and light) shows – especially around the Loire – tell the stories of châteaux with fabulous special effects.

Harvesting the grapes is still done largely by hand

WINE

The French have a Word for it...

All wine is made from grapes, but French wine has a very special principal ingredient: *Terroir*. It is what makes every wine different from its neighbour harvested in the next valley, the very essence of that catch-all phrase *je ne sais quoi*. *Terroir* is the indefinable ingredient that a wine gets from its own soil, its home town and the sweat and toil of the people whose lives are dedicated to raising and nurturing the grape from the vine to the bottle.

Every region claims that its *terroir* makes its wines special. And, whether you are talking about a *grand cru* from one of the better houses in Bordeaux or a simple table wine from a co-op in the foothills of the Pyrenees, it will be special to the locals, since age-old family recipes will have been created around the particular flavours of the tipple.

While waiters in Paris and on the money-making strip of the Riviera might be tempted by snobbery or profit to nudge diners to overspend on the wine list, in the regions you can unsually trust restaurant staff to recommend just the right accompaniment to the meal – and it generally pays to

Wine is left to mature in traditional wooden barrels

follow the local taste in wine. So, if you find yourself eating barbecued mussels at a Languedoc *brasucade* opt for a humble, local *vin de pays* rather than a pricier or more exotic Alsatian *gewürztraminer*. Likewise, stick with a good Burgundy with your *boeuf bourguignon*. The one exception to every rule is, of course, Champagne – to be celebrated anywhere, any time.

Know Your Regions

Alsace: produces refreshing white wines. Unusually for France, bottles name the grape variety, perhaps Riesling (crisp), Pinot Gris (dry) or Gewürztraminer (more complex).

Beaujolais: *nouveau* may be a triumph of marketing over winemaking, but check out the *crus* – fruity red wines including Morgan, Moulin à Vent and Juliénas.

Bordeaux: arguably the greatest wines of France. Better known as claret, the classic reds such as Margaux or Petrus are for

Taste before you buy at local suppliers – it's all part of the fun

the wealthy, and come in various grades, with *premier cru* at the top of the range. White dessert wines from Sauternes include the famed Château d'Yquem. Neighbouring Bergerac provides good budget alternatives.

Burgundy: the Côtes de Nuits and de Beaune boast many of the world's most popular quality wines. Nuits-St-Georges, Chablis and Mâcon are firm Burgundian favourites.

Champagne: top fizz any time, anywhere.

Jura: the yellow *vins jaunes* are full-flavoured treats.

Languedoc-Roussillon: France's biggest wine region revived with many skills from the New World. The region now produces palatable everyday wines and some robust southern classics such as St-Chinian, Corbières and Fitou.

Loire: produces more than 100 wines, mainly white (such as the crisp Muscadet and sparkling Saumur), but also a famous Rosé d'Anjou and respectable red Gamay.

Provence: wine to enjoy on site rather than elsewhere. Good summery choices include Bellet rosé and whites.

Scraping a barrel clean for the next time

Rhône: vineyards along the river from Avignon offer good local wines and such reputable classics as the quality red Châteauneuf du Pape.

Designer Labels?

As every fashion victim knows, your label says more about you than anything else, and wine bottles are no different. So check whether your wine is high street or catwalk quality.

Vin du pays is simply honest country wine, flaunting the name of the region and often proving a true and good-value reflection of the *terroir*. **AOC** (or *Appellation d'Origine Contrôlée*) meets the strictest standards before being allowed to be sold under the regional or vineyard name.

Vin de table is ideal for washing down your meal or a snack, but don't enquire too much about its family background, since it is often a blend from various regions or even countries.

> **Small-scale vineyards can join together as co-operatives**

Villagers often don't bother with labels, or even bottles. They take a 5-litre (1.3-US-gallon) can to the winery and fill up with the local stuff from a pump.

Vin de High Rise

Everyone has heard of house wine (**vin maison**), but France also produces the odd bottle of **vin d'appartement**, thanks to its smallest wine growing area: Montmartre, the Parisian hill once dotted with vineyards. Just one small vineyard remains. However, neighbours living in apartments on the hill cultivate vines on their balconies and have formed a co-operative, making wine in the tiny apartments above the Moulin Rouge.

When to Say "Non"

Travelling through France, look out for *dégustation* signs by the roadside – these are open invitations to stop at a vineyard or winery and sample the full range of wines before you buy. Tourist offices produce maps of wine routes for planning serious shopping or tasting trips, and the experience will stand you in excellent stead when it comes to negotiating the wine list in the evening's restaurant.

In other areas, you may spot signs offering a taste of home-made cider (in Brittany or Normandy) or beer (the north), which bear little relationship to the industrial fizzy stuff sold in supermarkets. If you say *non* to the offer of wine with your meal in a bistro, and instead order the

> **Local wines are usually the best accompaniment for local food**

village's artisanal *cidre* or *bière*, you will truly be accepted by the locals.

Paris's Bibliothèque Nationale, renamed in honour of François Mitterand

Mention contemporary architecture in France and certain images spring instantly to mind – that daring glass pyramid in the courtyard of the Louvre, and the vast angular arch at La Défense.

It's not just Paris – across the country avant garde municipal art galleries have sprung up, and extraordinary, beautiful high-tech projects such as the Musée de la Préhistoire in the Gorges du Verdon or the bizarre concrete canopy of the tram terminus at Hoenheim North, Strasbourg. What is it about the French and modern architecture? How come they seem to have more innovative, visually stunning ultra-modern buildings than the rest of Europe?

There's a long tradition of fine building – look no further than the Renaissance palaces of the Loire, where wealthy neighbours vied to outdo each other. And France has always found a home for the unusual – Le Corbusier's mushroom-like church at Ronchamp (1955), for example. Not that the French always approve immediately of their more challenging structures – the Eiffel Tower (▶ 50) was scorned when first unveiled in 1889, and the inside-out Pompidou centre (▶ 56) regarded as folly of the first order 1976.

Political leaders in France have seen building on a monumental scale as the way to immortality. The current wave is thanks to the vision of the late president, François Mitterand, who commissioned architects from around the world to build big in Paris – from Dominique Perrault (France, the four-cornered Bibliothèque Nationale) to Carlos Orff (Uruguay, the impressive curves and angles of the Opéra Bastille) and Johann Otto von Spreckelsen (Finland, La Grande Arche, ▶ 59).

The national pride generated by such big thinking has spread far. The latest commission is the multi-million-euro Zenith concert hall at St-Étienne, an aerodynamic and ecologically responsible structure designed by Sir Norman Foster. The rest of Europe should watch and learn.

the magazine

Marianne

Marianne, the personification of the slogan *Liberté, Egalité, Fraternité*, is the symbol of the French Republic. Her face is on the stamps and a bust of her in every town hall. Celebrities who have modelled for the figure in recent years include:

Brigitte Bardot – 1960s sex kitten and symbol of St Tropez glamour, most recently an animal rights activist and supporter of the far right National Front.

Catherine Deneuve – the ultimate French movie star and glamour icon.

Laeticia Casta – supermodel, face of l'Oréal cosmetics and Marianne for the millennium, who caused a scandal when she decided to live in London.

After controversy came political correctness. "Beurette", the latest incarnation, is a composite idealised Frenchwoman of north African extraction.

Brigitte Bardot, model for an icon

FAMOUS IN FRANCE

Heroines, Ancient and Modern

Jeanne d'Arc (c1412–1431) – Joan of Arc, the sainted Maid of Orléans who rode into battle against the English and was burnt at the stake.

Marie Antoinette (1755–93) – frivolous and misquoted Austrian Hapsburg princess whose pampered lifestyle as Louis XVI's queen embodied the downfall of the monarchy.

George Sand (1804–76) – pseudonym of cross-dressing baroness Amandine Dupin, feminist writer, lover of Chopin and head of a famous literary salon.

Josephine Baker (1906–75) – black, American-born singer and dancer who worked for the Résistance during World War II, adopted a rainbow tribe of children of many races and became Châtelaine of Les Milandes, in the Dordogne region.

Edith Piaf (1915–63) – diminutive, gutsy chanteuse known as the "Little Sparrow" of Paris, whose life echoed the tragic torch songs she sang.

Joan of Arc, the Maid of Orléans

Josephine Baker, a great performer

Heroes, Ancient and Modern

Charlemagne (745–814) – king of the Franks who, as Holy Roman Emperor, became the first leader of a united Christian Europe.

Louis XIV (1638–1715) – château and empire-building "Sun King".

Napoléon Bonaparte (1769–1821) – short in stature, big on ambition, the emperor who conquered much of Europe.

Charles de Gaulle (1890–1970)– wartime general and peace time president.

Jean Moulin (1899–1943) – chief of the French Résistance in World War II, tortured by the Gestapo.

Johnny Hallyday (1943–) – France's ultimate ageing rock star.

Gérard Depardieu (1948–) – top international movie star who owns a vineyard in the Loire and a restaurant in Paris.

Jean-Paul Gaultier (1952–) – once shocking fashion designer, now lovable media figure.

The Grimaldi Royal Family of Monaco – Princesses Caroline and Stephanie and Prince Albert are France's socialising royals of paparazzi choice.

Napoléon
Bonaparte

Political Names to Drop into Conversations...

José Bove – Roquefort cheese producer who, in 1999, led a national protest against fast food and whose status rose from angry farmer to national icon.

Right-wing leader Jean Marie
Le Pen on the campaign trail

Harlem Désir – his SOS Racisme campaign of the 1980s turned the tide of public opinion against the far right. His chosen logo of a dayglo-coloured palm with the slogan *"Touché pas à mon pote!"* ("Hands off my mate!") united the black, white and Arab communities behind him. He went on to become a member of the European Parliament.

Jack Lang – the government minister who became a cool party animal and reinvented French cultural pride. As minister for heritage and the arts, he supervised restoration of national monuments and invented National Music Day (► 14).

Bertrand Delanoë – socialist Mayor of Paris. Openly gay, he famously survived an attack by a knife-wielding would-be-assassin during a Nuits Blanche all-night cultural party at the Hôtel de Ville.

Jean Marie Le Pen – leader of the ultra-right-wing National Front party. Shockwaves shot through French political life when voter apathy led to his coming second in the presidential elections of 2002.

Famous Foodies

Auguste Escoffier (c1847–1935) – chef, inventor of haute-cuisine and leading light of the Paris Ritz and London Savoy hotels.

Paul Bocuse – Mr Big of Lyon dining, and 1970s pioneer of Cuisine Nouvelle.

Alain Ducasse – creator of fusion food in the 1980s.

Jacques and Laurent Pourcel – top-notch twin chefs who reinvented the food of the south of France as the new gastronomy for the 21st century.

Gardens Galore

It would seem that there is nothing quite so French as a Jardin Anglais – but don't expect rambling roses and hollyhocks dancing above clusters of forget-me-nots and daisies: France's favourite "English" gardens are regimented with geometric formality.

In a country where nature defines its every region and determines the food, drink and family lifestyle of each village, gardens are seen as a defiant expression of power against a backdrop of rampaging, untameable landscape. And throughout history, it has been natural for any wealthy landowner to want to stamp his authority on his own plot of ground.

So, just as great architects were hired to build grand houses and châteaux, landscape gardeners such as André le Nôtre (1613–1700) were commissioned to discipline and conquer all growing things. The gardens at **Versailles** present the classic Le Nôtre project, complete with precision topiary, avenues and fountains, although time has modified the original concept. The master's true visions were recently evoked by the mega-rich interior designer Jacques Garcia outside his own grandiose **Château du Champ de Bataille** in Normandy.

Le Nôtre's precision planting at Versailles

Public parks grew in popularity after the Revolution, making gardens accessible to everyone. The formality of a Jardin Anglais corner remained a vital element, if only to demonstrate the professionalism of local workmen. However, Baron Haussmann, who designed the great boulevards of Paris in the mid-19th century, turned the concept on its head. Excavating stones for his new roads from the hills of **Buttes Chamont** in north-east Paris, he then land-scaped the quarry as a wild and savage evocation of the French countryside within the city limits. Ravines and gorges, hills and valleys mark this as one of the capital's hidden gems.

In the 21st century, gardens and parks continue to reflect and define their age. Paris's **Parc Citroën** is the most loudly-sung hymn to modernism, but its contemporary, the **Promen-ade Plantée**, is a delightful re-invention of an urban scene. It came about when the original railway lines heading east out of the city from the Gare de Lyon, perched high above the streets, were replaced by underground tracks and became obsolete. It was the cue for a fabulous serpentine garden, as narrow as the viaduct that supports it, and which provides an oasis of calm and verdant tranquility above the city traffic. A sliver of countryside, it stretches on to the sprawling **Bois de Vincennes** at the city limits. The Bois is the venue for the springtime Foire du Trône – the centuries-old funfair, which featured in the recent movie *Amélie*.

Across the city another great park, the **Bois de Boulogne**, has race courses, *belle-époque* restaurants and an often overlooked **Shakespearean garden** planted with every flower mentioned in his plays. Meanwhile, each region of France has its own distinctive

gardens, from stepped and tiered terraces on the Riviera to the elegant formality of the château gardens of the Loire. Garden pilgrimages are promoted by the tourist office in Rouen, and just outside the city you'll find a real rarity: the **Jardin d'Angélique**, an English-style garden with hundreds of roses and shrubs, newly planted by the owners of a manor house in memory of their daughter.

Normandy is the most popular region for garden lovers, thanks to the vision of Impressionist artist Claude Monet (1840–1926). Monet painted waterlilies and irises, and all summer visitors queue to see them flowering in his **garden at Giverny** (▶ 86).

An artistic riot of colour in Monet's garden

The Best of

TOP 5 STEWS

Boeuf Bourguignon – beef in wine, Burgundy
Bouillabaisse – fish and seafood, Provence
Cassoulet – pork, goose and beans, Midi-Pyrénées
Carbonnade flamande – beef in beer, the North
Choucroute – cabbage, pork and sausages, Alsace

Best Snapshots

- Mont-St-Michel at dawn
- Chateau d'Ussé, Loire
- Cliffs on the beach at Étretat
- Pont d'Arc, Ardèche
- Lion of Belfort
- Place Stanislas, Nancy
- Pont de Gard
- Hospices de Beaune
- Canal du Midi
- Christmas markets

5 BEST...UNEXPECTED MUSEUMS

France is fabulous at museums. It helps that the country has probably the world's finest art collection, thanks to its producing many of the greatest artists – and to Napoléon, who stole the best of the rest as he conquered Europe in the 19th century. However, some of the most enjoyable museums to be found across the country are not actually the traditional art galleries. Try these for an entertaining diversion:

La Piscine, Roubaix – just outside Lille, this converted art-deco swimming pool is a spectacular building that almost upstages the art it houses.
Nausicaa, Boulogne-sur-Mer – more than a seaworld show, this is an eco-aware tour through the blue planet.
Vulcania, Clermont-Ferrand – set amid a green landscape of real volcanos, and the virtual reality tour through recreated lava floes is a must.
Musée de la Contrafaçon, Paris – celebrate the joy of fakes, with rip-off Barbie and dodgy Rolexes at the ultimate counterfeit museum.
Piper Heidsiek, Rheims – this champagne cellar visit is a veritable theme park ride in motorised corks through winemaking to Hollywood.

Top 5 Ways to Say..."Je t'Aime"

- At the **Mur Je t'Aime**, Paris – a Montmartre wall inscribed with "I Love You" in every known language under the sun.
- Being punted along the **Gorges du Tarn**, from La Malène in Lozère.
- Sipping the €400 **Side Car**, the world's most expensive cocktail, which features 100-year-old cognac, and is exclusive to the Paris Ritz hotel.
- Enjoying a plate of aphrodisiac **Bouzigues oysters** in a fishermen's bistro by the shores of the Thau lagoon, Languedoc.
- Taking inspiration from Rodin's famous sculpture of **The Kiss** in the gardens of his museum in Paris.

Finding Your Feet

First Two Hours

France has international gateways all around its national borders, which are shared with Belgium, Luxembourg, Germany, Switzerland, Italy, Spain and Andorra la Vella. In addition, there is ready access through the northern coastal ports, such as Calais, via rail routes including the Eurotunnel and Eurostar links with the UK, and to numerous airports.

Arriving in Paris

By Air

■ Most international flights come into **Roissy–Charles de Gaulle Airport** (tel: 01 48 62 22 80; www.adp.fr), 23km (14 miles) from the heart of Paris. There are three terminals, with information desks, shops, restaurants, banks, bureaux de change and car-rental firms.

■ **Taxis** to the city centre take 30 minutes to 1 hour, and cost around €43.

■ **Trains** into the city centre (Gare du Nord, Châtelet or St-Michel), on RER line B, are the cheapest option at round €7.70. They operate between 5 am and 11:40 pm and take 35 minutes.

■ Air France **shuttle buses** run from T1 and T2 to Montparnasse, Gare de Lyon and the Arc de Triomphe (€10–€11.50, 45 minutes to 1 hour). A Roissybus goes from all terminals to Opéra, between 6 am and 11 pm (€8:20, 50 minutes).

■ **Orly Airport** (tel: 01 49 75 15 15; www adp.fr) is 14km (8.5 miles) south of the centre, and deals with domestic and some international flights. It has two terminals, with the usual facilities. A **taxi** into Paris will cost around €25 and take 15 to 30 minutes. The Orlyval **train** connects to RER line B at Antony; the fare to the centre is €8.80, and the journey time 35 minutes. The Orlybus links to the **Métro** at Denfert-Rochereau (€5.70, 30 minutes), while the Air France **shuttle bus** takes you to Les Invalides and Montparnasse (€7.50, 30 minutes).

■ **Beauvais Tillé Airport** (tel: 0892 682 066; www.aeroportbeauvais.com) is 56km (35 miles) north of Paris, and used by low-cost airlines. The distance means a **taxi** into Paris will cost around €120, and take 1 hour 20 minutes. There is **no train** link into the centre, but there is a **bus** to Porte Maillot (€10, 1 hour 15 minutes).

By Train

■ **Eurostar** direct trains from southern England (in UK tel: 08705 186 186; www.eurostar.com) arrive in Paris's Gare du Nord station. A **taxi** from here into the centre costs around €12. The station is also on the Métro lines 4 (purple) and 5 (orange), and on the RER railway lines D (green) and B (blue).

■ **Paris City Centre Tourist Office** ✉ 25–27 rue des Pyramides, 75001
☎ 0892 683 000 (€0.34 per minute); www.paris-touristoffice.com
🕐 Daily 9–8, May–Oct; 10–7 Nov–Apr; closed 1 May, 25 Dec
Ⓜ Métro: Pyramides

Arriving in Marseille

■ **Marseille-Provence Airport**, also known as Marseille-Marignan (tel: 04 42 14 14 14; www.marseille.aeroport.fr), lies 30km northwest of the city, with the usual facilities.

■ A **taxi** into Marseille will cost around €37 and takes 30 minutes. There's
no rail link, but **buses** run every 15 minutes to the Gare St-Charles railway station in the city (€8.50, 30 minutes).

■ **Marseille Tourist Office** ✉ 4 La Canebière, Marseille
☎ 04 91 13 89 00 ◉ Mon–Sat 9–7, Sun 10–5 (longer hours in
peak season)

Arriving in Toulouse

■ **Toulouse-Blagnac Airport** (tel: 0825 380 000; www.toulouse.aeroport.fr)
lies 8km (5 miles) northwest of Toulouse, with all main facilities.
■ A **taxi** into the city costs around €20 and takes 20 minutes. There's **no
rail** link, but **buses** into the city go every 20 minutes (€3.70, 20 minutes).

■ **Toulouse Tourist Office** ✉ Donjon du Capitole, 31080
☎ 05 61 11 02 22 ◉ Mon–Sat 9–7, Sun 9–1, 2–5:30, May–Sep;
Mon–Fri 9–6, Sat 9–12:30, 2–6, Sun 10–12:30, 2–5, Oct–Apr

Arriving in Strasbourg

■ **Strasbourg Airport** (tel: 03 88 64 67 67; www.strasbourg.aeroport.fr) is
12km (7.5 miles) southwest of the city, with all main facilities.
■ A **taxi** into the city costs around €25 and takes 15 minutes. The airport
is a five-minute walk from the Gare Entzheim, from where you can catch
a **train** into the city centre (5 am–8:30 pm, 15 minutes). A regular **bus**
service links up to the Baggersee train station, from where you can take
a **tram** into the centre (€4.80, 30 minutes).

■ **Strasbourg Tourist Office** ✉ 17 place de la Cathédrale, 67082
☎ 03 88 52 28 28 ◉ Mon–Sat 9–7, Sun 9–6

Arriving in Lyon

■ **Lyon St-Exupéry Airport** (tel: 04 72 22 72 21; www.lyon.aeroport.fr) lies
28km (17 miles) east of Lyon, with all main facilities.
■ A **taxi** into the city centre will cost around €33, and takes 30 minutes.
There's **no rail** link, but **buses** leave every 20 minutes for the centre
(€8.20, 40–50 minutes).

■ **Lyon Tourist Office** ✉ place Bellecour, 69002
☎ 04 72 77 69 69 ◉ Mon–Sat 9–7, Sun 9–6, mid-Apr to mid-Oct;
Mon–Sat 10–6, Sun and holidays 10–5:30, mid-Oct to mid-Apr

Arriving in Calais

■ **Ferries and catamarans** from Dover arrive at Calais. The main *autoroutes*
from here are the A16/E40 north towards Dunkerque, then the
A26/A1/E15 towards Paris; and the A16/E40 south down the coast.
■ The **Shuttle** train from Folkestone, travelling via the Eurotunnel (from
UK tel: 08705 35 35 35; www.eurotunnel.com), delivers cars and their
passengers to Calais/Coquelles. Main routes are as above.

■ **Calais Tourist Office** ✉ 12 boulevard Clemenceau, 62102
☎ 03 21 96 62 40; www.ot-calais.fr ◉ Mon–Sat 9–7, Sun 10–1, 3–6,
Jun–Aug; Mon–Sat 10–1, 2–6:30, Sun 10–noon, 3–6, Sep–May

Getting Around

France is a big country, but an excellent network of fast trains and *autoroutes* (motorways/expressways) means that you can usually travel between regions quickly and easily.

Domestic Air Travel

■ France's national airline, **Air France** (in UK tel: 0845 0845 111; www.airfrance.co.uk; in US tel: 1 800 237 2747; www.airfrance.com) operates flights across a wide network of towns, linking 16 to Paris Roissy-Charles de Gaulle and 14 to Paris Orly. The longest flight takes around 1 hour. For information on regional airports, see www.aeroport.fr

Trains

■ Train services within France are run by the state railway company, the Société Nationale des Chemins de Fer (**SNCF**, tel: 0892 353 535; www.sncf.com), and are generally fast, comfortable and efficient.

■ The **TGV** (*Train à Grande Vitesse*) high-speed train links major towns and cities at speeds of up to 300 kph/186 mph. A journey from Paris to Bordeaux or Marseille takes around 3 hours. **CORAIL** trains provide regular long-distance services (*Grandes Lignes*), and the **TER** (*Transport Express Régional*) provide the local service (*Lignes Régionales*).

■ There are many **overnight sleeper trains** between major cities, offering reclining seats (in second class only), *couchette* berths (four or six to a compartment) or a sleeper car (two or three to a compartment). *Auto-Trains* can also take your car at the same time – the most useful services link Calais with Brives, Toulouse, Narbonne, Avignon and Nice.

■ **Buy tickets** at the railway stations, at SNCF offices or through some travel agents. **Ticket machines** can also be used to collect tickets ordered in advance on the internet, by telephone or Minitel. It is essential to **reserve tickets for TGV trains** in advance, and **book ahead** for any rail travel in the peak season (June to mid-September) to be sure of your place. Most trains have first and second class options, and fares are split into normal (blue) and peak (red) times. **You must stamp your ticket** in the orange machine on the platform before boarding the train at the start of your journey, to validate it.

■ Under-26s can get a 25 per cent **discount on travel** (*Découverte 12–25*), and discounts are also available for older people and by booking well ahead (*Découverte J30*). A variety of discount rail passes is available for travel within France, or within the whole of Europe, and should be bought before arrival in France from travel agents or Rail Europe (in the UK www.raileurope.co.uk; in the US www.raileurope.com).

■ With a minimum of 24 hours notice, the **SNCF luggage service** will pick up your luggage from your hotel and deliver it to your final destination for you. The service operates Monday to Friday, 7–9. To contact them, tel: 0825 845 845.

Buses

■ **Long-distance bus routes** within France are generally slightly less expensive than the trains, but much slower. You'll usually find the **bus station** (*gare routière*) close to the railway station (*gare SNCF*). **Eurolines** (tel: 0892 695 252; www.eurolines.fr) operates services between major towns and cities within France and to other destinations within Europe. **SNCF** (tel: 3635) also runs services as extensions to rail links.

Taxis

- **Taxis** are a convenient way to get around, but generally an expensive option. You'll pay a pick-up charge and a charge per kilometre, plus extra for items of luggage and travel in the evening or on Sundays. All taxis use a **meter** (*compteur*), and **taxi stands** in towns and cities are marked with a square blue sign.
- Some taxis accept bank cards, but it is best to **have cash available**. It is usual to give a **tip** of around 10 per cent.

Driving

- An excellent system of motorways/expressways (*autoroutes*, marked A on maps and road signs) fans out from Paris, making it fairly straight-forward to drive between destinations. **Tolls are charged** on most *autoroutes*, so have some cash to hand, as foreign credit cards are not always accepted. Key routes include the A1 north, the A13 to Normandy and the northwest, the A4 east, the A6 to the Alps and the Riviera, and the A10 west and southwest.
- There's a comprehensive network of other roads across the country, including main highways (*route nationale*, marked N), lesser highways (*route départementale*, marked D), and minor country roads. Surfaces are generally good at all levels.
- **Driving in Paris** is a nightmare so avoid it if possible, especially during the rush hour (7–9:30 am and 4:30–7:30 pm, weekdays). Bear in mind that a car can be a positive hazard in some other big cities, with congested traffic, confusing one-way systems and expensive parking.
- If **bringing your own car** to France, you must always carry the following documentation in addition to your passport: a full, valid national driver's licence, a certificate of motor insurance and the vehicle's registration document (plus a letter of authorisation from the owner if it is not registered in your name). Third-party motor insurance is the **minimum requirement**, but fully comprehensive cover is strongly advised. Check that your **insurance** covers you against damage in transit, and that you have adequate **breakdown cover** (for information contact the AA, tel: 0800 444 500; www.theAA.com, or your own national breakdown organisation). You must also display an **international sticker** or distinguishing sign plate on the rear of the car by the registration plate. **Headlights** of right-hand-drive cars must be adjusted for driving on the right.

Driving Know-How

- Drive on the **right-hand side** of the road (*serrez à droite*).
- Drivers must be **18 or over**, and you'll need to be **20 or over to hire** a car.
- **Speed limits** are 50kph/31mph on urban roads, 90kph/56mph outside built-up areas (80kph/49mph in rain), 110kph/68mph on dual carriage-ways/divided highways and non-toll motorways (100kph/62mph in rain), and 130kph/80mph on toll motorways (110kph/68mph in rain). Visiting drivers who have held a licence for less than two years must follow the wet-weather limits **at all times**, even when it's dry. Drivers from within the EU who **exceed the speed** limit by more than 25kph/15mph may have their licences confiscated by the police on the spot.
- **Yield** to vehicles coming from the right (*priorité à droite*). At round-abouts/traffic circles with signs saying *Cédez le passage* or *Vous n'avez pas la priorité*, traffic already on the roundabout has priority. On roundabouts without signs, traffic entering has priority.
- **Do not overtake** where there is a solid single line in the centre of the road.

- The **blood alcohol limit** is 0.5 percent (US blood alcohol content 0.05). If you drink, don't drive.
- **Fuel** (l) comes as unleaded (95 and 98 octane), lead replacement petrol (LRP or *supercarburant*), diesel (*gasoil* or *gazole*) and LPG. Many filling stations **close on Sundays** and at 6 pm during the week.
- Before you take to the road, familiarise yourself with the **French highway code** on www.legifrance.gouv.fr. For information on **road signs**, see www.permisenligne.com.

Renting a Car

- Cars can be rented by **drivers over 20** who have held a full driver's licence for a year, but some companies require a minimum age of 25. The average maximum age limit is 70.
- Most major **car rental firms** such as Europcar, Avis and Hertz have outlets at airports, main railway stations and in large towns and cities throughout France. Most will let you return your car to other cities and even countries, but agree this ahead; there may be a surcharge.
- Most rental cars in France are manual, so **if you want an automatic**, make sure you specify this and reserve ahead.

Urban Transport

- You can walk around the main sights in most French cities; historic centres are usually small, many are pedestrianised, and walking gives a great "feel" for any new place. Several cities have métro systems or trams, including Paris, Lyon, Marseille, Toulouse and Lille, and all towns have efficient bus services.

In Paris

- The **Métro and buses** use the same tickets and travel cards, which are also valid for RER trains within the city centre. **Buy them** at Métro stations, on buses (one-way tickets only) and some news-stands. Children under four travel free, and age four to nine, half price. The city is divided into **fare zones**, and most of the major sights are in Zone 1.
- The **Métro** underground train runs from 5:30 am to 12:30 am, and is a fast, efficient way of getting around. Lines are **colour-coded** and numbered on maps (free), and stations are identified by a large M. Maps show the suburban RER train lines too, which are lettered and usually run off the map.
- **Buses** travel slowly in the Paris traffic, but are a great way to see the city as you go. Most run from 7 am to 8:30 pm, with some late services until 12:30 am. Remember to **stamp your ticket** in the machine next to the driver, to validate it.
- **RER** (*Réseau Express Régional*) trains provide a local service around the Paris suburbs, with five main lines named A to E. Trains run from around 5:30 am to 12:30 am.
- The **Batobus** is a river shuttle boat, with regular services from 10 am–7 pm between April and October, and to 9 pm in midsummer. Stops include the Eiffel Tower, Musée d'Orsay, Notre-Dame and the Louvre.

Admission Charges

The cost of admission for museums and places of interest mentioned in the text is indicated by the following price categories:
Inexpensive under €5   **Moderate** €5–€8   **Expensive** over €8

Accommodation

There's a wide variety of accommodation available to visitors throughout France, and you should find something to suit your budget and your taste. The international hotel chains such as Best Western, Hilton and Holiday Inn are well represented, but for a more authentic experience of France, you may like to try a campsite, a rented *gîte* or perhaps a family-run *auberge*.

Types of Accommodation

Hotels

- Hotels in France are regularly inspected and are **classified into six categories**, from no stars (at the bottom) to four stars and four-star luxury hotels. Charges are usually **per room** rather than per person, and breakfast is generally charged separately. If you're travelling with a family on a budget, note that for a little extra, many hotels will put another bed in your room.
- Family-run inns and small hotels, the **Logis de France** usually offer some of the best accommodation if you're exploring on a budget. All have a basic standard of comfort, and some are in particularly quaint or charming locations. Most have their own restaurant, serving good local food. By prior arrangement, **luggage can be transported** between Logis for you – very useful if you're planning a hiking break. As well as star gradings, Logis also have their own chimney symbol of classification. Find them listed on the website www.logis-de-france.com, or get a complete list from the tourist office.
- There are some great **luxury hotels**, if you want to treat yourself to a very special experience. The Paris Ritz is one of the best-known, and the traditional *belle-époque* hotels of the Riviera have a cachet which is hard to beat. For something with a more modern twist, look at designer hotels such as the Hi-Hotel in Nice, where rock pools and plasma screens are part of the fun. Boutique hotels – small but chic – are becoming more popular. And if you fancy staying in a luxurious château setting, contact Relais & Château (tel: 0825 32 3232/ 01 58 18 30 00; www.relaischateau.com).

Bed-and-Breakfast

- **Chambres d'hôte** offers a taste of life in a real French household, anywhere from a farm to a château. Ask at the tourist offices for local availability. Many of the best are affiliated to the Gîtes de France organisation, which grades them with one to four ears of corn (*épis*) according to the level of comfort and facilities.
- For the **top end** of the scale – perhaps a room in a privately owned Loire château – contact Bienvenue au Château (2 rue de la Loire, BP20411, 44204, Nantes; www.bienvenueauchateau.com).

Self Catering (Gîtes)

- Self-contained cottages, villas and apartments (***gîtes***) are widely available in towns, villages and country areas across France, and offer particularly good value for families. They are usually **rented by the week or fortnight**, and facilities may range from simple and basic (bring your own linen) to more elaborate, with swimming pools and other facilities thrown in.

■ Many *gîtes* are administered through the **Gîtes de France** organisation, which also inspects and grades them according to comfort and facilities (www.gites-de-france.fr). Local tourist offices also generally hold this information for their area.

Youth Hostels

■ There are around 200 youth hostels (*auberges de jeunesse*) across France, which are open to members from other countries if they have a membership card with photo. For a complete list and details, contact the **Fédération Unie des Auberges de Jeunesse**, 9 rue Brantome, 75003 Paris (tel: 01 48 04 70 40; www.fuaj.org).

Camping

■ This is hugely popular in France, with a roll-call exceeding **9,000 fully equipped campsites**, plus around 2,300 farm campsites. Sites are **inspected and graded** with a star system like that of the hotels, and range from basic (electricity, showers, lavatories) to luxurious, with swimming pools and other family sports activities, restaurants and bars, and kids clubs. You don't even have to take your own tent – many have **pre-pitched tents and mobile homes** on site, complete with cooking equipment, fridge and beds.
■ Expect to **book well ahead**, especially in high season, which runs from May to September in the north, and April to October in the south. For more information, contact the **National Federation of Campsites** (tel: 01 42 72 84 08; www.campingfrance.com).
■ Note that camping or overnight parking of caravans and motorhomes is **not permitted** on the beach or at the roadside. If you get caught out and need to find a campsite, the local tourist office should be able to advise you, and in case of an emergency, police stations can also let you have a list of local campsite addresses.

Finding a Room

■ If you haven't booked ahead, visit the **local tourist office**, as they will have a list of accommodation with prices. In towns or villages without a tourist office, head for the main square or centre of town, where you're likely to find the greatest concentration of hotels.
■ When you **check in**, you'll need to complete a registration form and show your passport. Ask to see the room first, especially in cheaper accommodation.
■ **Check-out times** are usually around 10 or 11 am.

Seasonal Rates

■ Accommodation prices are likely to **vary widely throughout the year**, according to the season. In the resort areas of southern France, higher prices may be charged between April and October, while in northern France the summer season is generally shorter – July to September. Paris hotels often charge lower rates during July and August, when the sticky heat of the city coincides with the mass-exodus of Parisians on annual holiday.

Prices
Expect to pay per double room per night:
€ under €100   €€ €100–200   €€€ over €200

Food and Drink

Few nations enjoy their food with quite the pride and relish of the French. Eating out is one of the "must do" experiences on any French holiday, and there's no better way to discover the wealth of local dishes and culinary twists than at a local bistro. Fine dining is fun to try too, and you'll find top-class restaurants in many towns and cities, not just the capital.

Regional Menus

Sample the specialities of the region for an insight into the locale.

■ For example, around **Brittany, Normandy and the Loire**, *crêpes* and *galettes*(buckwheat pancakes), both sweet and savoury, are the fast-food of choice, freshly prepared with fillings such as chocolate or ham and cheese. *Moules marinières* (mussels in white wine) are delicious, and other seafood treats include *coquilles St-Jacques* (hot scallops in a creamy sauce topped with melted cheese or breadcrumbs, served in the shell), *langouste* (crayfish), *crevettes* (prawns) and *huîtres* (oysters). Look out, too, for *châteaubriand* (thick, tenderloin steak cooked with a white wine, herb and shallot sauce) and pork cooked in a *sauce normande* (cider and cream). Desserts include the upside-down apple pie, *tarte tatin*.

■ In the **north and Alsace Lorraine**, the influences are more Germanic, with hearty dishes such as *choucroute garnie* (pickled cabbage cooked in wine with pork, sausage and smoked ham, served with boiled potatoes), and meaty stews such as *bäeckeoffe* (cooked in wine) and *carbonnade flamande* (in beer and spices). It's also the home of *quiche Lorraine* (egg custard tart with bacon, onion and herbs) and the *salade de cervelas* (cold sausage in vinaigrette sauce).

■ Around **Burgundy and the northern Rhône** area, sample different meats cooked in red wine, from *boeuf bourguignon* (beef with onions and mushrooms) to *coq au vin* (chicken with mushrooms and onions). *Escargots à la bourguignon* are snails served in garlic and parsley butter, and local sausages include *boudin* (blood pudding/sausage).

■ Throughout **Jura and the Alps**, try a fondue, either *au fromage* (bread cubes are dipped into melted cheese mixed with wine) or *bourguignonne* (meat cubes are cooked in oil then dipped into various sauces). *Gratin dauphinois* (potatoes, sliced and baked with cream and nutmeg) and *gratin savoyard* (sliced potatoes with cheese, cooked in stock) are also favourites of this region.

■ In the **Pyrenees and the southwest** you'll taste dishes cooked *à la landaise* (in goose fat with garlic), *à la bordelaise* (with red wine sauce and mixed vegetables), *à la périgourdine* (with a truffle or *foie gras* sauce or stuffing) and *à la basquaise* (with Bayonne ham, *cèpe* mushrooms and potatoes). Duck is a particular favourite, with *magret de canard* (boned duck breast, grilled or fried), *confit de canard* (salted duck pieces cooked and preserved in their own fat) and of course, *foie gras* (the enlarged liver of maize-fed ducks or geese, served in slices hot or cold).

■ The flavours in the **southeast** and around the **shores of the Mediterranean** are those of the sunny climes, from the classic *salade niçoise* (any combination of tomatoes, green beans, anchovies, olives, peppers and boiled egg) to *ratatouille* (a stew of tomatoes, onions, courgettes/zucchini, aubergines/eggplant and garlic in olive oil). Stewed meats include *cassoulet* (a thick, rich stew of haricot beans and garlic with goose and pork sausage), and the ultimate fish stew – *bouillabaisse*.

Where to Eat

- You'll find a decent **restaurant** or several in every town, where the glasses are polished and the linen and waiters starched, and where the locals will go for a special occasion, a formal encounter or a top treat. Expect to **reserve your table in advance, dress smartly, and allow plenty of time** for the full gastronomic experience. Michelin stars and Gault et Millau *toques* help to identify the top eating places, and if the dinner price is beyond your budget, look out for better value set menus at lunchtime. The *menu dégustation* offers a selection of the restaurant's signature dishes with accompanying wines at a fixed price. Logis de France hotels are also associated with good local restaurants.

- **Brasseries** are **informal** establishments, generally open long hours, where you can sample local dishes alongside staples such as *steak-frites* (steak with chips/fries) and *choucroute* (sauerkraut).

- **Bistros** tend to be **small, informal, family-run** restaurants serving traditional and local dishes, with a modest wine list.

- Lunchtime menus tend to offer the **best value**, when a *menu du jour* (daily menu) of two or three courses with wine is likely to cost much less than an evening meal. *Prix-fixe* meals of three or four courses also generally offer good value.

- Restaurants mostly keep to **regular opening hours**: noon–2:30 and 7–10, although some may stay open longer during a holiday period. They generally **close** at lunchtime on Saturday and Monday, and Sunday evening. Some Paris restaurants may close completely in July and August, and those along the south coast may shut between November and Easter.

- **Service** is usually **included in the bill** (*l'addition*) – look for the words *service compris*, or *s.c.* If the service is exceptional, you may like to leave your loose change or a tip of around 5 per cent.

Where and What to Drink

- Relaxing in a **café** and watching the world go by is one of the pleasures of France. As a rule, you'll pay more for your drink if you're sitting outside on the terrace. Cafés and bars serve coffee, soft drinks, alcohol, snacks and often traditional and herbal teas.

- Cafés and bars sometimes open as early as 7 am to serve breakfast, and may close any time between 9 pm and the early hours of the next morning. Licensing hours when alcohol may be sold vary according to the individual establishment.

- A *citron pressé* (freshly squeezed lemon), to which you add your own sugar, can be particularly refreshing on a hot day. Bottled water (*eau*) comes as *gazeuse* (carbonated) or *non-gazeuse* (still). Beer (*bière*) is usually the light European lager, and cider (*cidre*) is found particularly around the apple-growing areas of Normandy. White and red wine (*vin blanc, vin rouge*) is widely available, and it is worth seeking out the local wines (▶ 16–18). If in doubt, try the house wine (*vin ordinaire or vin de table*).

- There is also a wide variety of regional liqueurs and spirits to try, including Benedictine, Calvados, Cognac, Armagnac and Chartreuse.

- The **legal age** for drinking alcohol is 16. Children aged 14 to 16 may drink wine or beer if accompanied by an adult.

Prices
Expect to pay per person for a meal, excluding drinks:
€ up to €25   €€ €25–50   €€€ over €50

Shopping

Shopping in France can be a real pleasure, whether it's hitting the boutiques for *haute couture*, choosing the chocolatiest cake in the *pâtisserie*, conversing with the small-scale cheese producers in the *marché* (market), or strolling through the varied delights of a *hypermarché* (hypermarket). Prices may not be cheap, but quality is usually high.

Opening Hours

■ Opening times vary according to the type of shop, the season and the location, and there are no hard and fast rules. For example, **smaller shops** often **close at lunchtime** between noon and 2:30 pm, but this may extend to 4 pm in the south during summer, with later opening into the evening to compensate.

■ **Department stores** and larger shops are open from Monday to Saturday, 9 am to 6:30 pm.

■ **Food shops** usually open from Tuesday to Saturday, between 7 or 8 am and 6:30 or 7:30 pm, and may close for lunch. Some may open on a Monday afternoon, and they may open on Sunday morning. *Boulangeries* (bakers) usually open on Sunday morning.

■ **Supermarkets and hypermarkets** generally open from 9 am to 9 or 10 pm, Monday to Saturday; the main names include Carrefour, Auchan, Champion and E. Leclerc.

■ Daily and weekly **markets** are a feature of cities and towns, and usually operate from around 7 am to noon. Often the people who produced or grew the food are the people selling it, too, and can tell you about their range of cheeses or whatever.

Payment

■ Shops in towns and major tourist areas usually accept payment by **credit or debit card**. For markets and smaller outlets, carry euros **in cash**.

■ Visitors from outside the European Union can **reclaim a 12 percent tax** on certain purchases. You'll need a *détaxe* form from the shopkeeper, which must be shown with the receipts and stamped at customs, then returned to the shop by post for a refund.

What to Buy

■ France is known world-wide for its stylish **fashion**, which is by no means limited to the capital. Check out the chic clothes stores in any of the bigger cities, and in resorts such as Cannes, Biarritz and Chamonix.

■ France is also the heart of a fabulous **perfume** industry, with names such as Dior and Chanel. You'll find fragrances and soaps in shops all across the country; Grasse, in Provence, is where much of it originates.

■ It is difficult to come away from France without a shopping bag or two of your favourite **food**, whether it's *galettes* (buttery biscuits) from Brittany, *saucisson* (sausages) from the northeast, *pâté* and sugared walnuts from the Dordogne, or *fromage* (cheese) from just about anywhere.

■ There are various options for buying **wine**. Hypermarkets usually stock a wide range of excellent French wines. Go for a tasting at a vineyard and you will be expected to buy at least one bottle – and, of course, more if you find something you really like. And in wine-growing districts, ask in the tourist offices about co-operatives, where you can sample the locally-produced AOC (*Apellation d'Origine Contrôlée*) wines.

Entertainment

France's rich cultural heritage means that you're rarely far from a venue for music, theatre and cinema, whether that's a small, smoke-filled club, a 15,000-seat Roman amphitheatre or something a little more conventional. Performances are likely to be in French, but some cinemas show movies in their original language; look for the symbol "VO" (*version originale*). From top sporting events to outdoor opera extravaganzas, tourist offices can usually tell you what's on and how to obtain tickets.

Music and Dance

- Paris is naturally the centre of high culture, including the famous **Comédie Française** theatre group (www.comediefrancaise.fr) and the Opéra de Paris ballet company (www.balletdelopera.com). Several other cities have ballet companies, and contemporary dance finds a focus at Montpellier's **Centre Choréographique National** (www.ville-montpellier.fr).
- France lacks a world-class national orchestra, but top-class recitals of classical music by smaller ensembles such as the **Orchestre de Paris** (www.orchestredeparis.com) are held across the country, often in historic settings such as châteaux and cathedrals.
- More than 300 **music festivals** are held around the country every year. They include the famous **International Celtic Festival** of folk music in Lorient, Brittany, at the start of August (www.festival-interceltique.com).
- **Jazz** has a great following in France, with annual festivals in Paris, Nice, Antibes, Vienne and Grenoble.

Nightlife

- Inevitably, the quality and quantity of nightlife varies according to where you are. In **Paris** you'll be spoilt for choice, with cabaret revue shows, bars and clubs galore. Other big cities such as **Marseille, Lyon and Toulouse** also have a vibrant night scene. Particularly in rural districts, however, you may find that the pool table in the local café-bar is as exciting as it gets.
- **Casinos** are part of the French entertainment scene: most resorts have them, and the most famous of them all is in **Monte Carlo** (➤ 172).
- For some of the best **gay and lesbian nightlife**, head for the Marais district of Paris. Other lively spots are found along the Côte d'Azur and around St-Tropez – check out local listings magazines for details.

Sports and Outdoor Activities

- France is a great **winter sports destination**, with resorts in the Alps, the Massif Central and the Pyrénées. Chamonix and Courcheval are the places to be seen, but there are plenty of more affordable options.
- The sport of cycling is a national obsession which reaches fever pitch around the time of the gruelling annual **Tour de France**, a race around the country held over three weeks in July. Renting bicycles for **leisure cycling** is also popular – they are available from more than 200 railway stations, at a cost of around €10 per day.
- **Motor racing** fans will look forward to the **Le Mans** 24-hour rally (www.lemans.org), and the glamorous Formula One **grand prix** races at Monte Carlo (www.monte-carlo.mc) and Magny Cours (www.magnyf1.com).
- **Walkers** can head for the hills or stride the plains on over 30,000km (18,600 miles) of footpaths, marked on maps as *Grandes Randonnées* (long-distance) and *Petites Randonnées*.

Paris and the Île de France

Getting Your Bearings 38 – 39
In Three Days 40 – 41
Don't Miss 42 – 57
At Your Leisure 58 – 61
Walk 62 – 64
Further Afield 65 – 67
Where to… 68 – 72

Getting Your Bearings

The Arc de Triomphe and the place de la Concorde, at either end of the broad, straight avenue des Champs-Élysées, are the twin traffic hubs of this vibrant capital. Through its heart curves the River Seine.

The Left Bank, or Rive Gauche, is the southern sector and contains many of the best-known attractions, including the Musée d'Orsay and the Tour Eiffel. East of here, the Latin Quarter is a bohemian student district. The mid-river Île de la Cité was home to the earliest settlers, the *Parisii* tribe (hence the city's name), and here you'll find Notre-Dame. North of the Seine, the area around the Louvre has elegant squares and fashion emporia. Head northwest for the Jardin des Tuileries, the Arc de Triomphe and La Défense. East of this lies the Beaubourg district, with Les Halles shopping centre and the eccentric Centre Georges Pompidou. Overlooking all is Montmartre, which retains its village identity.

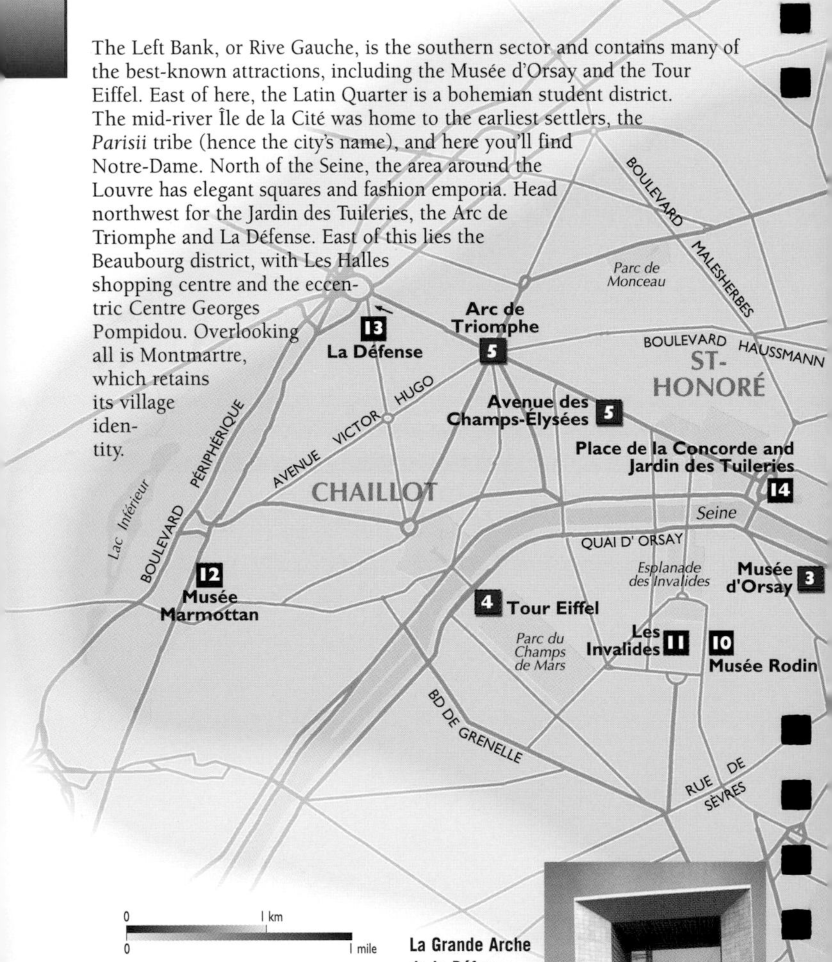

BOULEVARD MALESHERBES

Parc de Monceau

13 La Défense

Arc de Triomphe **5**

BOULEVARD HAUSSMANN

ST-HONORÉ

BOULEVARD PÉRIPHÉRIQUE

AVENUE VICTOR HUGO

Avenue des Champs-Élysées **5**

Place de la Concorde and Jardin des Tuileries **14**

CHAILLOT

Seine

QUAI D' ORSAY

Lac Intérieur

Esplanade des Invalides

Musée d'Orsay **3**

12 **Musée Marmottan**

4 **Tour Eiffel**

Parc du Champs de Mars

Les Invalides **11** **10** **Musée Rodin**

BD DE GRENELLE

RUE DE SÈVRES

0   1 km
0   1 mile

La Grande Arche de la Défence, complete with a suspended "floating cloud"

Previous page: The city by night

The Tour Eiffel, the city's most famous landmark

★ Don't Miss

1 Île de la Cité ➤ 42
2 Quartier Latin ➤ 45
3 Musée d'Orsay ➤ 47
4 Tour Eiffel ➤ 50
5 Champs-Élysées and Arc de Triomphe ➤ 52
6 Musée du Louvre ➤ 54
7 Centre Georges Pompidou ➤ 56

At Your Leisure

8 Île St-Louis ➤ 58
9 St-Germain-des-Prés ➤ 58
10 Musée Rodin ➤ 58
11 Les Invalides ➤ 59
12 Musée Marmottan ➤ 59
13 La Défense ➤ 59
14 Place de la Concorde and Jardin des Tuileries ➤ 60
15 La Villette ➤ 60
16 Musée Picasso ➤ 60
17 Place des Vosges ➤ 61
18 Cimetière du Père-Lachaise ➤ 61

MONTMARTRE

PIGALLE

La Villette **15**

BOULEVARD LA FAYETTE

RUE LA

BD DE SEBASTOPOL

MAGENTA

Canal St-Martin

Parc de Belleville

RÉPUBLIQUE

AV DE LA RÉPUBLIQUE

LES HALLES

RUE DE RIVOLI

Centre Georges Pompidou **7**

6 Musée du Louvre

Musée Picasso **16**

LE MARAIS

BOULEVARD VOLTAIRE

Cimetière du Père-Lachaise **18**

9 St-Germain-des-Prés

Sainte-Chapelle

Conciergerie

1 Île de la Cité

Notre-Dame

17 Place des Vosges

8 Île St-Louis

BASTILLE

RUE ST-MICHEL

RUE ST-JACQUES

Musée National du Moyen Âge

Jardin du Luxembourg

BOULEVARD

2 Quartier Latin

Jardin des Plantes

BOULEVARD DIDEROT

QUAI D'AUSTERLITZ

BOULEVARD ARAGO

Further Afield

19 Chantilly ➤ 65
20 Disneyland® Resort Paris ➤ 65
21 Chartres ➤ 66
22 Fontainebleau ➤ 66
23 Versailles ➤ 67

Three days is not long enough to explore a capital city as rich as Paris, but it is just enough to see the main sites and to get a feel for different districts, before heading out to explore its major outlying attraction, the royal palace of Versailles.

Paris and the Île de France in Three Days

Day One

Morning
Take the métro to Cité to explore **1 Île de la Cité** (➤ 42–44). Be first in the queue to climb the 387 steps of the tower of **Notre Dame** cathedral (right, ➤ 42–43) for fantastic views over the heart of Paris, and of the roof gargoyles. Relish the blacker side of Parisian history in a guided tour of the **Conciergerie** (➤ 43–44) before crossing the Pont de l'Archevêché for lunch at **La Rôtisserie du Beaujolais** (➤ 44).

Afternoon
Walk south through the streets of the **2 Quartier Latin** (➤ 45–46) and make your way to the **Musée National du Moyen Âge–Thermes de Cluny** (➤ 45–46) for a discovery of some of Paris's finest early treasures. Chill out afterwards in the nearby **Jardin du Luxembourg** (➤ 45).

Evening
Stroll back towards the river through the bohemian district of **9 St-Germain-des-Prés** (➤ 58) and pick out a restaurant that takes your fancy for dinner.

Day Two

Morning
Start the day at the **3 Musée d'Orsay** (➤ 47–49), a magnificent art gallery on the south bank of the Seine. In summer, catch the **Batobus** (➤ 30) west to the **4 Tour Eiffel** (left, ➤ 50–51), and take the lift to the top for outstanding views. Dine in the **café** on level 1 or the **restaurant** on level 2 (➤ 51).

Afternoon
Take a taxi across the river to the **5 Champs-Élysées** (➤ 52–53), making sure the driver includes a circuit of the **Arc de Triomphe** (left below, ➤ 52–53) before dropping you off on the famous avenue for some shopping. Visit the **main tourist office** at no. 127.

Evening
Book ahead for a glamorous night out at a **dinner and cabaret show** (➤ 72), maybe at the **Moulin Rouge** in **Montmartre** (Walk, ➤ 62).

Day Three

Morning
Get to the **6 Musée du Louvre** (➤ 54–55) as it opens to beat the crowds, and check out the *Mona Lisa*. If there's time, catch the métro to the **7 Centre Georges Pompidou** (centre, ➤ 56–57), for the contrast of modern art.

Afternoon
Take a picnic and eat it on the train to **23 Versailles** (right, ➤ 67). Spend the afternoon exploring the gardens and admiring the gilded interior.

Evening
Head back into town and seek out one of the great views of **Paris by night** – from the **Tour Eiffel** (➤ 50–51), perhaps.

▯ Île de la Cité

The history of this small, boat-shaped island in the Seine is the history of Paris. Here, in around 300 BC, the Parisii tribe settled, and it was here two centuries later that the Romans built the town of Lutetia, meaning "settlement surrounded by water". This was to become the seat of the ancient kings of France, the centre of political power, and the home of the church and the law. There's lots to see, and you can easily spend a whole day here, enjoying attractive parks and the flower market (Marché aux Fleurs), which on Sundays becomes a bird market (Marché aux Oiseaux).

Notre-Dame-de-Paris

Below and detail: Notre-Dame cathedral, beside the River Seine

Despite the inevitable crowds of tourists, the grandeur of this landmark cathedral, with its impressive sculpture-encrusted façade, its distinctive flying buttresses and its soaring nave, never fails to inspire.

Notre-Dame is one of the world's most beautiful examples of early Gothic architecture. The façade seems perfectly proportioned, with its two towers narrower at the top than at the base, giving the illusion of great height. Look closer, however, and you will notice the north (left) tower is wider than the south tower and that each of the three main entrances is slightly different in shape. On a sunny day, the nave is bathed in multi-coloured light, filtered through the superb stained-glass windows.

In the early 12th century the Bishop of Paris decided to build an immense church here, on a site where the Romans had earlier built a temple to Jupiter. It took over 150 years to complete (1163–1345). Over the centuries, the cathedral has fulfilled many roles, serving as a place of worship, a community hall, and even the setting for lavish banquets and theatrical productions. At one point it was abandoned altogether but, thanks largely to Victor Hugo's Hunchback of Notre-Dame, it was finally restored under Napoléon III.

Sainte-Chapelle

Sainte-Chapelle is surely Paris's most beautiful church – a veritable Sistine Chapel of shimmering stained glass, and a remarkable fusion of art and religion. The chapel is split into two levels, and the most striking feature of the upper chapel is its transparency. It seems as though there are no walls – only glowing stained-glass windows and clusters of slender columns rising to the vaulted ceiling. The gigantic rose window is best seen at sunset.

The church was built in 1248 by Louis IX to house the Crown of Thorns and a fragment of the Holy Cross. He had paid the outrageous sum of 1.3 million francs (the chapel itself only cost 400,000 francs) for these relics. He wanted the edifice to have the light, lacy aspect of a reliquary, and the result, in just five years, was this bejewelled Gothic masterpiece.

> **Notre Dame: Did You Know...**
> •The **interior** is 130m (430 feet) long, 48m (160 feet) wide and 35m (115 feet) high.
> •**387 spiral steps** lead to the top of the 75m (245-foot) high north tower.
> •**12 million people visit** each year, of whom 6,000 attend services.
> •The main bell, the "Emmanuel", rang out in 1944 to **celebrate the liberation** of France.

Left: The rose window of Notre-Dame

The Conciergerie

The imposing buildings stretching the entire width of the island at its western end were once a royal palace, and today house the city's law courts. The Conciergerie occupies part of the lower floor of the complex. Originally a residence, it served as a prison between 1391 and 1914. Guided tours make the most of its lurid history and include the Salle de la Toilette, where prisoners handed over their last possessions and were prepared for the guillotine. During the Revolution, 2,780 people were guillotined in place de la Révolution (today's place de la Concorde), including Marie-Antoinette, who spent 76 days in a humble cell here before losing her head in 1793.

Above: Inside the Conciergerie

Right: Browsing amid the colours and scents of the Marché aux Fleurs

Place du Parvis Notre-Dame

Not only is the Île de la Cité the heart of Paris, but it is also **the heart of France**. Set into the pavement on the square outside the main portal of Notre-Dame, a **bronze star** marks the *point zéro des routes de France*, the point from which all distances are measured to and from Paris throughout the whole of France.

TAKING A BREAK

Cross the Pont de l'Archevêché to enjoy a traditional French meal at **La Rôtisserie du Beaujolais**, at 19 quai de la Tournelle (tel: 01 43 54 17 47, closed Mon).

Île de la Cité
✚ 204 C2
🚇 Cité

Marché aux Fleurs and Marché aux Oiseaux
✚ 204 C2
✉ place Louis-Lépine
🕐 Daily 8–7
🚇 Cité
Ⓡ St-Michel

Notre-Dame
✚ 204 C2
✉ 6 place du Parvis Notre-Dame
☎ 01 42 34 56 10
🕐 Daily 8–6:45; sacristy: Mon–Sat 9:30–11:30, 1–5:30. Closed some religious feast days
🚇 Cité Ⓡ RER St-Michel–Notre Dame
✋ Free; sacristy inexpensive; tower moderate

Sainte-Chapelle
✚ 204 B2
✉ 4 boulevard du Palais
☎ 01 53 40 60 80
🕐 Daily 9:30–6 (last entry 30 mins before closing). Closed 1 Jan, 1 May, 25 Dec
🚇 Cité/St-Michel
Ⓡ Châtelet-Les-Halles, St-Michel–Notre-Dame
✋ Moderate

(combined Ste-Chapelle/Conciergerie ticket is available)

The Conciergerie
✚ 204B2
✉ Palais de la Cité, 2 boulevard du Palais
☎ 01 53 40 60 80
🕐 Daily 9–6. Closed 1 Jan, 1 May, 25 Dec
🚇 Cité
Ⓡ Châtelet
✋ Moderate

ÎLE DE LA CITÉ: INSIDE INFO

Top tips Visit Notre-Dame early in the morning, when the cathedral is **at its brightest and least crowded.**

• If you plan to climb the tower of Notre-Dame to admire the gargoyles and the views, **remember to wear sensible shoes** and be prepared to queue (daily 9:30–7:30, Apr–Jun; Mon–Fri 9–7:30, Sat–Sun 9 am–11 pm, Jul, Aug; daily 10–5:30, rest of year. Last admission 45 minutes before closing).

• There are **free guided tours** of Notre-Dame in English on Wed and Thu at noon, on Sat at 2:30, and weekdays at 2:30 in August.

• For a magical experience, attend one of the **regular candlelit chamber music concerts** at Ste-Chapelle. Ask for details at the ticket office or the tourist office.

One to miss Don't bother with the **lower chapel of Ste-Chapelle.** It pales into insignificance beside the upper chapel.

2 Quartier Latin

The Latin Quarter has been the centre of learning in Paris for more than 700 years, with the Sorbonne at it heart. Its highlight is the Musée National du Moyen-Âge–Thermes de Cluny, though the nearby formal Jardin du Luxembourg is a favourite rendezvous for students and residents. The grand Palais du Luxembourg overlooking the gardens was built for Marie de' Médicis, widow of Henri IV, in 1627.

Musée National du Moyen-Âge–Thermes de Cluny

Even if you're not a fan of medieval art and history, this out-standing museum, with exhibits spanning 15 centuries, is a must, if only for the remarkable building, which in itself is the architectural embodiment of this period.

The collections are housed in two adjoining buildings. Around AD 200 the guild of Paris boatmen built a complex of Roman baths here. The remains of the well-preserved *frigidarium* form a kind of basement gallery, exhibiting Roman items. In the 15th century, monks of the abbey of Cluny in Burgundy built a mansion here to house visiting abbots. With its ornate turrets, gargoyles and cloistered courtyard, it's the finest example of medieval civil architecture in Paris.

Its treasures reflect the richness and diversity of life in the Middle Ages, including furnishings,

Tapestry (top) and buildings at the Cluny

stained glass, jewellery, statuary, carvings, illuminated manuscripts, paintings and, most famous of all, the *Dame à la Licorne* (*Lady and the Unicorn*) tapestries. This exquisite series of six embroidered panels portraying a lady flanked by a lion and a unicorn, set against a pink flower-strewn background, provides a reflection of the chivalrous world of courtly love.

Above and right: Enjoying the Jardin du Luxembourg

TAKING A BREAK

Have lunch at **La Gueuze**, close to the Jardin du Luxembourg at 19 rue Soufflot (tel: 01 43 54 63 00).

➕ 204 C1

Musée National du Moyen-Âge–Thermes de Cluny
➕ 204 B2 ✉ 6 place Paul Painlevé ☎ 01 53 73 78 00
🕐 Wed–Mon 9:15–5.45. Closed Tue, public holidays
🚇 St-Michel, Cluny–La

Sorbonne 🚆 RER B or C St-Michel–Cluny-Sorbonne
🎫 Moderate

Jardin du Luxembourg
➕ 204 A1 ✉ boulevard St-Michel 🕐 Daily 7:30–dusk, Apr–Oct; 8–dusk, Nov–Mar
🚇 Odéon 🎫 Free

QUARTIER LATIN: INSIDE INFO

Top tips Even if you don't have time to visit the museum, **step inside the courtyard** to admire its ornate turrets, gargoyles and friezes.
• Pick up a leaflet at the ticket desk which **details the key sights** and provides a plan of the floors of the museum.

Must-sees As well as the **Roman baths**, *Lady and the Unicorn Tapestry* and the monks' chapel, don't miss:
• **Statues of the Kings of Judaea** fromNotre-Dame's façade (ground floor, room 8).
• The Flamboyant Gothic **chapel of the monks of Cluny** (first floor, room 20).

❸ Musée d'Orsay

If you visit only one art gallery during your stay, make it the Musée d'Orsay, a feast of 19th-century art and design, including a hugely popular collection of Impressionist paintings. The originality of this amazing museum lies in its presentation of a wide range of different art forms – painting, sculpture, decorative and graphic art – all under the lofty glass roof of a former Industrial Age railway station.

The museum occupies the former Gare d'Orsay, built by Victor Laloux on the site of the Palais d'Orsay. The station was inaugurated in 1900 but ceased operating in 1939 with the dawn of electric trains. It was subsequently used as an auction room, then as a theatre, and was saved from demolition in 1973, to be finally converted into a museum in 1986. Much of the original architecture has been retained.

Top: The gallery is housed in a vast former railway station

Above: Van Gogh's painting of his bedroom at Arles

Seeing the Museum

The art collections span the years from 1848 to 1914, conveniently starting where the Louvre (▶ 54 – 55) leaves off and ending where the Centre Georges Pompidou (▶ 56 – 57) begins. They are organised chronologically on three levels, with additional displays throughout.

The skylit upper level houses the biggest crowd-puller – a dazzling collection of Impressionist and post-Impressionist treasures. It would be impossible to list all the star attractions, but favourites include Monet's *Coquelicots (Poppies)* and *La Rue Montorgueil – Fête du 30 juin 1878*, Renoir's *Danse à la ville (Town Dance)* and *Danse à la campagne (Country Dance)*, Van Gogh's *La Chambre à Arles (Room at Arles)* and Matisse's pointillist *Luxe, calme et volupté*. Montmartre fans will especially enjoy Renoir's *Bal du Moulin de la Galette*,

Degas' *L'Absinthe* and Toulouse-Lautrec's *Danse au Moulin Rouge*, all inspired by local scenes.

The close juxtaposition of paintings and sculptures on the ground floor illustrates the huge stylistic variations in art from 1848 to 1870 (the key date when Impressionism first made its name). Look out in particular for Courbet's *L'Origine du monde (Origin of the World)* and early Impressionist-style works such as Boudin's *La Plage de Trouville (The Beach at Trouville)*.

The middle level has objects reflecting the art nouveau movement, which display the sinuous lines – epitomised in jewellery and glassware by Lalique – that led the French to nickname the movement *style nouille* (noodle style). And throughout the museum you will find priceless sculptures at every turn, with works by Rodin on the middle floor and Degas on the top floor.

Above and opposite: A light and airy space for a fabulous art collection

Below: Statue by Carpoux

203 F3
1 rue de la Légion d'Honneur
01 40 49 48 14; www.musee-orsay.fr
Tue–Sat 10–6 (Thu until 9:45 pm), Sun 9–6, opens 9 mid-Jun–Aug. Ticket sales stop 45 minutes before closing time. Closed Mon, 1 Jan, 1 May, 25 Dec
Self-service cafeteria; café; restaurant
Solférino
RER Musée d'Orsay
Moderate. Free on first Sunday of the month.

MUSÉE D'ORSAY: INSIDE INFO

Top tips Be sure to **pick up a plan of the museum** as the layout is not clearly signed and can be rather confusing.

- Buy a copy of the excellent ***Pocket Guide***. It provides a succinct outline of the most important works of the collection. For a more comprehensive look at the collection, the beautifully illustrated ***Guide to the Musée d'Orsay*** is a must for all self-respecting art-buffs.
- If you are pressed for time, **ignore the lower floors** and head straight to the upper level to see the famous Impressionists on the river side of the gallery.

Tickets and tours Tickets for the permanent exhibits are valid all day, so **you can leave and re-enter** the museum as you please.

- **English-language tours** (charge: moderate) begin daily (except Sun and Mon) at 11:30 am. Ask for a ticket at the information desk.
- **Audioguides** – cassette tours (charge: inexpensive, available in six languages from just beyond the ticket booths on the right) – steer you round the major works. Both these and the English-language tours are excellent.

4 Tour Eiffel

Strange to think that Gustave Eiffel's famous tower, the universally beloved symbol of France, was considered a hideous eyesore when it was constructed over 100 years ago. Yet since its inauguration in 1889, over 200 million people have climbed the tower, and today the "iron lady" attracts 6 million visitors annually, making it one of the world's premier tourist attractions.

The lacy wrought-ironwork of this masterpiece of engineering is amazing and most visitors find soaring skywards in a double-decker glass lift both exciting and alarming. No visit to Paris is complete without seeing this awesome structure of gleaming brown metal, and the views from the top are unforgettable.

In 1885, Paris held a competition to design a 300m (985-foot) tower as the centre-piece for the Centennial Exhibition of 1889. Gustave Eiffel, nicknamed the "magician of iron", won the contest with his seemingly functionless tower, beating 107 other proposals, including one for a giant sprinkler and another for a monster commemorative guillotine. It took less than two years to build, and for years

the finished product remained a world-record breaker (until New York's Chrysler Building of 1930), but it was not without its critics. Local residents objected to this "overpowering metal construction" that straddled their district, fearing it would collapse onto their homes. Author Guy de Maupassant was a regular at the second-floor restaurant, swearing that it was the only spot in Paris from which you could not see the tower! He launched a petition against its erection, describing it as a "monstrous construction", a "hollow candlestick" and a "bald umbrella". On the other hand, playwright Jean Cocteau described it as the "Queen of Paris".

The tower was designed to stand for 20 years. Fortunately, its height was to be its salvation – the tall iron tower proved to be a marvellous antenna. The first news bulletin was broadcast from the Eiffel Tower in 1921, and the first television broadcast in 1935.

TAKING A BREAK

Try the impressive regional cooking at **Altitude 95**, advance booking essential (1st floor Tour Eiffel, tel: 01 45 55 20 04).

Vital statistics
WEIGHT: 7,000 tonnes
TOTAL HEIGHT: 320m/1,050 feet (15cm/6 inches higher on hot days due to metal expansion)
NUMBER OF METAL SECTIONS: 18,000
NUMBER OF RIVETS: 2.5 million
NUMBER OF RIVET HOLES: 7 million
NUMBER OF STEPS: 1,710
VISIBILITY FROM THE TOP: 75km (47 miles)
MAXIMUM SWAY AT THE TOP: 12cm (5 inches)

➕ 202 B3
✉ quai Branly
☎ 01 44 11 23 23; www.tour-eiffel.fr
🕐 Daily 9:30 am–11 pm, Sep to mid-Jun; 9 am–midnight, mid-Jun to

Aug. Last access 30 minutes before closing
🍴 Café (Level 1); Jules Verne restaurant (Level 2)
Ⓜ Bir-Hakeim
🚆 RER Champ-de-Mars
By elevator: 1st floor

(57m/185 feet) inexpensive; 2nd floor (115m/375 feet) moderate; 3rd floor (276m/905 feet) expensive. On foot (1st & 2nd floors only) inexpensive

---

TOUR EIFFEL: INSIDE INFO

Top tips Visit early in the morning or late at night to avoid the worst of the queues. **For the best views**, arrive one hour before sunset.
• **Forget the third level** unless it's an exceptionally clear day – the views can be disappointing as you're very high up and Paris is so flat.
• The tower itself looks at its **best after dark** when every girder is illuminated.
• Get your postcards stamped with the famous **Eiffel Tower postmark** at the post office on level one (daily 10–7:30).

Fast Track Skip the long queues for the lifts and **climb the stairs to the first level** (it takes about 5 minutes and isn't as tough as it looks). Catch your breath in the cineiffel (a short film recounts the tower's history), then walk or take the lift to level two. Tickets for both stages are available at the ticket office at the bottom of the southern pillar – Pilier Sud.

5 Champs-Élysées and Arc de Triomphe

The Arc de Triomphe rises majestically at the head of the city's most famous avenue, the Champs-Élysées. Planned by Napoléon I as a monument to his military prowess, the colossal arch was not finished until 15 years after his death, in 1836. The Tomb of the Unknown Soldier beneath the archway makes it also a place of remembrance.

Two hundred and eighty-two steps up a narrow spiral staircase will lead you to the 55m (180-foot) high terrace. Here, the breathtaking view highlights the city's unmistakable design – the Voie Triomphale from the Louvre to La Défense, and the 12 avenues radiating out from the arch itself like the points of a star (hence the name place de l'Étoile, which stubbornly persists despite being changed officially to place Charles-de-Gaulle).

Above: Busy traffic passes around Napoléon's triumphal arch, day and night
Right: Frieze detail on the Arc

It is hard to believe that the broad and busy thoroughfare of the avenue des Champs-Élysées was just an empty field before André Le Nôtre converted it into parkland as an extension of the Tuileries. For centuries it was a popular strolling ground, reaching its zenith in the mid-1800s, when a constant flow of horse-drawn carriages paraded up the street in order to allow ladies to show off their finest fashions. Today, with its brash shops, cinemas and fast food joints, the avenue that was once the "most beautiful street in the world" has lost much of its magic, glamour and prestige, yet it still retains an aloof grandeur and unique appeal.

Street Celebrations

The avenue des Champs-Élysées has always been associated with grand parades and parties. In 1810 Napoléon I organised a lavish procession here (complete with life-size mock-up of the Arc de Triomphe, then under construction) to celebrate his marriage to his second wife, Marie Louise.

The avenue's patriotic status was confirmed by the World War I victory parade of 14 July, 1919. Twenty-five years later, Charles de Gaulle followed the same triumphal route at the end of World War II. It remains the venue for national celebrations – the last leg of the Tour de France cycle race every July ends here, and it is the scene of great pomp on Bastille Day (14 July) and Armistice Day (11 November).

TAKING A BREAK

Have lunch or dinner at the bar or terrace of **Le Fouquet's** – the place to see and be seen – well placed at 99 avenue des Champs-Élysées (tel: 01 47 23 70 60).

Arc de Triomphe
🔛 202 B5
✉ place Charles-de-Gaulle-Étoile
☎ 01 55 37 73 77;
www.monum.fr
🕐 Daily 10 am–11 pm, Apr–Sep; 10 am–10:30 pm, Oct–Mar
Ⓜ Charles-de-Gaulle-Étoile
♿ Moderate

Avenue des Champs-Élysées
🔛 203 D4
Ⓜ George V, Franklin D Roosevelt, Charles-de-Gaulle-Étoile

ARC DE TRIOMPHE: INSIDE INFO

Top tips The best time to visit the Arc de Triomphe is early in the day, when the **morning light emphasises the details** of the sculptures, or late afternoon as the sun sets over the roof-tops. Glittering lights map out the city on an evening visit.

• **Don't try to cross the road** to reach the arch. Access is via a subway at the top of the Champs-Élysées.

• Take plenty of film with you as the **views are stupendous**. An orientation table at the top of the arch makes spotting the key landmarks easy.

• The **main tourist office** is a short walk away, at 127 avenue des Champs-Élysées.

One to miss The **small museum at the top of the arch** tracing its history is not particularly inspired.

6 Musée du Louvre

The centuries-old Musée du Louvre contains one of the largest, most important art collections in the world – more than 35,000 works of art are displayed. Whether you find your visit here breathtaking, overwhelming, frustrating or simply exhausting, one thing's for sure – you would need a lifetime to see everything. The key to a successful visit is to pace yourself, be selective and enjoy: you can always return tomorrow for more. Allow at least half a day, and be patient.

The museum buildings were originally a 12th-century hunting lodge, which later became a royal residence. A succession of rulers improved on and enlarged the complex. François I replaced the imposing keep with a Renaissance-style building and also started the Louvre's collections with 12 stolen Italian works of art, including the *Mona Lisa*.

In the 17th century, Louis XIV added works by Leonardo da Vinci, Raphael and Titian, and Napoléon filled the palace with artworks looted during his victorious years. The art collections were first opened to the public after the Revolution, in 1793.

Recent architectural additions include the glass pyramid entrance by Chinese-American architect Ieoh Ming Pei (1989), and the stunning renovation of the Richelieu wing (1993). With exhibition space almost doubling to 60,000sq m (645,900 square feet), it has become the largest museum in the world.

Below and right: Outside and inside the glass pyramid, added in 1989

The Wings – Finding Your Way

The collections are divided between three main wings – the Sully, the Richelieu and the Denon. Each has four levels, on which are arranged seven departments, each represented by a colour: yellow for Oriental

Antiquities/Arts of Islam; green for Egyptian Antiquities; blue for Greek, Roman and Etruscan Antiquities; red for Paintings; pink for Prints and Drawings; purple for Decorative Arts; light brown for Sculpture; dark brown for the History of the Louvre/Medieval Louvre.

TAKING A BREAK

The **Café Marly** at the Louvre makes a pleasant lunch stop.

🚼 204 B3
✉ 34–6 quai du Louvre
☎ 01 40 20 51 51 (recorded message); 01 40 20 53 17 (information desk); www.louvre.fr

🕐 Wed–Mon 9–6; evening opening Mon (part of the museum only) and Wed (the whole museum) until 9:45 pm. Closed Tue
🚇 Palais Royal-Musée du Louvre, Louvre Rivoli
💶 Moderate (reduced rate daily after 3 pm and on Sun). Free first Sun of the month

7 Centre Georges Pompidou

Known to Parisians as "le Beaubourg", the avant-garde Centre Georges Pompidou is one of the city's most distinctive landmarks and one of its most visited attractions. An X-ray-style extravaganza of steel and glass, striped by brightly coloured pipes and snake-like escalators, it looks as if someone has turned the whole building inside out. What's more, it contains one of the largest collections of modern art in the world.

Above and right: The famous inside-out building Below: Modern sculpture displayed within

It was in 1969 that President Georges Pompidou declared "I passionately want Paris to have a cultural centre which would be at once a museum and a centre of creation." The building caused an outcry when it was opened in 1977, in the heart of the then run-down Beaubourg district, and it has been the subject of controversy ever since, but it is generally acknowledged as one of the city's most distinctive landmarks – a lovable oddity, and far more popular as a gallery than anyone anticipated.

Before you go inside, pause to admire the centre's unique external structure, designed by Richard Rogers and Renzo Piano. Glass predominates, giving the entire edifice a transparency that abolishes barriers between street and centre. Steel beams cross-strutted and hinged over the length and width of the entire building form an intriguing external skeleton. Inside, walls can be taken down or put up at will, enabling the interior spaces to change shape for different displays.

On the outside, the building reveals all its workings by way of multi-coloured tubes, ducts and piping in "high-tech" style. Far from being merely decorative, they are carefully colour-coded: green for water, blue for air-conditioning and yellow for electricity.

Musée National d'Art Moderne

The Centre Georges Pompidou's main attraction is this collection of more than 50,000 works of contemporary art (of which about 2,000 are on display at any one time), starting from the early 20th century, roughly where the Musée d'Orsay (➤ 47–49) leaves off. Among the artist represented are Matisse, Derain, Chagall, Braque and Picasso. The collection also covers the futurists, surrealists, minimalists – you name it, it's here.

Displays change annually, so if there's a particular piece you're eager to view, visit the website to check that it's on show.

TAKING A BREAK

There is a **café** on the 1st floor and the ultra-cool restaurant, **Georges**, with sweeping views over the roof-tops of Beaubourg on the 6th floor.

Finding Your Way Around

There are six main floors:
• The **1st and 2nd floors** house an information library and a cinema.
• The **4th and 5th** floors house the permanent collections of the Musée National d'Art Moderne (MNAM). Works from 1905 to 1960 – the Collection Historique – are on the 5th, with the 4th reserved for more recent art – the Collection Contemporaine (1960–present) – and a room for viewing video-art. (Note that to reach the 5th floor you must enter the museum on the 4th floor.)
• The **1st and 6th** floors are for temporary exhibitions.
• The **basement and remaining floors** are used for all types of shows, films, meetings and documentation.

✚ 204 C3
✉ 19 place Georges-Pompidou
☎ 01 44 78 12 33;
www.centrepompidou.fr
🕓 Wed–Mon 11–10; MNAM and exhibitions close at 9 (11 Thu)
🚇 Rambuteau, Hôtel de Ville
✋ MNAM and exhibitions:
moderate–expensive

CENTRE GEORGES POMPIDOU: INSIDE INFO

Top tips If you are limited by time, stick to the exhibits on the **4th floor**, which tend to be the more frivolous, outrageous and highly entertaining works.
• Entrance to some of the temporary exhibitions is free, but for most you will need a ticket. If you are planning on spending several hours here, consider an **"all-gallery pass"**, which you validate in a Métro-style machine in each gallery. For details, ask at the information desk on the ground floor.

Hidden Gem *Josephine Baker* by sculptor Alexander Calder (1898–1976) is an early, elegant example of the mobile – a form that he invented.

At Your Leisure

8 Île St-Louis

When you tire of urban life, head for the Île St-Louis – an oasis of tranquillity at the heart of the city. The smaller of Paris's two islands, it has a village-like atmosphere, with tree-lined quays, matchless views of Notre-Dame and peaceful streets of grey stone mansions, built in the 17th century as an annexe to the fashionable Marais district.

One of the attractions of the island is its main street, rue St-Louis-en-l'Île, with its luxury shops, including Maison Berthillon – an ice-cream bought here is sure to be a highlight of your day.

➕ 204 C2
Berthillon ✉ 31 rue St-Louis-en-l'Île,
☎ 01 43 54 31 61 🕐 Wed–Sun 10–8.
Closed Mon, Tue (and mid-Jul to Aug)
🚇 Pont Marie

9 St-Germain-des-Prés

St-Germain is the literary and artistic heart of Paris, bursting with cafés, restaurants, antiques shops, art galleries and fashion boutiques, and is peopled by students, arty types, the wealthy socialist intelligentsia, and the simply rich, who come here to sample bohemian life. The area is now a luxury shopping district, with a spotlight on fashion, and such designers as Giorgio Armani, Christian Dior and Christian Lacroix have moved in from the Rive Droite.

The main artery, boulevard St-Germain, stretches from the Latin Quarter to the government buildings of the Faubourg St-Germain. Between the two world wars just about every notable Parisian artist, writer, philosopher and politician frequented three cafés on boulevard St-Germain – the Café de Flore (No 172), Brasserie Lipp (No 151) and Les Deux Magots (No 170). The Benedictine Abbey of St-Germain-des-Prés was founded in the 6th century, but only the Romanesque church – the oldest in Paris – survived the Revolution.

➕ 204 A2 🚇 St-Germain-des-Prés

Rodin's masterpiece, The Thinker, in the garden at Musée Rodin

10 Musée Rodin

Nowhere is more pleasurable on a sunny day than the sculpture-studded gardens of this open-air museum dedicated to the best-known sculptor of the modern age.

Rodin lived and worked in the adjoining elegant mansion – Hôtel Biron (1730), now the Musée Rodin – alongside Cocteau and Matisse. Inside are 500 sculptures, including such masterpieces as *The Kiss*, and *The Age of Bronze*, whose realism so startled the critics that they accused him of having imprisoned a live boy in the plaster. See Rodin's most celebrated work, *The Thinker*, in deep contemplation in the garden he loved.

➕ 203 E2 ✉ 77 rue de Varenne
☎ 01 44 18 61 10; www.musee-rodin.fr
🕐 Tue–Sun 9:30–5:45 (last entrance 5:15, park closes at 6:45), Apr–Sep; Tue–Sun 9:30–4:45 (last entrance 4:15, park closes at 5), Oct–Mar. Closed Mon, 1 Jan, 25 Dec 🍴 Café (9:30–6:30, Apr–Sep; 9:30–4:30, rest of year)
🚇 Varenne 💰 Moderate (garden only inexpensive)

The altar in the Église du Dôme

mansion near the Bois de Boulogne, it contains the world's largest collection of Monets, including *Impression – Soleil Levant* (the work that gave the Impressionist movement its name) and such celebrated series as *Cathédrale de Rouen* and *Parlement de Londres*, as well as paintings by other Impressionists such as Gauguin and Renoir.

🔢 202 A3 ✉ 2 rue Louis-Boilly
☎ 01 44 96 50 33 🕐 Tue–Sun
10–5:30 🚇 La Muette 💰 Moderate

🔟🔟 Les Invalides

The Hôtel National des Invalides was built in the 17th century as a convalescent home for wounded soldiers. Still a home to war veterans, it is now a memorial to the endless battles and campaigns that have marked French history, all vividly portrayed in the Musée de l'Armée.

Admission to the museum also buys a visit to the Musée de l'Ordre de la Libération and the 17th-century Église du Dôme. The golden dome of this church symbolises the glory of the Sun King, Louis XIV, who built the complex. Inside, the centre-piece is Napoléon's mausoleum: a circular crypt containing six coffins within a red porphyry sarcophagus. Adjoining the Dôme, the Soldiers' Church is more tasteful, decorated only by a row of poignantly faded tricolore pennants.

🔢 203 D2 ✉ esplanade des Invalides
☎ 01 44 42 37 72; www.invalides.org
🕐 Daily 10–5, Oct–Mar; 10–6,Apr–Sep.
Closed 1 Jan, 1 May, 1 Nov, 25 Dec, first
Mon of the month 🍴 Café 🚇 La
Tour Maubourg, Varenne, Invalides
🚉 RER Invalides 💰 Moderate

🔟🔟 Musée Marmottan

If you have visited the Musée d'Orsay (► 47–49) and thirst for more Impressionist art, this museum is a must. Set in an elegant 19th-century

🔟🔟 La Défense

This modern skyscraper district on the western outskirts of Paris bristles with around 60 ultra-modern highrise office buildings which create an atmosphere so different from the rest of the city that it's worth a brief visit.

The Grande Arche dominates La Défense

The highlight, designed by Danish architect Otto von Spreckelsen, is the

Napoléon Bonaparte

Napoléon is strongly associated with **Les Invalides**. Here he celebrated his military successes, staging grandiose parades on the Champ-de-Mars. He used the esplanade outside Les Invalides to show off his war spoils – guns captured in Vienna in 1803 and a lion statue plundered from St Mark's Square in Venice – and he honoured his victorious armies in Les Invalides and the nearby École Militaire, where he himself had trained as a young officer.

Grande Arche de la Défense (1989) – a hollow cube of white marble and glass symbolising a window open to the world and measuring 112m (368 feet) on each side.

La Grande Arche ✚ 202, off A5
✉ Parvis de La Défense ☎ 01 49 07 27 57 🕐 Daily 10–8, in summer; 10–7, in winter; last entry 30 minutes before closing 🚇 La Défense–Grande Arche 🚊 RER La Défense–Grande Arche 💰 Moderate

14 Place de la Concorde and Jardin des Tuileries

The vast, traffic-encircled square of place de la Concorde was laid out between 1755 and 1775, with a 3,300-year-old pink granite obelisk from the Temple of Rameses at Luxor in Egypt at its centre and eight female statues representing France's largest cities at its four corners. In 1793 the square was the scene of the execution of Louis XVI, and in the next two years a further 1,343 "enemies of the Revolution" were guillotined here. At the end of this Reign of Terror, the square was renamed to evoke peace.

On the east side, bordering the Seine, the Tuileries is one of the oldest and most beautiful public gardens in Paris. It was created in the 16th century by Catherine de' Médicis, and transformed in the 17th century by André Le Nôtre (of Versailles fame, ➤ 67) into a formal and symmetrical garden, studded with statues and embellished with box-edged flower beds, topiarised trees and gravel walkways.

Place de la Concorde
✚ 203 E4 🚇 Concorde

An Egyptian obelisk stands at the heart of Paris's main square

Jardin des Tuileries ✚ 203 F4
☎ 01 40 20 90 43 🕐 Daily 7 am–9 pm, Apr–Sep; 7:30–7, Oct–Mar
🚇 Tuileries, Concorde

15 La Villette

La Villette was for many years a livestock market, but in 1984 its 55ha (135 acres) were turned into a spectacular urban park and science city. The chief crowd-puller is the Cité des Sciences et de l'Industrie – a vast science and technology museum. In the main part, Explora, you can experience optical illusions, chat to a robot, and fly a flight simulator. On the ground floor, La Cité des Enfants introduces under-12s to basic scientific principles through games and dazzling hands-on displays. Don't miss La Géode, a giant, shiny steel marble with the world's largest hemispherical movie screen inside.

La Géode, at La Villette

✚ 204, off C5 ✉ Parc de la Villette
☎ Musique: 01 44 84 44 84; www.cite-musique.fr; Sciences: 01 40 05 12 12; www.cite-sciences.fr 🕐 Musique: Tue–Sun noon–6; Sciences: Tue–Sun 10–6. Closed Mon 🍴 Several cafés
🚇 Porte de la Villette 💰 Moderate

16 Musée Picasso

Hidden in a back street in one of the finest 17th-century mansions in the Marais, this outstanding museum contains an unparalleled collection of works by the most acclaimed artist of modern times. Picasso kept the majority of his works himself, and on his death in 1973, his heirs donated to the State 3,500-plus paintings, drawings, sketch books, collages, reliefs, ceramics and sculptures, which form the basis of this museum. A second contribution, after his wife died in 1986, enhanced the museum further. Together with numerous key works by Picasso himself, treasures from his private collection include works by Cézanne, Matisse, Miró, Renoir, Degas and Braque.

➕ 204, off C3 ⊠ Hôtel Salé, 5 rue de Thorigny ☎ 01 42 71 25 21 ⏰ Wed–Mon 9:30–6 (until 5:30 Oct–Mar). (Last entrance 45 minutes before closing.) Closed Tue, 1 Jan, 25 Dec ⓂSt-Paul, Chemin Vert, St-Sébastien-Froissart 🎟 Moderate

🔟 Place des Vosges

The oldest and most gracious square in Paris, place des Vosges' stately 17th-century town houses, laid out by Henri IV, are arranged symmetrically around an immaculately kept park, once a popular venue for duels. Novelist and poet Victor Hugo lived at No 6 from 1832 to 1848, and it is now a museum in his memory. Otherwise, the arcades house a variety of up-market galleries, antiques shops and elegant *salons de thé*.

After the Revolution the Marais district sank into decay, but following a major face-lift in the 1960s it has become one of the most lively and fashionable quartiers of central Paris, a magnet for elegant shops, fine restaurants and bars. Some of its restored mansions house museums, from the Musée Picasso (➤ above) to the Maison Européenne de la Photographie (5–7 rue de Fourcy).

➕ 204, off C2 Ⓜ St-Paul, Bastille, Chemin Vert

🔟 Cimetière du Père-Lachaise

This must be the world's most fascinating cemetery – a silent village with countless occupants in higgledy-piggledy tombs, and the

Mansions and gardens in place des Vosges

final resting place of Paris's most prestigious names: painters Corot, Delacroix, Pissaro and Ernst; composers Bizet and Chopin; writers Apollinaire, Daudet, Balzac, Molière and Proust; singers Maria Callas, Edith Piaf and former Doors lead vocalist, Jim Morrison, to name but a few. Oscar Wilde's grave is marked by a massive statue of a naked Egyptian flying skywards. Pick up a map at the entrance to see where the famous are buried.

➕ 204, off C2 ⊠ boulevard de Ménilmontant ☎ 01 55 25 82 10 ⏰ Mon–Fri 8–6, Sat 8:30–6, Sun 9–6, mid-Mar–5 Nov; Mon–Fri 8–5:30, Sat 8:30–5:30, Sun 9–5:30, 6 Nov–mid-Mar Ⓜ Père-Lachaise, Philippe Auguste, Gambetta

For Kids

• **Aquaboulevard** is an aquapark with waterslides and a wave machine, as well as other activities such as tennis and putting (4–6 rue Louis Armand, tel: 01 40 60 10 00, open daily, expensive).
• Take a walk through the **Jardin d'Acclimatation** park, with minigolf and playgrounds (boulevard des Sablons, Bois de Boulogne, inexpensive).
• The **Théâtre de la Mainate** offers puppet shows, story-telling and a kids' cabaret complete with clown, for children age two to eight (36 rue Bichat, tel: 01 42 08 83 33; performances Wed and Sat–Sun, Sep–May; moderate, credit cards not accepted).

MONTMARTRE AND SACRÉ-CŒUR

Walk

Explore the back streets of Paris's historic hilltop "village", with its leafy cobbled streets and steep stairways lit by iron lamps, its quaint whitewashed cottages and country gardens, its picturesque café-lined squares and its sweeping panoramas, and you will soon understand why so many generations of artists, writers and poets have fallen in love with this atmospheric neighbourhood.

DISTANCE 2 miles/3km **TIME** 2.5–3 hours
START POINT Place Blanche ➕ 204, off A5
END POINT Place des Abbesses ➕ 204, off A5

1–2
From **place Blanche** climb up **rue Lepic** past tempting delicatessens and cafés. Turn left at the top and branch right, still on rue Lepic. Van Gogh lived in an apartment at **No 54** from 1886 to 1888, taking his inspiration from the windmills and gardens of Montmartre.

2–3
Continue to climb rue Lepic, following the road round to the right. Note the steep flights of steps on your left leading up to countrified private villas, and high above you (opposite the junction with rue Tholozé), the **Moulin de la Galette**, once the venue for a notorious open-air cabaret. A few steps beyond (on the corner with rue Girardon), Montmartre's only other remaining windmill – **Moulin Radet** – is now part of a restaurant.

3–4
Turn left here, and cross **avenue Junot**, where artists Utrillo and Poulbot once lived at **Nos 11 and 13**. Soon after, turn left into **square Suzanne-Buisson**, a lovely secluded park where St Denis allegedly washed his decapitated head in a fountain. Today a statue of the saint marks the spot, overlooking a boules pitch.

4–5
Turn right at the statue, descend into **place Casdesus**, in rue Simon-Dereure and turn right

The Moulin Rouge, Montmartre's famous night spot

up several steps into **allée des Brouillards.** Here, the 18th-century Château des Brouillards on your right was once used as a shelter for homeless artists. Painter Pierre-Auguste Renoir lived and worked in one of the houses on the left from 1890 to 1897.

5–6
At the end of allée des Brouillards, carry straight on up the cobbled **rue de l'Abreuvoir**, once a country lane used by horses and cattle en route to the watering trough (*abreuvoir*) which stood on the site of No 15. **Number 14** was formerly the Café de l'Abreuvoir, frequented by many great artists

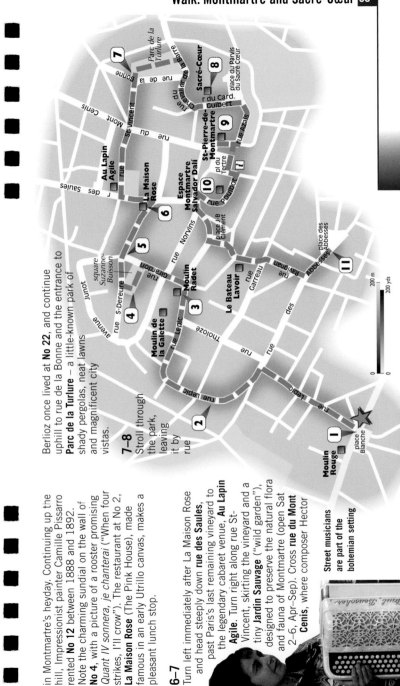

in Montmartre's heyday. Continuing up the hill, Impressionist painter Camille Pissarro rented **No 12** between 1888 and 1892. Note the charming sundial on the wall of **No 4**, with a picture of a rooster promising *Quant IV sonnera, je chanterai* ("When four strikes, I'll crow"). The restaurant at No 2, **La Maison Rose** (The Pink House), made famous in an early Utrillo canvas, makes a pleasant lunch stop.

6–7

Turn left immediately after La Maison Rose and head steeply down **rue des Saules**, past Paris's last remaining vineyard to the legendary cabaret venue, **Au Lapin Agile**. Turn right along rue St-Vincent, skirting the vineyard and a tiny **Jardin Sauvage** ("wild garden"), designed to preserve the natural flora and fauna of Montmartre (open Sat 2–6, Apr–Sep). Cross **rue du Mont Cenis**, where composer Hector

Berlioz once lived at **No 22**, and continue uphill to rue de la Bonne and the entrance to **Parc de la Turlure** – a little-known park of shady pergolas, neat lawns and magnificent city vistas.

7–8

Stroll through the park, leaving it by rue

Street musicians are part of the bohemian setting

crypt and dome is in rue du Cardinal Guibert.)

8–9

On leaving the Sacré-Cœur, head right along **rue Azaïs**, admiring the distant views of Paris as you go. A right turn up rue St-Eleuthère will lead you to the church of **St-Pierre-de-Montmartre**, consecrated in 1147.

9–10

As you leave the church, continue straight ahead into **place du Tertre**, once a delightful 18th-century village square, now a veritable tourist honeypot. Leave the square via **rue du Calvaire.** A right turn just before a descending flight of steps will lead you across cobbled place du Calvaire to rue Poulbot and the **Espace Montmartre Salvador Dalí,** which houses a permanent display of more than 300 works by the eccentric Spanish Surrealist artist, who died in 1989.

10–11

Follow **rue Poulbot** round to rue Norvins. Turn left, then almost immediately left again, and head downhill, passing the grassy square of place Jean-Baptiste Clément on your left. Turn right at the T-junction into **rue Ravignan,** and

follow the road round to the left into place Émile Goudeau, past Le Bateau-Lavoir on your right. Leave the square down a small flight of steps. Cross over rue Garreau and continue downhill on rue Ravignan. A left turn at the next T-junction will take you straight to the art nouveau Métro stop at **place des Abbesses** and the end of the walk.

Taking a Break

Avoid the pricey, tourist cafés in place du Tertre. Try **La Maison Rose** (tel: 01 42 57 66 75) on rue de l'Abreuvoir instead, or enjoy a leisurely picnic in the **Parc de la Turlure.**

When

This walk is best on a clear day, for the breathtaking views of the city. Avoid Sundays, when the district is always jam-packed.

Art noveau style at the entrance to the Métro

Steps in front of the basilica of Sacré-Cœur give a superb panorama over the city

du Chevalier de la Barre round the back of the **Sacré-Cœur,** and carrying on into **rue du Cardinal Guibert,** which runs alongside the basilica to its entrance on place du Parvis du Sacré-Coeur. (Note that the entrance to the

Further Afield

🔟 Chantilly

Chantilly, 48km (30 miles) north of Paris, has always enjoyed a reputation for fine cuisine, and the name of the town is indelibly associated with fresh whipped and sweetened cream, ordered in the best restaurants worldwide as *crème chantilly*.

Visitors today come not for the cream but for the impressive (albeit heavily restored) Renaissance **château**, with its exceptional art collection (including works by Corot, Delacroix and Raphael), and its palatial 17th-century stables which contain the **Musée Vivant du Cheval** (Living Horse Museum), known for dressage demonstrations.

➕ 219 E4 ☎ Château: 03 44 62 62 62; Musée Vivant du Cheval: 03 44 57 40 40 🕐 Château: Wed–Mon 10–6, Mar–Oct; Wed–Mon 10:30–12:45, 2–5, Nov–Feb. Musée Vivant du Cheval: Wed–Mon 10:30–5:30, Apr–Oct (and Tue May–Jun); Wed–Fri, Mon 2–5, Sat, Sun 10:30–5:30, Nov–Mar 💰 Château: moderate; Horse Museum: expensive 🚊 Numerous trains from Paris's Gare du Nord to Chantilly-Gouvieux.

🔟 Disneyland® Resort Paris

Despite a shaky financial start in 1992, this imported American theme park is now Europe's most popular

Snow White and Sleeping Beauty Castle

Further Afield

🔟 Chantilly ➤ 65
🔟 Disneyland® Resort Paris ➤ 65
2️⃣1️⃣ Chartres ➤ 66
2️⃣2️⃣ Fontainebleau ➤ 66
2️⃣3️⃣ Versailles ➤ 67

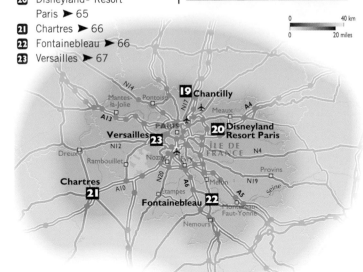

tourist destination. The Resort offers such thrilling rides as Big Thunder Mountain, Indiana Jones and the Temple of Peril: Backwards! (including 360-degree loops backwards) and, scariest of all, Space Mountain. Peter Pan, 'it's a small world' and Dumbo the Flying Elephant are geared to toddlers, and a whole host of American-style eateries, shops and parades ensure non-stop entertainment. There is also the Walt Disney Studios® Park.

While a visit to the Disneyland® Resort Paris is not an inexpensive option, for most children (and adults, too) it has to be the ultimate treat. Avoid weekends and mornings, when the queues are at their worst.

🚼 219 E3 ✉ Marne-la-Vallée
☎ 01 60 30 60 30 🕐 Times vary according to season; phone for the latest information 💷 Expensive (the 2- or 3-day "multipass" is good value)

The irregular towers of Chartres cathedral rise above the Beauce plain

🚇 The RER (line A) takes around 45 minutes–1 hour to reach Marne-la-Vallée or Chessy; the entrance to Disneyland is 100m (110 yards) from the station exit

21 Chartres

The wonder of Chartres is its cathedral, dedicated to Notre-Dame and rebuilt in the 13th century with uneven spires. Yet it is not the Gothic architecture which is the most memorable feature, but rather

Above: Topiary at Fontainebleau
Opposite: The formal gardens of Versailles

the glowing, jewel-like colours of its medieval stained glass. There are 176 windows in all, richly illustrating biblical scenes and activities of daily life, including shoemaking and weaving. They were designed to be read from bottom to top, and from left to right, starting with Old Testament scenes in the north wall, and ending with the Last Judgement on the east wall. There are no less than three rose windows.

If you can tear your eyes away from the rich glasswork, you'll discover an unusual labyrinth in the stone of the nave floor – a maze for devout pilgrims to crawl through on their knees.

A second church in the town centre, St-Pierre, also has fine medieval windows. More stained glass is on show in the Centre International du Vitrail, along with information about its preservation and restoration.

🚼 218 C3
Tourist Information Office ✉ place de la Cathédrale, BP289, 28005
☎ 02 37 18 26 26; www.ville-chartres.fr 🕐 Mon–Sat 10–6, Sun 10–1, 2:30–4:30 🚇 Trains from Paris's Gare Montparnasse take around one hour

22 Fontainebleau

If you can't face the crowds at Versailles (below), come to this château instead. It's equally grand

and surprisingly overlooked. This splendid royal residence, 65km (40 miles) southeast of Paris, started out as a hunting pavilion and ornamental fountain (hence the name) at the heart of a dense royal hunting forest – the Forêt de Fontainebleau. François I converted the lodge into the beautiful Renaissance château it is today: one of France's largest erstwhile royal residences (1,900 rooms), celebrated for its splendid interior furnishings and immaculate grounds.

🏛 219 E3 ☎ 01 60 71 50 70
🕐 Château: Wed–Mon 9:30–6, Jun–Sep; Wed–Mon 9:30–5, Oct–May. Gardens: daily 9–7, May–Sep; 9–6 Mar, Apr, Oct; 9–5, Nov–Feb. Closed 1 Jan, 1 May, 25 Dec 💶 Moderate 🚃 Trains leave Paris's Gare de Lyon approximately every hour for Fontainebleau-Avon. Then take Bus A to the château. Total journey time is about 1 hour

23 Versailles

This monumental palace, 23km (14 miles) southwest of Paris, is on every visitor's must-see list. And it's all thanks to one person – Louis XIV, the Sun King – whose extravagant taste, passion for self-glorification and determination to project both at home and abroad the absolute power of the French monarchy created one of France's great treasures.

Louis planned a palace large enough to house 20,000 courtiers. He commissioned the greatest artists and craftsmen of the day: architects Louis Le Vau and Jules Hardouin-Mansart planned the buildings; Charles Le Brun designed the interior; and the landscaper André Le Nôtre started on the 100ha (247 acres) of gardens. The building took 50 years, and as no expense was spared, it wrought havoc on the kingdom's finances.

The palace became the centre of political power in France and was the seat of the royal court from 1682 until 1789, when Revolutionary mobs massacred the palace guard and seized the despised King Louis XVI and Marie-Antoinette, dragging them to Paris and the guillotine.

The vast palace complex is divided into four main parts – the palace itself with its innumerable wings, sumptuous halls and chambers (only certain parts are open to the public), the extensive gardens and two smaller châteaux in the grounds, used as royal guesthouses – the Grand Trianon and the Petit Trianon.

The highlight is the grandiose **Galerie des Glaces** (Hall of Mirrors), where 17 giant mirrors face tall windows. In 1919 it was the scene of the ratification of the Treaty of Versailles, which ended World War I.

🏛 219 D3 ✉ 78000 Versailles ☎ 01 30 83 78 00; www.chateauversailles.fr
🕐 Grands Appartements: Tue–Sun 9–5:30 (Apr–Oct until 6:30). Grand Trianon and Petit Trianon: daily 12–5:30, Nov–Mar; 12–6:30, Apr–Oct (last admission 30 mins before closing). Gardens: 9–dusk. Closed some public holidays 💶 Palace: expensive; Grand Trianon and Petit Trianon (combined ticket): moderate (entrance to Versailles is free Oct–Mar on first Sun of the month); Gardens: inexpensive Mar–Oct, free rest of year 🚆 RER (Line C) to Versailles-Rive Gauche; main-line train from Gare Montparnasse to Gare des Chantiers; or train from Paris's Gare St-Lazare via La Défense to the Gare Rive Droite. All three stations are within walking distance of Versailles.

Where to... Stay

Prices
Expect to pay per night for a double room
€ up to €100   €€ €100–€200   €€€ over €200

Hôtel Franklin Roosevelt €€–€€€

Top-class shopping is just steps away from this smart hotel off the Champs-Élysées. Inside, you'll find thick carpets and rich red fabrics for a feel of luxury, along with a reading room and winter garden if you're looking for peace and quiet. Air-conditioning throughout.

✚ 202 C4 ⊠ 18 rue Clément Marot, 75008 Champs-Élysées ☎ 01 53 57 49 50; www.hroosevelt.com ⓜ Franklin D. Roosevelt, Alma Marceau

Pavillon de la Reine €€€

For serious luxury in a hotel fit for a queen, this former royal residence on the historic place des Vosges takes some beating. Louis XIII's queen, Anne of Austria, was responsible for the finest fittings, including the grand fireplace in the salon. Tapestries line the walls of the breakfast room. Style and a setting this good come at an appropriately breathtaking price.

✚ 204, off C2 ⊠ 28 place des Vosges, 75003 Le Marais ☎ 01 40 29 19 19; www.pavillon-de-la-reine.com ⓜ Notre-Dame-des-Champs, Montparnasse

Hôtel St-Merry €€–€€€

A former Renaissance presbytery close to the ultra-modern Centre Georges Pompidou is the intriguing location for this intimate hotel. Gothic touches in the public rooms include wood carvings and sculptures, and some of the ceilings display their original beams.

✚ 204 C3 ⊠ 78 rue de la Verrerie, 75004 Le Marais ☎ 01 42 78 14 15; www.hotelmarais.com ⓜ Hôtel-de-Ville, Châtelet

Hôtel Atlantis €€

There's a light, airy feel to this elegant two-star hotel, with sleek furniture and quilted bedspreads. Most of the 27 bedrooms overlook bustling place St-Sulpice, with its fountains and cafés, and all have satellite TV.

✚ 204 A2 ⊠ 4 rue du Vieux-Colombier, 75006 St-Germain-des-Prés ☎ 01 45 48 31 81; www.hotelatlantis.com ⓜ St-Sulpice

L'Atelier Montparnasse €€

The artistic enclave of Montparnasse in the 1930s gives this comfortable hotel its theme, with period furniture and paintings galore. Even the bathroom mosaics recall artwork of the age. Facilities are up-to-date, however, and include cable TV and minibars in the 17 bedrooms.

✚ 204 A1 ⊠ 49 rue Vavin, 75006 St-Germain-des-Prés ☎ 01 46 33 60 00; www.ateliermontparnasse.com ⓜ Notre-Dame-des-Champs, Montparnasse

Hôtel le Bouquet de Montmartre €

If you're looking for affordable, attractive accommodation in the heart of Paris, try this relatively simple, two-star hotel near the landmark basilica of Sacré-Cœur. Inside there's a comfortable blend of kitsch and classic Louis XVI styling, with candelabra wall lamps and small cupboards and alcoves in the 36 bedrooms making up for the lack of TV.

✚ 204, off A5 ⊠ 1 rue Durantin, 75018 Montmartre ☎ 01 46 06 87 54; www.bouquet-de-montmartre.com ⓜ Abbesses

Where to...
Eat and Drink

Prices
Expect to pay per person for a meal, excluding drinks
€ up to €25   €€ €25–€50   €€€ over €50

Bistro d'à Coté €€

Excellent regional cooking, especially that of Lyon, is the preserve of this, one of Michel Rostang's three successful and budget-conscious establishments serving modern versions of traditional dishes. Other branches are at 10 rue Gustave-Flaubert, 75017, tel: 01 42 67 05 81, and 16 avenue de Villiers, 75017, tel: 01 47 63 25 61. Specialities include fish, tempura of langoustines, chicken and foie gras tart, and calves' kidneys with red wine sauce. For dessert, try hot chocolate soufflé. There is a splendidly affordable wine list.

🚇 204 C2 ✉ 16 boulevard St-Germain, 75005 ☎ 01 43 54 59 10; www.michelrostang.com 🕐 Mon–Fri noon–2, 7.30–11.30, Sat 7.30–11.30 🚇 Maubert-Mutualité

Bofinger €€

A legendary brasserie, claiming to be Paris's oldest, close to place de la Bastille with an amazing turn-of-the-century belle époque interior that is a must on any visitor's list. The classic dishes here are oysters and a wealth of other shellfish, choucroute (sauerkraut), duck foie gras, steak tartare and grills with delicious home-made desserts and

ices to finish. The three-course fixed-price menu, including wine, is a popular choice and good value.

🚇 204, off C3 ✉ 5–7 rue de la Bastille, 75004 ☎ 01 42 72 87 82 🕐 Mon–Fri noon–3, 6:30–1 am, Sat, Sun noon–1 am 🚇 Bastille

Brasserie Flo €€

This famous brasserie has branches at the Printemps department store (▶ 70), Roissy airport and even in Tokyo and Beijing, but the original Flo still holds fort in this atmospheric location – along a narrow street off the colourful rue du Faubourg St-Denis. Banks of dripping shellfish outside and the bustling wooden-panelled interior tell you right away that you've come to a traditional Parisian brasserie. Friendly, efficient service complements the succulent steaks and fresh fish dishes – sole meunière is just one of the classic offerings – while the prune and armagnac vacherin (meringue and ice-cream dessert) is a perfect

finale to any meal. The wine list is faultless. Very busy at weekends until late.

🚇 204 C5 ✉ 7 cour des Petites-Écuries, 75010 ☎ 01 47 70 13 59 🕐 Daily noon–3, 7 pm–1:30 am 🚇 Château-d'Eau

Café de la Paix €

Famous customers have included Oscar Wilde, Emile Zola, Maurice Chevalier, Joséphine Baker and, not suprisingly given its Opéra-side location, Maria Callas and Placido Domingo. The interior was designed by the Opéra's architect, Charles Garnier, and the walls are decorated with fine Second Empire frescoes. Forget the fairly uninteresting restaurant and grab a terrace table (shielded by glass in the colder months) and indulge in the impeccable pâtisseries and mammoth ice-cream sundaes. Enormous baguette sandwiches filled with pâté, ham or salami should fuel your shopping sprees, while the coffee is also top quality, but expect to pay for the view of the opera house. A great place to observe the continuous flow of Parisian passers-by.

🕂 204 A5 ⊠ 12 boulevard des Capucines, 75009 ☎ 01 40 07 36 36 🕐 Breakfast 7 am; terrace 10 am–12:30 am; restaurant noon–12:30 am Ⓜ Opéra

La Rôtisserie d'En Face €€

Tucked away down a narrow street and across the road from his main restaurant at 14 rue des Grands-Augustins (tel: 01 43 26 49 39), this is one of Jacques Cagna's three cheaper dining options (the others are La Rôtisserie d'Armaillé and L'Espadon Bleu). The setting is lively and informal with a good choice of dishes bearing the Cagna hallmark of care and quality. The suckling pig and spit-roast chicken from the rôtisserie are particularly delicious. Look for game in season, and for dessert opt for the delicious fruit tart of the day.

🕂 204 B2 ⊠ 2 rue Christine, 75006 ☎ 01 43 26 40 98; www.jacques-cagna.com 🕐 Mon–Fri noon–2, 7–11, Sat 7–11:30. Closed Sat lunch, Sun Ⓜ Odéon/St-Michel

Taillevent €€€

Paris's most enduring "grand" restaurant, whose panelled walls and discreet service help to create a civilised and refined ambience favoured by the great and the good of the city's establishment. There is a wonderfully old-fashioned and classic basis to the cooking, with only a few modern trends. Specialities include *foie gras*, lobster and truffles. The chocolate dessert served with an unusual thyme ice-cream will round off your meal in style.

🕂 202 C5 ⊠ 15 rue Lamennais, 75008 ☎ 01 44 95 15 01; www.taillevent.com 🕐 Mon–Fri noon–2, 7:30–9:30. Closed Sat, Sun, Aug, public holidays Ⓜ George V

Where to...
Shop

Shopping is part of the fun of Paris – and if the stylish *haute couture* for which the city is famous is beyond your budget, at least there's no charge for window shopping.

At the other end of the scale, enjoy the markets – the floral displays of the *Marché aux Fleurs* near Notre-Dame (▶ 42); Montmartre's famous flea market, **Marché aux Puces de St-Ouen**, where you may find a bargain, after a bit of haggling; or the wonderful **Sunday organic market** (*marché biologique*) on boulevard Raspail, near Rennes Métro station.

DEPARTMENT STORES

No serious shopping trip would be complete without a visit to at least one of the great Paris department stores. **Bon Marché** (24 rue de Sèvres, tel: 01 44 39 80 00, Métro: Sèvres-Babylone) is the best department store on the Left Bank and houses the Grand Epicerie food hall. **Galeries Lafayette** and **Au Printemps** are glamorous neighbours offering perfumes, jewellery and ready-to-wear fashion. (Galeries Lafayette, 40 boulevard Haussmann, tel: 01 42 82 34 56, www.galerieslafayette.com, Métro: Chaussée d'Antin, Opéra, Trinité; Au Printemps, 64 boulevard Haussmann, tel: 01 42 82 50 00, www.printemps.fr, Métro: Havre-Caumartin).

La Samaritaine is in an art deco building, with a good view of Paris from the 10th-floor terrace (19 rue de la Monnaie, tel: 01 40 41 20 20, Métro: Pont Neuf). From the 11th floor you can observe the alignment of the Concorde Obelisk, the Arc de Triomphe and La Défense – and it's the only place in Paris where you can see this.

FOOD

Place de la Madeleine is home to two of the greatest luxury gourmet emporia, **Fauchon** at 26–30 (tel: 01 47 42 60 11, closed Sun, Métro: Madeleine) and **Hédiard** at 21 (tel: 01 43 12 88 88, closed Sun). These are a must for all *épicures*.

Alléosse, off avenue des Ternes, is one of the finest cheese shops in the city, where Camembert, *époisses*, *reblochon* and goat's cheese are brought to the peak of maturity (13 rue Poncelet, tel: 01 46 22 50 45, closed Sun afternoon, all Mon, Métro: Ternes). **La Ferme St-Aubin** (76 rue St-Louis-en-L'Île, tel: 01 43 54 74 54, closed Mon, Métro: Pont-Marie) has some 200 French and European cheeses on offer, all in peak condition. **Barthélémy (Sté)** is an old-fashioned cheese shop which supplies the homes of both the president and prime minister of France, well-stocked with Brie, Mont d'Or, Roquefort and many

other delights (51 rue de Grenelle, tel: 01 42 22 82 24, open Tue–Sat, Métro: rue du Bac).

For chocolate, try **Christian Constant** (37 rue d'Assas, tel: 01 53 63 15 15, Métro: Notre-Dame-des Champs-Elysées) and **Debauve et Gallais** (30 rue des Sts-Pères, tel: 01 45 48 54 67, Métro: St-Germain-des-Prés).

Les Caves Augé (116 boulevard Haussmann, tel: 01 45 22 16 97, Métro: St-Augustin) is the oldest wine shop in Paris.

FASHION AND ACCESSORIES

Colette, a relative newcomer, is the place to go for leading designs in both fashion and home furnishings – from Givenchy's Alexander McQueen to Tom Dixon and the latest from Sony (213 rue St-Honoré, tel: 01 55 35 33 90, www.colette.fr, Métro: Palais-Royal/Tuileries/Pyramides). The Water Bar, which has more than 100 brands of bottled water, in

the basement is a good place for a light snack.

The *crème de la crème of haute couture* and one of the most exclusive shopping streets anywhere, is **rue St-Honoré** in the 1st *arrondissement*. A stroll westwards from Palais-Royal reveals a roll-call of famous designer names. Rue Cambon, crossing rue St-Honoré, is where **Chanel** is based – the place for chic clothing, though the accessories are a little more affordable (31 rue Cambon, tel: 01 42 86 28 00, www.chanel.com, Métro: Concorde/Madeleine).

It's easy to spot **Louis Vuitton**'s store on the **Champs-Elysées** by the lengthy queues outside (101 avenue des Champs-Elysées, tel: 01 53 57 24 00, closed Sun, Métro: George). **Avenue Montaigne**, which crosses the Champs-Elysées, is a street of immense chic lined by the likes of **Christian Dior, Dolce e Gabbana, Celine, Nina Ricci, Ungaro** and **Valentino**.

Armani (149 boulevard St-Germain, tel: 01 53 63 33 50, Métro: St-Germain-des-Prés) has a store with a good coffee shop, not far from **Sonia Rykiel**'s ready-to-wear fashion house at No 175, with its excellent accessories and cosmetics (tel: 01 49 54 60 60).

Yves Saint Laurent for women is at 6 place St-Sulpice, tel: 01 43 29 43 00, www.ysl.com. The men's shop is at No.12 (tel: 01 43 25 84 40, Métro: Mabillon).

A small enclave of superior designer boutiques is located around **place de la Victoire**, which joins rue des Petits Champs and rue Étienne Marcel. A branch of innovative designer **Jean-Paul Gaultier**'s main store (30 rue du Faubourg St-Antoine, Métro: Bastille) is located here in Galerie Vivienne.

Agnès B, just northwest of the Forum des Halles, is an international chain of high repute offering sharply-cut clothes with original details (2–19 rue du Jour, tel: 01 45 08 56 56/01 42 33 04 13).

Where to...
Be Entertained

CINEMA

Mainstream and art house cinemas are numerous across the city, generally showing films in their original languages. Check out the listings pages in *Pariscope*.

UGC Ciné Forum Les Halles (7 place de la Rotonde, tel: 0892 70 00 00) is a 19-screen multiplex showing the latest releases. **La Pagode** (57 rue de Babylone, tel: 01 45 55 48 48, Métro: St-François Xavier) is probably the city's most charming cinema: shipped over in sections from Japan, it has velvet seats, painted screens and a Japanese garden. Cult classics and recent arty releases are shown in their original language on two screens. **La Géode** (26 avenue Corentin-Cariou, tel: 0892 68 45 40, Métro: Porte de la Villette) has a vast hemispheric screen, and shows movies specially adapted to its unusual technology.

THEATRE AND CONCERTS

The capital's greatest diversity of entertainment venues is located between the Louvre and the Arc de Triomphe on the Right Bank. Look out for concerts held in some of the most spectacular churches around the city, which are often free.

The Orchestre Nationale de France is based at **Maison de Radio-France** (116 avenue du Président-Kennedy, tel: 01 56 40 15 16), which also offers numerous free classical concerts and operas throughout the year. The elegant **Théâtre des Champs-Élysées** hosts opera, ballet, classical and chamber music orchestras. The imposing **Opéra Palais Garnier** offers a repertoire of beautifully staged operas and ballets (place de l'Opéra, tel: 0892 89 90 90, closed Aug, Métro: Opéra).

The **Comédie Française** presents quality productions by masters such as Molière and Shakespeare (2 rue de Richelieu, tel: 01 44 58 15 15, closed Jul–Sep, Métro: Palais Royal).

NIGHTLIFE

You'll find infinite variety in the city. The **Caveau de la Huchette** nightclub (5 rue de la Huchette, tel: 01 43 26 65 05, closed Sun, Métro: St-Michel), in medieval cellars, is always busy at weekends, with a lively mix of swing, boogie and rock. **Aux Trois Maillets** (56 rue Galande, tel: 01 43 54 00 79, Métro: St-Michel) is a terrific jazz café. **Le Saint** (7 rue St-Séverin, tel: 01 43 25 50 04, open Tue–Sat, Métro: St-Michel) is a small dance club playing music including techno and R&B.

If you speak some French, *Chansonniers* (singing cabarets) make a great night out with their mix of popular music and sharp-edged repartee. **Au Lapin Agile** (22 rue des Saules, tel: 01 46 06 85 87, closed Mon, Métro: Lamarck-Caulaincourt) is one of the best – book ahead. Montmartre is known for the rather risqué **Moulin Rouge** (82 boulevard de Clichy, tel: 01 53 09 82 82, Métro: Blanche). The **Lido de Paris** offers dinner and a spectacular show featuring the Bluebell Girls and special effects, twice nightly (116 bis avenue des Champs-Élysées, tel: 01 40 76 56 10).

Le Dépôt is a huge dance factory and a cult venue for the gay community in the heart of the Marais district (10 rue aux Ours, tel: 01 44 54 96 96, Métro: Étienne Marcel). Expect techno, house, disco and cabaret theme nights.

Northwest France

Getting Your Bearings 74 – 75
In Three Days 76 – 77
Don't Miss 78 – 85
At Your Leisure 86 – 88
Drive 89 – 90
Where to… 91 – 94

Getting Your Bearings

A coastline riddled with little sandy bays and dotted with fishing ports marks out the northwest corner of France. To the west, around Brittany's rugged peninsulas, the landscape is rockier and rougher, with ancient stones set upright in endless rows at Carnac. Eastwards through Normandy and Picardy the sands sweep more generously, and the holiday resorts are correspondingly more chic.

Of the bigger cities, Rouen and Rennes hold considerable historic interest, but the major harbour ports such as Brest and Le Havre are more workaday places, rebuilt after World War II. Motorways make for quick access inland and along the coast from Calais and other main Channel ports, but the real pleasure of this area is to be found away from the main roads, in the little towns and villages of rural Normandy and Brittany.

Inland from the sheltered bays, picturesque harbours and fishing ports you'll discover an ancient landscape in the west, where small communities such as St-Thégonnec take pride in their local tradition of carved stone calvaries and enclosed cemeteries. The rolling farmland of Normandy is a richer landscape, with timbered houses and great abbeys set amid orchards of cider apples and pears.

This land has been fought over for centuries, and you can follow trails of recent history – the battlefields of World War I around Amiens, and the D-Day beaches of World War II to the north of Caen.

Previous page:
Sauzan harbour
Below: Lighthouse
at Goury

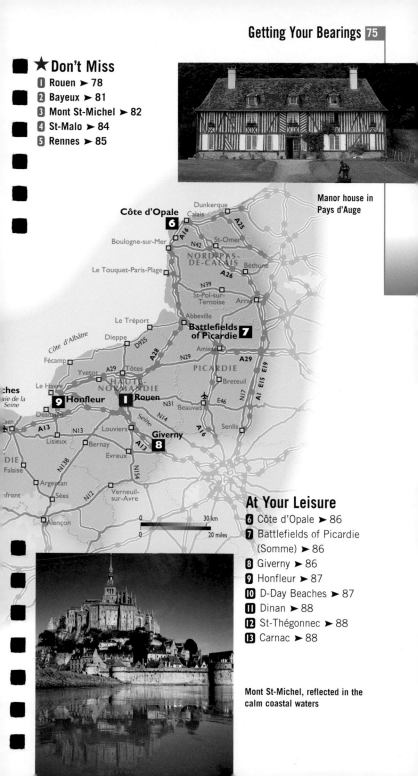

★ Don't Miss

1 Rouen ➤ 78
2 Bayeux ➤ 81
3 Mont St-Michel ➤ 82
4 St-Malo ➤ 84
5 Rennes ➤ 85

Manor house in Pays d'Auge

Côte d'Opale
6

Dunkerque
Calais
A25
Boulogne-sur-Mer
N42 St-Omer
NORD-PAS-DE-CALAIS
Béthune
A26
Le Touquet-Paris-Plage
N39
St-Pol-sur-Ternoise
Arras
Abbeville
Le Tréport
Battlefields of Picardie 7
Côte d'Albâtre
Dieppe
D925
Amiens
Fécamp
A28
N29
PICARDIE
A29
Yvetot
A29 Tôtes
Breteuil
ches
aie de la
Seine
Le Havre
HAUTE-NORMANDIE
9 Honfleur 1 Rouen
N31
Beauvais
A1 E15 E19
N17
E46
Deauville
A13
N13
Louviers
Giverny
8
Senlis
A16
Lisieux Bernay
A13
N14
Seine
DIE
N138
Evreux
N154
Falaise
N12
Verneuil-sur-Avre
nfront
Argentan
Sées
Alençon

0   30 km
0   20 miles

At Your Leisure

6 Côte d'Opale ➤ 86
7 Battlefields of Picardie (Somme) ➤ 86
8 Giverny ➤ 86
9 Honfleur ➤ 87
10 D-Day Beaches ➤ 87
11 Dinan ➤ 88
12 St-Thégonnec ➤ 88
13 Carnac ➤ 88

Mont St-Michel, reflected in the calm coastal waters

Three days is enough for a quick taste of the northern coast
of this diverse region – allow more time to make the
most of Brittany, and an extra day to include the scenic
drive to Cap Fréhel.

Northwest France in Three Days

Day One

Morning

Plan to spend most of your day exploring **⊞Rouen** (below, ➤78–80). Start
at the **tourist office** on place de la Cathédrale (➤80), look into the **cathedral** (➤79), and stroll around the **old quarter** to the northeast of here.

Afternoon

After a light lunch at the **Salon de Thé Marianne** (➤80), visit the **Musée
des Beaux Arts** (➤79).

Evening

Take the D982 west towards Le Havre, then the N15 and turn south on
the D929 to spend the evening in one of the restaurants around the
picturesque harbour at **⊡Honfleur** (➤87).

Day Two

Morning
Head west on the minor coastal roads, passing through Ouistreham and the **10 D-Day Beaches** (➤ 87). Turn inland on the D516 for **2 Bayeux** (left, ➤ 81) and its famous tapestry. Dine at the historic inn, **Le Lion d'Or** (➤ 81).

Afternoon
Take the D572 to St-Lô, then head south towards Avranches via the coast roads, then the minor D43 to the unmissable island-bound abbey of **3 Mont St-Michel** (➤ 82–83).

Evening
Stay here into the evening, and enjoy the peace when the day-trippers have moved on, before taking the D797 and D155 to **St-Malo** for the night.

Day Three

Morning
Explore the historic port of **4 St-Malo** (➤ 84), enjoying the views from the ramparts, and consider whether to take an extra day here and include the **Cap Fréhel Drive** (➤ 89–90) in your itinerary. Lunch on crêpes at **La Gallo** (➤ 84).

Afternoon
Head west along the coast, then south from Ploubalay on the D2 to visit the medieval town of **11 Dinan** (right, ➤ 88). Continue south on the D68, joining the N137 into **5 Rennes** (➤ 85), where the old masters in the **Musée des Beaux-Arts** and the timbered buildings of **rue de Psalette** are the must-see attractions.

ⓘ Rouen

Rouen, the capital of the Normandy region, is a thriving city with a compact historic heart. Despite severe bomb damage sustained during World War II, the centre of the old city has been restored with care and sensitivity, making it a fascinating place to explore. Rouen straddles the River Seine, and its two outstanding landmarks are the magnificent medieval Gothic cathedral, and the place du Vieux Marché, where Joan of Arc, the heroine who led the French army successfully against the occupying English, was burned at the stake on 30 May, 1431 at the age of just 19.

A port at Rouen was established in Roman times, but the city's fortunes were made with the arrival of the Dukes of Normandy in the Middle Ages. The magnificent medieval timbered buildings bear witness to its later success as France's fourth major port. The cathedral of **Notre-Dame** was built between the 12th and 16th centuries, and is a highlight of any tour. Its distinctive spire stands 151m (495 feet) high.

Above: Cascading geraniums adorn
a timbered hotel in the old city

Just along the pedestrianised rue du Gros Horloge is another famous landmark, a huge **one-handed clock**, which is mounted on a carved Renaissance arch above the street. The clock dates back to the 14th century, and was moved to this highly visible location in the 16th century.

West again from here is **place du Vieux Marché**, where a large cross marks the spot where Joan of Arc was martyred. In the north-east corner stands a remarkable modern church (1981) dedicated to the saint, which incorporates stained glass from a much older church that was destroyed during the bombing raids of World War II.

Two sites to the northeast of the cathedral are worth a look. One is the 14th-century church of **St-Ouen**, with its superb truncated, lacy Gothic spire. In the churchyard here, Joan of Arc recanted when first threatened with being burned to death, on 24 May. The other is a pretty courtyard of timbered buildings called the **Aître St-Maclou**, on rue Martainville (open 8–8, free). It was built on the site of a charnel house, in use after the Great Plague of 1348 swept through the town, and is now occupied by the School of Fine Arts.

There's an impressive collection of paintings to see in the **Musée des Beaux-Arts**, including works by Renoir and Monet.

Above: Overview of the city
from Vista Point

Left: Joan of Arc, the city's
celebrated martyr – statue in
the place du Vieux Marché

Right: Carvings on the Portail
des Marmousets gateway

Gustave Flaubert (1821–80)

Flaubert is the city's most famous son. The great novelist and scourge of bourgeois society, notorious for keeping a parrot on his desk while writing *Un coeur simple* (1877), was born at 51 rue de Lecat. His best-known novel was his first, *Madame Bovary* (1857), about the adulterous life and eventual suicide of a provincial doctor's wife. The tale was condemned and the author prosecuted unsuccessfully for immorality, causing a great scandal of the day.

Gustave Flaubert was the son of a noted surgeon in the town, and his birthplace doubles as an intriguing museum dedicated to the history of medicine.

TAKING A BREAK

The centrally placed **Salon de Thé Marianne**, at 6 rue Massacre, is perfect for a breakfast top-up, a light lunch or an afternoon snack (tel: 02 35 89 33 36).

A superb carved staircase rises above the Portail des Libraires, in the cathedral

✚ 218 C4

Tourist Information Office
✉ 25 place de la Cathédrale, BP 666, 76008
☎ 02 32 08 32 40; www.rouen.fr;
www.rouentourisme.com ◷ Mon–Sat 9–7,
Sun and public hols 9:30–12:30, 2–6,
May–Sep; Mon–Sat 9–6, Sun and public hols
10–1, Oct–Apr

Musée des Beaux-Arts
✉ esplanade Marcel-Duchamp, 76000
☎ 02 35 71 28 40 ◷ Wed–Mon 10–6
🎟 Inexpensive

Musée Flaubert et d'Histoire de la Médicine
✉ 51 rue de Lecat, 76000 ☎ 02 35 15 59 95
◷ Wed–Sat 10–noon, 2–6, Tue 10–6

ROUEN: INSIDE INFO

Top tips The old centre of Rouen is compact enough to **explore easily on foot**, so don't worry about métro maps and bus routes. The railway station is also central and has good connections to Paris.

• Start any visit by calling in to the tourist office, opposite the cathedral. Dating from 1509, it's **an attraction in its own right** as Rouen's oldest Renaissance building, and the place where Monet sat to paint his famous series of images, *Cathédrales de Rouen* (1892–93).

• The **Bon Weekend en Ville** two-for-one promotion means that weekend visitors to Rouen can get discounts on accommodation and museum entry.

• For extra events, time your visit to coincide with the **annual Joan of Arc cultural festival**, in the last week of May. On the last Sunday of that month, children throw flowers from the Boïeldieu Bridge in memory of the saint, whose ashes were scattered from the same spot. Her feast day is celebrated on 30 May.

Hidden gem In local antiques shops you're likely to see the distinctive local blue-and-white pottery or faïence, known as Rouenware. It gets a museum all to itself, the **Musée de la Céramique** (1 rue de Faucon, tel: 02 35 07 31 74, open Wed–Mon 10–1, 2–6, inexpensive).

One to miss Unless you're a particular fan of 17th-century dramatist Pierre Corneille, skip the **Musée Corneille** at 4 rue de la Pie.

2 Bayeux

An extraordinary account of the invasion of England in 1066, Bayeux's famous tapestry reads like a medieval cartoon, as fresh today as when it was stitched in the 11th century. It's the highlight of this preserved small town: visit out of season or be prepared to wait in line for this top attraction.

See the tapestry around the walls of its own museum, well signed in the town centre. It's actually an embroidery, using wool on linen, and the accompanying exhibition gives an insight into its design and creation. The margins at the top and bottom of the tapestry repay closer study – while some of the designs are purely ornamental forms such as dragons and whimsical curls, other sections depict side-aspects to the main action, such as fallen warriors. Multi-lingual audioguides help to pick out notable events including the arrival of Halley's Comet and the assassination of King Harold.

Elsewhere in the town, the 11th- to 15th-century **cathedral** is worth a look for the relief carving which depicts the murder of English archbishop Thomas à Becket in Canterbury in 1170. The Normandy Landings of 1944 are commemorated in the **Musée Mémorial**.

Tapestry Facts
Commissioned by Bishop Odo, half-brother of William the Conqueror
Length 70m/230 feet
Width 50cm/20 inches
Stitched by nuns from 1070 to 1080
Made in England

TAKING A BREAK

For a top-notch lunch of regional specialities, try the 18th-century former coaching inn, **Le Lion d'Or** (71 rue St-Jean, tel: 02 31 92 06 90, closed Jan).

➕ 217 F4

Tourist Information Office
✉ Pont St-Jean, 14400 ☎ 02 31 51 28 28; www.bayeux-tourism.com
🕐 Mon–Sat 9–7, Sun 9–1, 2–7, Jun–end

Aug; Mon–Sat 9:30–12:30, 2–5:30, Jan–end Mar, Oct–Dec; daily 9:30–12:30, 2–6, Apr, May, Sep

Bayeux Tapestry
✉ Centre Guillaume Le Conquérant, rue

de Nesmond ☎ 02 31 51 25 50 🕐 Daily 9–6:30, mid-Mar to end Apr, Sep–Oct; 9–7, May–Aug; 9:30–12:30, 2–6, Nov to mid-May 👣 Moderate

Musée Mémorial de la Bataille de

Normandie
✉ boulevard Fabien Ware, 14400
☎ 02 31 51 46 90
🕐 Daily 10–12:30, 2–6, mid-Sep to Apr; 9:30–6:30, rest of year; closed mid-Jan to end Jan
👣 Moderate

Mont St-Michel is a must-see sight on every visitor's itinerary, an unmistakable vision rising from the shallow waters of its own bay on the north coast. The site, perched high on a rock, just off-shore, has been drawing pilgrims since the first century. Although the sheer number of visitors threatens to choke it at the height of summer, the fairytale appearance of the mount, with a village huddled below and the rock topped by the 157m (515-foot) Gothic spire of the abbey church, cannot fail to delight the eye.

The first chapel was built here by St Aubert, Bishop of Avranches, in 708. Benedictine monks built a Romanesque church on the rock between the 11th and 17th centuries, transporting the granite blocks across the quicksands from the Îles Chausey to the north. A guided tour of the **abbey** reveals a treadmill which operated a pulley system to haul the building materials up to the site. The gold statue of St Michael on the tip of the spire was added in 1897. There's still a monastic community here, which helps

Above: Mont St-Michel, with a statue of St Michael inside the abbey
Below: The mount is a high point in this flat landscape

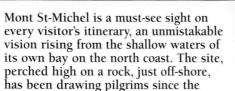

to counterbalance the touristy feel of the village below.

The Mount is linked to the mainland by a causeway, north of Pontorson, but a project to dig out the silt and return the sea to this part of the bay means this will be replaced by a bridge (due to complete in 2007). Buses go to the Mount from Rennes and St-Malo, the former connecting in the morning with the TGV rail link at Rennes. The nearest railway station, Pontorson, is 9km (5.5 miles) away. The present car park by the causeway is to be replaced with a bigger one, 1km (0.5 mile) south of the coast road, on the mainland. The parking charge will include a free shuttle bus service (and eventually rail link) to the Mount.

Ready-Seasoned Lamb

Mouton pré-salé is naturally pre-salted lamb, considered a delicacy throughout France. It comes from the sheep which graze the salty pastures and samphire at the margins of the Baie du Mont St-Michel, and is usually served lightly grilled, without need for further seasoning.

TAKING A BREAK

Enjoy the seafood and the views over the bay from **Du Guesclin**, on Grande Rue. There's even a kids' menu (tel: 02 33 60 14 10, closed Nov–Mar).

➕ 217 E3

Tourist Information Office
✉ BP4, Mont St-Michel 50170
☎ 02 33 60 14 30; www.ot-montsaintmichel.com 🕐 Mon–Sat 9–7, Sun 9–6, Jul–Aug; Mon–Sat 9–12:30, 2–6:30, Sun 9–noon, 2–6, May–Jun, Sep; Mon–Sat

9–noon, 2–6, Sun 10–noon, 2–5, Apr, Oct; Mon–Sat 9–noon, 2–5:30, Sun 10–noon, 2–5, Nov–Mar

The Abbey
☎ 02 33 89 80 00; www.monum.fr
🕐 Daily 9–7, May–Aug; 9:30–6, rest of year
🎫 Moderate; audioguide available

MONT ST-MICHEL: INSIDE INFO

Top tips Entry to the Abbey costs €7 except at midday mass, when you can get in and **explore for free**.
• If the Grand Rue is choked with visitors, make your way straight up the steps to the **abbey ramparts**, from where the views are superb.

④ St-Malo

The most magnificent and appealing of the Channel ports, St-Malo has a rich background of adventurers and pirates to discover, along with 1.6km (1 mile) of walls around the immaculately restored old town centre. This area, known as the Intra Muros (within the walls), includes lively outdoor cafés and some stylish shops.

Top: The harbour entrance

Right: Gardens in the Marché aux Légumes
Below: Sun-bathing below the ramparts

✚ 217 E3
Tourist Information Office
✉ esplanade St-Vincent, 35400 ☎ 02 99 56 64 48; www. saint-malo-tourisme.com
🕐 Mon–Sat 9–7:30, Sun 10–6, Jul–Aug; Mon–Sat 9–12:30, 1:30–6, Sep–Jun

Cathédrale St-Vincent
✉ place Jean de Châtillon
☎ 02 99 40 82 31 🕐 Daily 9–6

Musée d'Histoire
✉ Château de St-Malo
🕐 Closed Mon, Sep–Jun
🎫 Inexpensive

The heart of St-Malo was bombed out during World War II, and what you see today is a careful reconstruction, including the **Cathédrale St-Vincent** with its medieval stained glass. A mosaic here recalls the navigator Jacques Cartier (1491–1557), who discovered and first explored Newfoundland, in Canada. The massive grey fort holds a **museum of local history**, including information about nautical heroes and villains such as privateers René Dugay-Trouin and Robert Surcouf, who brought such wealth to the town.

Climb the steps on to the 14th-century **ramparts** for the best views, with the old town on one side, the sea on the other, and Dinard on the opposite bank of the Rance estuary. You can also follow the causeway out to the rocky tidal island of **Grand Bé**, where the romantic writer Chateaubriand (1768–1848) is buried.

TAKING A BREAK

Tuck into the local speciality – freshly made *crêpes*, with savoury or sweet fillings, at **La Gallo**, a venerable *crêperie* in the old part of town (21 rue de Dinan, tel: 02 99 40 84 17).

5 Rennes

The Breton capital is a fine old mixture of 15th-century timbered houses and grand 18th-century architecture in the classical style, imposed after a devastating fire all but destroyed the city in 1720. Today it's a bustling, sprawling place with its own (single) métro line and a wide industrial hinterland that includes the headquarters of the famous car manufacturer Citroën, but the centre has some notable features which make it well worth exploring.

Start at the tourist office, for a quick overview of the history, and pick up a walking tour leaflet (in French only). The tourist office also has a free leaflet detailing the history of the city.

Top of the attractions is the **Musée des Beaux-Arts**, with a host of paintings by the old masters, including Rubens and da Vinci, as well as more modern works by the likes of Gauguin and Picasso. Look out for the 16th-century carved wooden altar panels in the **Cathédrale St-Pierre**, and admire the restored timber-framed roof of the **Palais du Parlement de Bretagne**. When you've looked in the cathedral, stroll along the **rue de la Psalette** just behind it for some of the best medieval houses in Rennes. Saturday is market day in the place des Lices, with fresh vegetables galore (ends 1 pm).

The hilltop **Parc du Thabor** is a public park where you can break for a picnic or just enjoy the open green spaces.

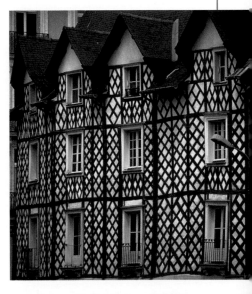

Decorative timbering on houses in the old town

TAKING A BREAK

Treat yourself to roast sausage with apple *compote* at the popular **Le Bocal-P'ty Resto** (6 rue d'Argentré, tel: 02 99 78 34 10, Métro: République).

➕ 217 E2

Tourist Information Office
✉ 11 rue St-Yves, 35000
☎ 02 99 67 11 11;

www.tourisme-rennes.com
🕐 Mon–Sat 9–7, Sun 11–6, Apr–Sep; Mon–Sat 9–6, Sun 11–6, Oct–Mar

Musée des Beaux-Arts
✉ 20 quai Émile Zola, 35000
☎ 02 99 28 55 85
🕐 Mon–Wed 10–noon, 2–6
💷 Inexpensive

At Your Leisure

6 Côte d'Opale

The Opal Coast lies between Le Crotoy and Dunkerque, an area of cliffs, sand dunes and beaches studded with busy commercial ports and seaside resorts. **Cap Gris-Nez** (45m/147 feet) is at the northwest corner, and on a clear day you can see all the way to England. Louis Blériot made the first flight across the Channel from the beach at Calais in 1909, and the glamour of aviation in the early 20th century helped to establish **Le Touquet** as one of the finest resorts along here. **Dunkerque**, now France's third largest port, was almost totally destroyed in World War II. Find out more about the famous events of 1940, when 350,000 Allied troops were evacuated by sea from here, at the **Mémorial du Souvenir**.

➕ 222 B3
Tourist Information Office ✉ rue de l'Admiral Ronarc'h, 59140 Dunkerque ☎ 03 28 66 79 21; www.ot-dunkerque.fr ⏱ Mon–Sat 9–12:30, 1:30–6:30, Sun 10–noon, 2–4
Mémorial du Souvenir ✉ rue des Chantiers de France ☎ 03 28 66 79 21 ⏱ Daily 10–noon, 2–5:30, May–Sep

7 Battlefields of Picardie (Somme)

Fields of white crosses across the Somme commemorate the fallen of World War I

The gentle farmland around the River Somme today seems a world away from the muddy trenches of World War I, but the vast, neatly tended graveyards are a poignant reminder that more than one million young men died in the appalling fighting here. The 60km (37-mile) **Circuit de Souvenir**, starting from the town of Albert and signed with a poppy, takes in the key battlefields, cemeteries and museums. Sites include the dramatic **Mémorial**

The familiar bridge over the lily pond in Monet's garden at Giverny

Franco-Britannique at Thiepval, which recalls 73,367 French and British soldiers whose bodies were never found, and the Canadian **Vimy Parc Memorial** at Vimy Ridge.

➕ 222 C1
Tourist Information Office ✉ 9 rue Léon Gambetta, Albert, BP 82, 80300 ☎ 03 22 75 16 42; www.ville-albert.fr ⏱ Mon–Fri 9–12:30, 1:30–6:30, Sat 9–noon, 2–6:30, Sun 10–12:30, Apr–Sep; Mon–Fri 10–12:30, 1:30–5, Sat 9–noon, 3–5, Oct–Mar

8 Giverny

Claude Monet's home and the garden which inspired his series of water lily paintings are well worth a detour, especially in early summer when the gardens look their best. Monet, born in Paris in 1840, was a founder of the Impressionist school of painting, capturing light and colour in his landscapes. He lived here from 1895 until his death in 1926, by which time he was a recluse. The gardens, willow-fringed ponds and wooden bridge will be familiar to anyone who has admired his paintings, and the interior of the house reflects the artist's delight in colour and pattern. Come early to avoid the crowds.

➕ 218 C4
Tourist Information Office ✉ 36 rue Carnot, 27201 Vernon ☎ 02 32 51 39 60; www.ville-vernon27.fr
🕐 Tue–Sat 9:30–12:15, 2:15–6:30, Sun 10–noon, May–Aug; Tue–Sat 10–noon, 2–5, Sep–Apr
Fondation Claude Monet
✉ rue Claude Monet, 27620 ☎ 02 32 51 28 21; www.fondation-monet.com
🕐 Wed–Mon 9:30–6, Apr–Oct
💵 Moderate

🟨 Honfleur

Honfleur is the picturesque old harbour town that artists love to paint, and with its tall slate-fronted and timbered buildings, fishing craft and romantic corners, it's easy to see why. Eugène Boudin (1824–98) was born here and became one of the first artists to paint outdoors. You can catch his work, including local views, in the **Musée Eugène Boudin**, in place Erik Satie. The square is named after the composer and Honfleur's second famous son, who is celebrated in the **Maison Satie** on boulevard Charles V. There are lots of good fish restaurants to explore at leisure, too.

➕ 218 B4
Tourist Information Office
✉ place Arthur Boudin, 14602
☎ 02 31 89 23 30 🕐 Daily 9:30–7, Jul–Aug; 10–12:30, 2–6:30, Sep; Mon–Sat 9:30–12:30, 2–6:30, Sun 9:30–12:30, 2–5, Easter–Jun; Mon–Sat 9:30–noon, 2–6, Oct–Easter
Musée Eugène Boudin
✉ place Erik Satie ☎ 02 31 89 54 00
🕐 Wed–Mon 10–noon, 2–6, mid-Mar to Sep; Mon, Wed–Fri 2:30–5, Sat–Sun

10–noon, 2:30–5, mid-Feb to mid-Mar and Oct–Dec 💵 Moderate
Maison Satie
✉ boulevard Charles V ☎ 02 31 89 11 11 🕐 Wed–Mon 10–7, May–Sep; Wed–Mon 11–6, mid-Feb to May and Oct–Dec 💵 Moderate

🔟 D-Day Beaches

The beaches of the Normandy coast along the Baie de la Seine became the focus of the war in Europe on the night of 5 June, 1944, when Allied troops began a massive invasion from England to kick-start the liberation of France. Parachute and glider forces of the American 88th and 101st Airborne Division led the way, followed by 4,000 landing craft which arrived on the five key beaches at dawn, codenamed Sword, Juno, Gold, Omaha and Utah. A free

Cafés on the waterfront at Honfleur

booklet from local tourist offices, *The D-Day Landings and The Battle of Normandy*, outlines events and locations, including Arromanches, the American cemetery at Colleville-sur-Mer, and the Mémorial Pegasus museum in Ranville.

➕ 218 A4
Tourist Information Office ✉ place St-Pierre, 14000 Caen ☎ 02 31 27 14 14; www.caen.fr/tourisme 🕐 Mon–Sat 9–7, Sun 10–1, 2–5, Jul–Aug; Mon–Sat 9:30–6:30, Sun 10–1, Apr–Oct; Mon–Sat 9:30–1, 2–5, Sun 10–1, Nov–Apr

Boats along the River Rance, Dinan

🌀 Dinan

The cobbled **rue de Jerzual**, at the heart of this medieval town, is one of the most photographed streets in all Brittany. Explore the narrow lanes of the old quarter on foot, past timbered merchants' houses (the best are on **place Merciers**) and the Gothic **Église St-Malo**, and the **Basilique St-Sauveur**, where the remains of a 14th-century soldier and local hero, Bertrand du Guesclin, lie entombed. Sections of the town's ramparts can still be followed, and you can climb the 16th-century **clock tower**, presented to the town by Duchesse Anne in gratitude for refuge, for great views over and beyond the town.

➕ 217 D3
Tourist Information Office ✉ 9 rue du Château, 22105 ☎ 02 96 87 69 76; www.dinan-tourisme.com ⏰ Mon–Sat 9–7, Sun 10–12:30, 2:30–6, Jun–Sep; Mon–Sat 9:30–12:30, 2–6:30, Oct–May

🌀 St-Thégonnec

If you only see one traditional Breton **parish close**, then this is the one to go for – St-Thégonnec has one of the finest, most exuberantly carved examples in the country. The calvary dates from 1610, and its many stone figures are in medieval dress. They portray the events of Christ's Passion, but slightly out of order – the cross was dismantled and hidden for safety during the Revolution, and may have been wrongly reassembled. The interior of the church is an ostentatious revelation of the wealth of this parish in the 17th and 18th centuries, with statues and altar-pieces, and a magnificent carved wooden pulpit.

➕ 216 B3 ⏰ Daily 9–6 (no visits during Sunday mass at 10:30)

🌀 Carnac

More than 3,000 standing stones and other prehistoric monuments are found in and around Carnac, dating to between 5000 to 2000 BC. Three of the biggest groups of stones (*menhirs*) are carefully set in long parallel lines (*alignements*) to the north of the town, and their purpose – religious, astrological or ritual – is a total mystery. Wander among the stones at **Kermario** and discover the extent of this extraordinary site from the scale model in the information centre there, open daily.

The nearby resort of **Carnac-Plage** offers a choice of six beaches, with plenty of bars, restaurants and smart villas.

➕ 216 C1
Tourist Information Office ✉ place de l'Église, Carnac ☎ 02 97 52 13 52 (Carnac-Plage); www.carnac.fr ⏰ Mon–Sat 9–12:30, 2–7, Sun 9–12:30, Apr–Sep

For Kids

• **Carnac:** When gazing at standing stones tires, buy them a *niniche*, or long, thin lollypop from the sweet shop of the same name, at 7 avenue du Parc (open daily 9:30–12:30, 2:30–7, Apr–Sep).

• **Dinan:** Discover the zoo and play-ground in the grounds of the Château de Bourbansais, east of town at Pleugueneuc (tel: 02 99 69 40 07, open daily 10–7, Apr–Sep; 2–6 Oct–Mar, expensive).

• **Plailly:** Cartoon heroes Astérix and Obélix star at Parc Astérix, with all the rides, shows and attractions you could hope for. The park is signed off the A1 between Paris and Lille (tel: 03 44 62 30 30, www.parcasterix.fr, open Apr–Oct, expensive).

CAP FRÉHEL AND THE CÔTE D'EMERAUDE

Drive

Pristine sandy beaches, a medieval bastion set on high cliffs, fabulous views from a historic lighthouse, and the inland contrasts of the Forêt de la Hunaudaye are just some of the riches on offer on this easy day's route. The Côte d'Emeraude, or Emerald Coast, is a rugged corner on the northern coastline, just west of St-Malo, which gives way to the pink sandstone cliffs and sandy bays of the Côtes d'Armor to the west.

DISTANCE 92km (57 miles) **DRIVING TIME** 2–3 hours, but allow most of a day to give yourself plenty of time to enjoy the beaches along the route
START/END POINT Lamballe ⊞ 217 D3

1–2

Start near the splendid Gothic church in the hillside village of **Lamballe**. This area is known throughout France as the home of the national stud farm, or *haras national* (tours daily Jul–Aug, Wed, Sat, Sun pm Sep–Jun). Head east out of the village on the D28, then bear right on to the D52a, signposted to Plédéliac. Turn left on to the D55 and continue for 4km (2.5 miles), to reach the

ruined **Château de la Hunaudaye** (open daily 11–6:30, Sat pm only, Jul–Aug). It dates from the 12th century, and became a victim of the Revolution. Look out for the spiral stair in the 15th-century keep.

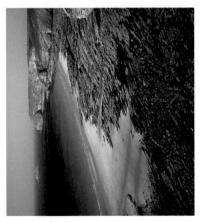

The coast at Cap Fréhel

2–3

Turn left and left again along the D2ε, passing through the **Forêt de la Hunaudaye** to the tiny village of St-Aubin. Continue on the D52 and turn right. Follow the D13 and D43 towards Pléboulle and the coast, and continue north beside the Baie de la Frénaye to the rocky tip. A massive 14th-century castle, **Fort la Latte**, guards the end, built high on a lump of rock and surrounded by thick stone battlements. To the west the spectacular views are to the point of Cap Fréhel, while the Emerald Coast spreads down to the east.

3–4

Return to the main road, turn right and drive around the coast for 4km to reach **Cap Fréhel**, a dramatically sculpted headland 70m (230 feet) above sea-level. According to local lore, the giant Gargantua created the rocky point by throwing a lump of stone over his shoulder. The elegant, square lighthouse is open daily 2–7, Jul–Aug. Continue on the sinuous

5–6

Continue on the D786 towards Le Val-André, and after about 3km (2 miles) pass the splendid medieval pink-sandstone **Château de Bienassis** (daily 10:30–12:30, 2–6:30, mid-Jun to mid-Sep), which was rebuilt in the 17th century with pepperpot towers.

6–7

Stay on the D786 to reach the coast again at **Le Val-André**, which is one of the sandy beaches in Brittany. Follow the D34 to **Planguenoual**, then take the D59 back to **Lamballe**.

When

With its views and beaches this tour is of interest on any day, but note that the châteaux and lighthouse are only open in high summer.

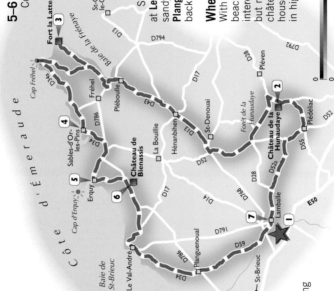

Fishing boats face the tide at Erquy

D34, through heathland to **Sables-d'Or-les-Pins**. **Pléhérel-Plage** is a wonderful beach of golden sand, but strong currents make it unsafe for swimming.

4–5

Continue on the D34 and detour right on to the D786 to explore the fishing port and resort of **Erquy**, which is set on a curving bay. Scallops are the local speciality, and there are plenty of tempting eating places along the seafront. The harbour is sheltered by the protective arm of the Cap d'Erquy, and is home to both a sailing school and a dive centre.

Where to... Stay

Prices

Expect to pay per night for a double room

€ up to €100   €€ €100–€200   €€€ over €200

Hôtel des Abers €-€€

This friendly hotel lies within the walls of the old city, behind a 16th-century façade. There are 14 rooms, each equipped with a queen-sized bed, TV and safe. Coffee and tea is on tap in the reception area, and for a change of menu, why not try the Indonesian restaurant next door, which is part of the hotel.

🏠 217 E3 ⊠ 10 rue de la Corne-du-Cerf, 35400 St-Malo ☎ 02 99 40 85 60; www.abershotel.com

L'Absinthe €€

For a small hotel with great character, try this former presbytery, which offers just six rooms and one suite. There's lots of wooden panelling, stained glass in the reception area, beamed ceilings and luxuriously draped curtains. The facilities are up to date, however, and each room has its own Jacuzzi. Breakfast can be included for an extra €10.

🏠 218 B4 ⊠ 1 rue de la Ville, 14600 Honfleur ☎ 02 31 89 23 23; www.absinthe.fr

Hôtel Victoria €

This is an ideal spot to stay if you want to explore the D-Day beaches. The hotel is in a 19th-century manor house in Arromanches-les-Bains, adorned with gracious furniture and paintings of the period. There are 14 rooms of different sizes, which overlook either the gardens or the charming flower-filled courtyard.

🏠 217 F4 ⊠ 24 chemin de l'Église, 14117 Arromanches-les-Bains ☎ 02 31 22 35 37; www.hotelvictoria-arromanches.com ☺ Closed Oct–Mar

La Butte de St-Laurent €

Joselin is a pretty village to the southwest of Dinan, and this cosy bed-and-breakfast stands on top of the *butte*, or small hill, which gives it its name. It also gives it superb views over the village and the nearby château. There are just four bedrooms, and the large garden makes it a delight for children as well as adults. Rooms are located under the eaves (no smoking). Note: credit cards are not accepted here.

🏠 217 D2 ⊠ 56120 Josselin ☎ 02 97 22 22 09; www.chambres-bretagne.com ☺ Closed mid-Sep to mid-Apr

Ars Prebital Coz €

Enjoy the simple but comfortable accommodation on offer in this historic house. There's no TV, but who needs it when you're in one of Brittany's most picturesque villages, St-Thégonnec. What was once the presbytery now offers bed-and-breakfast in six good-sized rooms (no smoking). An excellent and reasonably priced evening meal can be served by prior arrangement. Note: credit cards not accepted.

🏠 216 B3 ⊠ 18 rue du Gividic, 29410 St-Thégonnec ☎ 02 98 79 45 62

Le Relais de Fréhel €

Cap Fréhel is a rugged point on the Emerald Coast (▶ 89), and this restored farmhouse is a great place from which to explore this northern shore. The building is a *longère* – a long, narrow farmhouse typical of this part of Brittany, with an extensive garden and even a tennis court. There are five bedrooms.

🏠 217 D3 ⊠ route du Cap, Plévenon, 22240 Fréhel ☎ 02 96 41 43 02; www.lerelaisdefrehel.com ☺ Closed mid-Nov to April

Where to...
Eat and Drink

Prices
Expect to pay per person for a meal, excluding drinks
€ up to €25   €€ €25–€50   €€€ over €50

Le Catelier €–€€

You'll find this restaurant close to the botanic garden in Rouen, with the cane chairs of its stylish interior reflected in a big mirror. Daniel Atinhault acts as sommelier and front-of-house, while his wife Anne-Marie is the chef behind the scenes. Take your pick from the prix-fixe menus, but seafood is at the top of the bill here, with fresh lobster served in a salad with cider-butter and fried apples, or perhaps turbot in a white wine sauce.

➕ 218 C4 ⌂ 134 bis avenue des Martyrs de la Résistance, 76100 Rouen ☎ 02 35 72 59 90 🕔 Tue–Sat noon–2, 7–9; closed 2 weeks in Aug

La Pêcherie €€–€€€

In sunny weather you can dine out on the tiny terrace of this relaxed brasserie, in the heart of Rouen. The menu is dominated by fresh fish and seafood as you might expect, but there are some interesting twists and flavour combinations to discover here, including lobster served in a cider reduction, and *crème brûlée* scented with Earl Grey tea. Portions are generous.

➕ 218 C4 ⌂ 29 place de la Basse Vieille Tour, 76000 Rouen ☎ 02 35 88 71 00 🕔 Mon–Fri noon–2:30, 7:30–9:30, Sat 7:30–10

Les Embruns €€

Look out for this restaurant among the hotels close to the beach in St-Malo, which doubles as an art gallery – the paintings on the walls are for sale. You can pick your own lobster from the display tank, or sample scampi with mayonnaise, or perhaps salmon with asparagus. And it's not all fish and seafood – lamb's kidneys served with purple Brive mustard are another gastronomic highlight.

➕ 217 E3 ⌂ 120 chaussée du Sillon, 35400 St-Malo ☎ 02 99 56 33 57 🕔 Tue–Sat noon–2, 7–10, Sun noon–2; closed Jan

La Ferme St-Siméon €€€

For a gourmet treat, book a meal at this classy restaurant overlooking the sea. It is housed in a 19th-century mansion which is also a hotel and beauty spa – and it is said that Claude Monet and fellow artists enjoyed its comforts in years gone by. The menu is pricey but the quality of the preparation makes it all worthwhile, with mouth-watering dishes such as lobster risotto, fresh oysters, and langoustines served with caviar.

➕ 218 B4 ⌂ rue Adolphe Marais, 14600 Honfleur ☎ 02 31 81 78 00 🕔 Wed–Sun 12:30–2, 7:30–9:30, Tue 7:30–9:30

Les Marissons €€–€€€

An ancient shipyard on the banks of the River Somme is an unusual location for a restaurant, but Les Marissons is well worth seeking out. There's a lovely garden, and the 15th-century buildings with their blue and yellow décor make an attractive setting for dining. The menu varies according to season, but you might find locally caught eels (smoked, or perhaps stewed in a fragrant sauce of herbs), duck pie and *gâteau battu* – a sugared brioche. On fine days, dining extends on to the terrace.

Leclerc, tel: 02 31 98 11 42, open daily 9–1, 3–7, may close Tue–Wed). The shop also stocks other local delicacies such as preserved meat and caramels.

Striped nautical sweaters are a Breton classic, and you'll find them in lots of places. One of the best is **Armor Lux** in Quimper (60 bis rue Guy Autret, tel: 02 98 90 05 29, open Mon–Fri 8:30–12:30, 1:30–6), where you can also book ahead for a tour of the factory where they've been making these popular garments for more than 60 years.

Nautical clothing is also sold at **Gallerie de Ker-Ilez** (8 rue du Général de Gaulle, Perros-Guirec, tel: 02 96 91 01 62, open daily 10–noon, 2:30–7, Apr–Sep; closed Sun pm and Mon am, Oct–Mar). It's an extensive mall which specialises in Breton crafts, and you'll also find locally made porcelain, Celtic jewellery and wood carving here.

---

open daily 8–8, Jun to mid-Sep, 8–1, 3–7 mid-Oct to May).

Saturday markets are a feature across France, and always good places to source local cheeses and other distinctive produce. For a great setting amid the historic, timbered houses of Honfleur, try its **Marché Traditionnel** (place de l'Eglise Ste-Catherine, Sat 9:30–12:30), where locally caught fish is sold alongside the more usual fruit and vegetables.

There's also a great **Farmer's Market** on Friday mornings at Dury, in Picardie, where you can pick up home-made delights from *foie gras* to preserves, as well as local honey, flowers and organic vegetables (facing IME, route de Paris, Fri 8:30–1:30).

Apple growing is a regional speciality, and at Villerville, just west of Honfleur, you'll find cider, Calvados and *pommeau* (a blend of Calvados and apple juice) from local orchards on sale at **Ma Pomme** (rue du Général

---

Where to...
Shop

Beyond the cities in this part of France, you'll discover a wealth of local suppliers of regional delicacies, which include cheeses and apple products, including the brandy-like spirit Calvados.

FOOD AND DRINK

Take the recommended drive to Cap Fréhel (▶ 89) and you'll come across one of the best *pâtisseries* in Brittany. **Pâtissier-Chocolatier R. Jouault** is located in a modest building in Fréhel, but has been awarded the European Lauriers d'Or for its *kouignamann*, an almond cake. *Palet de Fréhel* – a nougat made with almond and chocolate and depicting the Cap itself – is another speciality (place de Chamblis, tel: 02 96 41 41 31,

---

➕ 219 D5 🗺 Pont de la Dodane, Quartier St-Leu, 8000 Amiens ☎ 03 22 92 96 66 🕒 Mon–Fri noon–2, 7–10, Sat 7–10

La Marine €–€€

Enjoy the views over the river and the château from the terrace of this modern, airy restaurant, while you tuck into the local *crêpe*, La Josselinoise. It's filled with a fragrant concoction of black pudding and fried apples. If you prefer, L'Automne has a combination of sweet chestnut purée and apple and pear jam, and if this all sounds too much, then there are plenty of *crêpe*-free and vegetarian choices on the menu, too. Children are welcomed with their own menu, and it's no wonder this place is popular – expect to book ahead in summer.

➕ 217 D2 🗺 8 rue du Canal, 56120 Josselin ☎ 02 97 22 21 98 🕒 Daily noon–1:45, 7–9, Jul–Aug; daily noon–1:45 and Thu–Sun 7–9, Sep–Jun; closed for lunch 2 weeks in Feb

Where to...
Be Entertained

While families may prefer the traditional resorts such as **St-Malo**, younger visitors head for the bright lights of the bars and clubs in **Rennes**. With its racecourse, blackjack tables and film festival, **Deauville** is the place for gambling with the jet set.

CASINOS

If gambling is your thing, then try the **Casino Barrière** at Dinard (4 boulevard Wilson, tel: 02 99 16 30 30, www.lucienbarriere.com, open Sun–Thu 10 am–3 am, Fri–Sat 10 am–4 am, over-18s only), where you can play roulette, blackjack, stud poker, hit the one-armed bandits and enjoy the beach views from the cocktail bar.

Big shots will want to head for Deauville's famous seafront **Casino** (rue Edmond Blanc, BP 32400, tel: 02 31 14 31 14, www.lucienbarriere.com, open Mon–Thu 10 am–2 am, Fri 11 am–3 am, Sat 11 am–4 am, Sun 10 am–3 am), where the building is *belle-époque*, the dress code formal, and you can divide your time between the excitement of the gaming tables, the three restaurants and the nightclub.

THEATRE AND CINEMA

St-Malo has one of the biggest theatres in the area, with big touring productions, concerts and opera (6 place Bouvet, tel: 02 99 81 62 61, open Tue–Sat).

Rennes has the **Théâtre Nationale de Bretagne (TNB)**, which includes concert halls and a cinema in its complex (1 rue St-Hélier, tel: 02 99 31 12 31, www.t-n-b.fr, open Tue–Sat), and the **Péniche Spectacle**. This unusual venue occupies two barges, *L'Arbre d'Eau* and *La Dame Blanche*, which have been converted to host music, jazz and cabaret performances, and a variety of exhibitions (quai St-Cyr, tel: 02 99 59 35 38).

Le Théâtre du Pays de Morlaix is a great venue for local and world music events as well as plays, movies and dance, with Wednesday street performances in the height of summer (20 rue Gambetta, Morlaix, tel: 02 98 15 22 77, performances daily 8 pm).

The four-screen cinema at St-Lô, **Le Drakkar**, shows mainstream blockbusters and some independent films in their original language (29 rue Alsace-Lorraine, tel: 02 33 05 16 50, open daily).

CLUBS

If you want to boogie the night away in Paimpol, try the piano-bar **Le Pub**, with a bar on the ground floor and dancing upstairs, and music for all ages (3 rue des Islandais, tel: 02 95 20 82 31, open Thu–Sun 9 pm–5 am, Mon–Wed 9:30 pm – 4 am).

Quiberon has its own rum bar, **Bar le Nelson**, where you can taste up to 54 different sorts of rum to the retro-pop beat (20 place Hoche, tel: 02 97 50 31 37, open Mon–Sun noon–2 am, Feb–Nov; Fri–Sat Mar–Oct; closed mid-Jan).

At Blonville-sur-Mer, near Deauville, **Les Planches** is a lively nightclub with one dance floor (of two) dedicated to music from the 1960s to the 1990s (Les Longs Champs, 14910, tel: 02 31 87 58 09, closed Sun Sep–Jun).

Northeast France

Getting Your Bearings 96 – 97
In Four Days 98 – 99
Don't Miss 100 – 109
At Your Leisure 110 – 114
Drive 115 – 116
Where to... 117 – 120

Getting Your Bearings

The northeast is France's richest and
most varied border country, sharing
boundaries and influences with
Belgium, Luxembourg, Germany and
Switzerland. There is much to see,
and many gastronomic treats to
enjoy along the way.

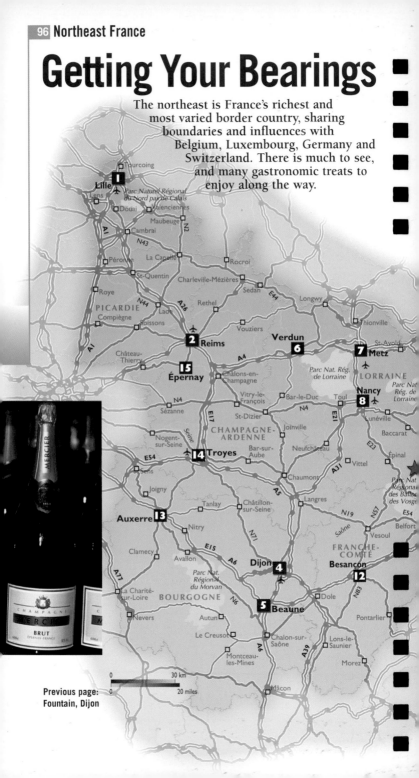

Tourcoing

Lille **1**

Lens

Parc Naturel Régional
du Nord par de Calais

Douai

Valenciennes

Maubeuge

Cambrai

N43

A1

N2

La Capelle

Rocroi

Péronne

St-Quentin

Charleville-Mézières

Roye

N44

Laon

A26

Sedan

E44

Longwy

Thionville

PICARDIE

Compiègne

Soissons

Château-
Thierry

Reims **2**

A4

Vouziers

Verdun **6**

Metz **7**

St-Avold

Épernay **15**

Châlons-en-
Champagne

Parc Nat. Rég.
de Lorraine

LORRAINE

Nancy **8**

Parc Nat
Rég. de
Lorraine

N4

Sézanne

Vitry-le-
François

Bar-le-Duc

Toul

Lunéville

E17

St-Dizier

N4

Baccarat

Nogent-
sur-Seine

Joinville

Neufchâteau

E21

Vittel

Épinal

CHAMPAGNE-
ARDENNE

Troyes **14**

Bar-sur-
Aube

E33

Parc Nat
Régional
des Ballon
des Vosge

E54

Sens

Chaumont

A31

Joigny

Tanlay

Châtillon-
sur-Seine

Langres

N19

N57

Belfort

Auxerre **13**

Nitry

A5

Saône

Vesoul

FRANCHE-
COMTÉ

Clamecy

E15

Avallon

A6

Dijon **4**

Besançon **12**

La Charité-
sur-Loire

A71

Parc Nat.
Régional
du Morvan

N6

Beaune **5**

Dole

N83

Pontarlier

Nevers

BOURGOGNE

Autun

Le Creusot

A6

Chalon-sur-
Saône

Lons-le-
Saunier

A39

Morez

Montceau-
les-Mines

Mâcon

0   30 km

0   20 miles

Previous page:
Fountain, Dijon

CHAMPAGNE

MERCIER

BRUT
ÉPERNAY FRANCE

The modern city of Lille

Lille, close to the seaport of Dunkerque, is the capital of the plains to the north of the region, while Strasbourg, home of the European Parliament, is queen of the south. In the middle come the chalky hills of the Champagne-Ardenne country, which spreads out to the south of the great cathedral city of Reims. Some of France's greatest waterways are found to the south of here, including the rivers Seine and Marne, and canals including the Canal de Bourgogne.

To the east, the lively cities of Metz and Nancy are the current and one-time capitals of the formerly independent Lorraine. In the southeast the verdant mountains of the Vosges form a natural barrier, with the River Rhine on the far side marking the German border. Dijon, with a medieval heart overlaying a Roman core, is the focus for the southwest corner, with nearby Beaune a must-see historic highlight.

A good network of motorways ensures easy access to all the major cities in this area, as well as west to Paris, south to Lyon and across international frontiers. The Route du Vin d'Alsace is a 170km (105-mile) driving route celebrating local wine production which goes from Marlenheim, just west of Strasbourg, south to Thann, which lies just west of Mulhouse.

Sarreguemines
A35
Haguenau
A4 Rhin
Strasbourg ✈ **3**
Château de Haut Kœnigsbourg
10
9 **Riquewihr**
11
Colmar
ALSACE
Mulhouse ✈

★ Don't Miss

1 Lille ➤ 100
2 Reims ➤ 102
3 Strasbourg ➤ 103
4 Dijon ➤ 106
5 Beaune ➤ 108

Vineyards at Reims

At Your Leisure

6 Verdun ➤ 110
7 Metz ➤ 110
8 Nancy ➤ 110
9 Riquewihr ➤ 111
10 Château de Haute Kœnigsbourg ➤ 112
11 Colmar ➤ 112
12 Besançon ➤ 113
13 Auxerre ➤ 113
14 Troyes ➤ 114
15 Épernay ➤ 114

Opposite: Champagne is produced in this region

This is an extensive area, with some major city highlights including Reims and Strasbourg. However, the *autoroute* network means that travel between sites can be fairly efficient, and in four days you can see a great deal.

Northeast France in Four Days

Day One

Morning
Start your discovery of the region in **1** **Lille** (right, ➤ 100–101), with a morning dedicated to exploring the city on foot, and shopping at the massive **Centre Euralille** (➤ 101), Lunch at **La Chicorée** (➤ 101).

Afternoon
Take a break from shopping to wander through the outstanding collection of old masters at the **Palais des Beaux-Arts** (➤ 101). Then head south out of town, picking up the A26/E17 autoroute or the slower N43/N44, to spend the night near **Reims**.

Day Two

Morning
Make an early start and explore the heart of the historic city of **2** **Reims** (left, ➤ 102), with a tour of its World Heritage sites and a quick visit to a champagne cave. Lunch at **Le Grand Café** (➤ 102).

Afternoon
Head off southeast on the A4 autoroute towards **Metz**, stopping off to visit the World War I sites at **6** **Verdun** (➤ 110). Reach the attractive old city of **7** **Metz** (➤ 110), and either plan to stay here and perhaps catch a **concert** of classical music in the evening, or continue south on the A31 to see **8** **Nancy** (➤ 110).

Day Three

Morning
Continue southeast to reach ❸ **Strasbourg** (above and left, ➤ 103–105), a lively city at the heart of the European community. Visit the **tourist office** by the **cathedral** (➤ 105), and **hire bicycles** to travel around and get your bearings. Dine on local fare by the riverside (➤ 105).

Afternoon
Treat yourself to **modern art and folk art** in the city's top museums (➤ 104), and perhaps a 1-hour **river cruise** by *bateau-mouche* (➤ 105).

Evening
Try out the city's nightlife at a **themed bar** (➤ 120).

Day Four

Morning
Head southwest on the N83/E25, passing through ⓫ **Colmar** (➤ 112), pausing to see the Issenheim altar-piece in the **Musée d'Unterlinden**. Continue west on the A36/E60 via ⓬ **Besançon** (➤ 113) to reach ❹ **Dijon** (➤ 106–107) in time for lunch, perhaps washed down with a glass of *kir*.

Afternoon
Explore **Dijon** at leisure, before finally driving southwest to historic ❺ **Beaune** (right, ➤ 108–109), with its magnificent **Hôtel-Dieu**.

0 Lille

Lille is a major city with one of the country's most prestigious art museums, and a historic core that makes for enjoyable exploring. Add to that one of the best shopping centres at Euralille, a fun Sunday market at Wazemmes and a sprinkling of historic gems, and you've got the makings of a perfect short break destination.

Top and above: It's all happening in Lille's busy place Général de Gaulle

Lille has always been a prosperous trading town, and its prime location at a hub of main waterways and major land routes made it a valuable prize as it passed between French, Spanish, Burgundian, Flemish, Dutch and – during the two world wars – German hands. Its excellent transport links today make it highly accessible to visitors from all over Europe, including Britain.

At its heart is the handsome, broad square known as **Grand' Place**, surrounded by tall, 17th-century buildings in brick and white Lezennes stone, and little side-streets with cafés and bars. The square is officially named after the city's most famous son, Général Charles de Gaulle (1890–1970). His **birthplace** north of here is now a dedicated museum, celebrating the life of the wartime hero who led the country in the vital post-war period and rose to be the first president of the Fifth Republic in 1958.

Markets take place in different quarters on different days (► 119), and modern shopping is based around **Euralille**, between the two railway stations east of Grand' Place.

Palais des Beaux-Arts

It's well worth setting aside an hour or two of your visit to explore this world-class collection of fine art, amassed in a former palace to the south of the Grand' Place. The Flemish and Dutch masters are well represented, as you might expect so close to the Belgian border, and 40 Raphael cartoons are a highlight of the displays. There are many works by French artists, too, including Impressionists Monet and Renoir. For local interest, there are the great military engineer Vauban's models for the **Citadelle**, a star-shaped fortress of 1670 which lies west of Grand' Place.

The modern façade of the cathedral of Notre-Dame-de-la-Treille

Retail Therapy

Centre Euralille is a massive temple to the modern goddess of shopping, in the east of the Old Town and next door to the bizarrely ski-boot-shaped Gare Lille-Europe railway station. There are around 140 retail outlets in the mall, which opened in 1994 as part of a futuristic 70ha (173-acre) development designed by Dutchman Rem Koolhaas. There is also a massive concert hall here, a hypermarket and plenty of restaurants to collapse in when you've shopped 'til you've dropped.

TAKING A BREAK

Sample the onion soup or perhaps the rabbit at **La Chicorée**, an appealing brasserie in the town centre (15 place Rihour, 59000, tel: 03 20 54 81 52).

---

222 C2
Tourist Information Office
✉ Palais Rihour, place Rihour, BP 205, 59002
☎ 03 20 21 94 21; www.lille-tourism.com ⏰ Mon–Sat 9:30–6:30, Sun 10–noon, 2–5

Maison Natale du Général de Gaulle
✉ 9 rue Princesse
☎ 03 28 38 12 05
⏰ Wed–Sun 10–1, 2–5:30
💶 Inexpensive

Palais des Beaux-Arts
✉ place de la République
☎ 03 20 06 78 00
⏰ Mon 2–6, Wed–Thu, Sat–Sun 10–6, Fri 10–7. Closed first weekend in Sep
💶 Inexpensive

LILLE: INSIDE INFO

Top tips Lille is particularly **well connected**: just 40 minutes by train from Brussels, an hour by TGV from Paris, and only two hours from London on the Eurostar.
• A **City Pass** from the tourist office allows unlimited travel on buses, trams and the Métro within the city, and even free entry to some museums. Passes cost €15 for one day, €25 for two days and €30 for three.
• If you're not sure where you are, look out for the **town stewards** in their yellow jackets – they're there to help you with directions and advice.

One to miss Don't bother with the **guided tour inside the Citadelle** unless you're seriously into military history – you can admire Vauban's five-point design from the encircling Bois de Boulogne park for free.

2 Reims

A busy industrial city in the heart of France's champagne-producing country, Reims has witnessed great events in history including the crowning of 25 sovereigns and the surrender of the German army at the end of World War II, in 1945.

Before you start sight-seeing, consider investing in a *Pass Citadine Reims en Champagne*, from the tourist office (€12 for one day, €23 for two days). This gives you entry to six museums and a champagne house, plus a bonus box of local biscuits.

Then head straight for the town centre to see the top sights which have made it on to the World Heritage list: the 11th-century **Basilique St-Rémi**, and the restored **Cathédrale Notre-Dame** and its neighbouring **Palais de Tau museum**. The cathedral dates back to 1211, and its Gothic façade is encrusted with statues. Look out for the history of champagne-making depicted in the windows of the south transept (1954).

Book a tour and tasting (*dégustation*) at one of the top **champagne houses** (*maisons de champagne*) via the tourist office. You can visit the chalk storage caverns of familiar names such as Mumm & Cie, Taittinger and Piper-Heidsieck without prior appointment. Most champagne houses are open daily, though they may close at weekends out of season.

TAKING A BREAK

Le Grand Café, at 92 place Drouet d'Erlon, has a large terrace opening on to the square where you can try 13 different varieties of mussels, or tuck into pasta, salads and gâteaux (tel: 03 26 47 61 50).

➕ 220 A4
Tourist Information Office
✉ 2 rue Guillaume de Machault
☎ 03 26 77 45 25; www.reims-tourisme.com
🕐 Mon–Sat 9–7, Sun 10–6, mid-Apr to mid-Oct; Mon–Sat 9–6, Sun 11–5, mid-Oct to mid-Apr

Basilique St-Rémi
✉ place St-Rémi 🕐 Daily 8–7 or dusk if earlier; closed during services

Cathédrale Notre-Dame
✉ place du Cardinal-Luçon 🕐 Daily 7:30–7:30; closed during services

Top: The cathedral by night

Above: Chilling out in place d'Erlon

③ Strasbourg

Strasbourg is a city of brilliance, with a picturesque medieval quarter – La Petite France, a remarkable small Gothic cathedral and a vibrant attitude to life and culture which comes of its historically tenuous location on the border with Germany. It's a university city, the place where the talents of Gutenberg and Goethe were nurtured, and is now home to the Council of Europe and the ultra-modern architecture of the Palais des Droits de l'Homme (1995), where the European Court of Human Rights sits. Its ancient heart of timbered buildings lies on an island, Grand Île, and the city's blend of ancient and modern is bewitching.

Cathédrale de Notre-Dame de Strasbourg

The single spire of this red sandstone edifice towers above the roofs of the city, offering a great view from its platform, 332 steps and 142m (465 feet) up. Added in 1439, it was the crowning glory to a cathedral started in 1190, and paid for by the people of the town. Look out for a stork, symbol of Strasbourg, carved on the western façade. Lacy stonework on the exterior is reflected in the elaborate design of the organ

Above: The Gothic cathedral fills the end of rue Mercière

Inset: A rose window in the cathedral

inside. In the south transept, behind the carved, three-sided Pillar of Angels, stands an elaborate astronomical clock – at 12:30 it comes to life as the Apostles parade before Christ, the rooster crows and flaps its wings, and Death strikes the hour.

Far right: Timbered buildings in Petite France

Below: Houses lean at interesting angles in the old town

Museum Choices

There are several excellent museums in the city, and three of the best are located under one roof in the 18th-century bishops' palace, **Palais Rohan**. Exhibits cover all periods from prehistory up to the 19th century, including art by Giotto, Boticelli, El Greco and Corot, and you'll find archaeology in the basement, decorative arts on the ground floor and fine art upstairs. The story is brought up to date with photography and graphic art, as well as paintings by Monet, Picasso, Gustave Doré and others, in the splendid **Musée d'Art Moderne et Contemporain**, west of Petite France. For a less sophisticated but thoroughly engaging view of Alsatian culture, cross the River Ill and walk south to the **Musée Alsacien**, dedicated to humbler folk art and crafts of the region.

Above: Imposing towers mark out the Ponts Couverts

City of Bridges

The bridges which criss-cross the river and canals are a distinctive feature of the city. The most famous are the three **Ponts-Couverts** (Covered Bridges) on the western tip of Grand Île, on the edge of the Petite France district, though they lost their wooden roofs in the 19th century. They are strung in a line, punctuated by four tall, severe square towers which were intended for defence, and later served as prisons.

Another bridge with a grim reputation is the **Pont de Corbeau** (Raven Bridge), on the south side near the 14th-century Customs House. In days gone by, unlucky criminals

were locked in cages and thrown from its stonework to drown in the river below.

For a taste of local Alsatian cuisine, call in at **À l'Ancienne Douane**, by the river, and sample the *flameküche* (thin-crust pizza) and *sauerkraut* (6 rue de la Douane, tel: 03 88 15 78 78).

🞣 221 F3

Tourist Information Office
✉ 17 place de la Cathédrale, 67082 (also offices at place de la Gare and Pont de l'Europe) ☎ 03 88 52 28 28; www.ot-strasbourg.fr
🕑 Mon–Sat 9–7, Sun 9–6

Cathédrale de Notre-Dame de Strasbourg
✉ place de la Cathédrale
☎ 03 88 43 60 32
🕑 Mon–Sat 7–11:30,

12:40–7, Sun 12:40–7.
Viewing platform: 🕑 Mon–Fri 9–5:30, Sat–Sun 10–5:30, Jan–Oct; closes 4:30 Nov–Dec
💷 Inexpensive

Palais Rohan (Musée Archaeologique, Musée des Arts Décoratifs, Musée des Beaux-Arts)
✉ 2 place du Château
☎ 03 88 52 50 00
🕑 Wed–Mon 10–6
💷 Inexpensive

Musée d'Art Moderne et Contemporain
✉ 1 place Hans-Jean Arp
🕑 Tue–Wed, Fri–Sat 11–7, Thu noon–10, Sun 10–6
💷 Inexpensive

Musée Alsacien
✉ 23–25 quai St-Nicolas
☎ 03 88 35 55 36
🕑 Wed–Mon 10–6
💷 Inexpensive, under 18 free

STRASBOURG: INSIDE INFO

Top tips The three-day **Strasbourg-Pass**, available from the tourist office (€10.60), offers free admission to one museum and reductions at other attractions, plus a free bateau-mouche river tour, access to the cathedral tower, and a day's cycle rental.
• You can visit the **European Parliament** during the week but only on a guided tour and by prior reservation, tel: 03 88 17 20 07. The building is 2km (1.2 miles) east of the centre, and tours last 1 hour.
• **Christmas street markets** bring the winter city to life. Catch them from late November through December at place Broglie, by the railway station and in front of the cathedral.
• **Boat trips on the River Ill** offer a different perspective of this vibrant city. Bateaux-mouche leave from a point near the Palais Rohan, and tours last around an hour.

Hidden Gem Seek out weekday tranquillity in the 3.5ha (8.5-acre) **botanic garden** on rue Goethe, part of the university, where more than 6,000 different plant species flourish. Access is free, and the site is open Mon–Fri 8–11:45, 2–5, plus occasional weekends.

One to miss Unless your time is unlimited, bypass the **Musée de l'Oeuvre Notre-Dame** on place du Château, which tells of the building of the cathedral and acts as an overspill for replaced statues and other relics.

4 Dijon

The city of Dijon is famed for its gastronomical delights, with a pleasantly walkable centre bursting with boutiques, bars, green parks, historic buildings and interesting galleries and museums. It's also the home of *kir*, an aperitif made from a blend of the local white wine and *crème de cassis* (blackcurrant liqueur).

Originally a Roman settlement, Dijon rose to prominence in the 14th century as the seat of the powerful dukes of Burgundy, and its medieval wealth can still be seen in the buildings at its heart. Seek out the little streets behind the Palais des Ducs, such as **rue Verrerie** and **rue des Forges**, which recall the trades – glass and ironworks – that once flourished there. **Rue de la Chouette** is named after the owl, a symbol of the town that you will also see carved on a sidewall of the Gothic **Église Notre-Dame**, on place Notre-Dame.

For contrast, the **place de la Libération** is an elegant crescent of houses dating from the 17th century. The arcades beneath are occupied by appealing little boutiques and restaurants. **Rue de la Liberté** is the main shopping street, its arteries filled with cafés and interesting food shops, and markets are held in and around the 19th-century covered market, **Les Halles**.

Above: A medieval house in the heart of Dijon

Below left: The Palais des Ducs

Below: A statue treads grapes in place François-Rude

Cutting the Mustard

Strong and flavoursome, **Dijon mustard** is known across the world, and a pot or two makes a great souvenir. Brown or black mustard seeds are crushed before being emulsified in verjuice – a wine made from unripe grapes. It's still produced to a standard set down by the Dijon Academy in the 19th century, but the name is not fiercely protected by a patent in the way that champagne is, so make sure you're buying the local stuff. **Moutarde Maille,** on rue de la Liberté, is a great place to find it.

Musée des Beaux-Arts

This outstanding museum shares a roof with the town hall, in the 18th-century ducal palace. There's a great collection of paintings and sculptures, including some modern and contemporary material. Don't miss the amazing carved 14th- and 15th-century tombs of Philip the Bold, first Duke of Burgundy, and his quarrelsome son John the Fearless, who was murdered in 1419.

TAKING A BREAK

Maison Millière, at 10 rue de la Chouette, sells regional products and gifts, and has a restaurant and a tea room offering 20 different teas to accompany its pastries (tel: 03 80 30 99 99). To find it, look for the animal figures on the roof.

Banners
bedeck the rue
de la Liberté

🔢 220 B1
Tourist Information Office
✉ place Darcy, 21000 (also a smaller office at 34 rue des Forges)
☎ 03 80 44 11 44; www.dijon-tourisme.com
🕐 Daily 9–7, Jun–Aug; 10–6 Sep–May

Musée des Beaux-Arts
✉ Palais des Ducs et des États de Bourgogne
☎ 03 80 74 59 31
🕐 Wed–Mon 9:30–6, May–Oct; 10–5, Nov–Apr
🎟 Inexpensive, under 18 free, free on Sun

DIJON: INSIDE INFO

Top tips The **Dijon à la Carte** visitor pass, available from the tourist offices, offers excellent value for money (€8 for one day, €11 for two, €14 for three days). It includes a guided walking tour, free entry to most of the museums, and unlimited bus travel.
• **Take your own tour** around the town's historic buildings for free by following the red arrows on the ground and reading the multi-lingual information boards at each site. The *Owl's Trail* guidebook, available from the tourist office (€2), gives more details.

5 Beaune

The irresistible wine capital of Burgundy, the lovely old town of Beaune has one of the most remarkable medieval buildings in France, whose tiled roof has become an icon of the area.

Beaune's prosperity was built on a foundation of trade in cloth, iron and wine, and today its ancient centre of narrow cobbled streets and pretty squares is a delightful distraction, as you while away the time and perhaps plan a visit to one of the famous wine cellars or a stroll around the ramparts. The **Musée du Vin**, in a former palace of the dukes of Burgundy, is worth a look.

Hôtel-Dieu

This is Beaune's must-see attraction, and if a charitable hospital for the poor founded in 1443 by Nicolas Rolin and his wife Guigone de Salins, sounds a dispiriting and worthy sort of place, don't be put off.

Rolin was the wealthy chancellor of Philip the Bold, and at the age of 67 felt the need to make an ostentatious gesture of bounty in this world, in order to bag his place in the next. Inspired by hospitals he had seen in Flanders, he commissioned this superb structure, sparing no expense.

Top: The tiled roofs of the inner courtyard

Above: An 18th-century hero celebrated in place Monge

The most notable feature is the steep roof around three sides of the interior coutyard, covered with coloured, glazed tiles in rich geometric patterns. An open gallery runs below, supported on slender pillars. Inside there are the vaulted wards, the great hall and the old kitchens. Among the tapestries, fine furniture and medical exhibits here, look out for the superb painted polyptych of the Last Judgement, by Flemish painter Rogier van der Weyden, which Rolin commissioned to hang in the chapel.

TAKING A BREAK

La Grilladine is a friendly restaurant between boulevard Bretonnière and rue Gardin, serving typical Burgundian fare including *boeuf bourguignon*, *oeufs en meurette* (poached eggs in red wine sauce) and snails (17 rue Maufoux, tel: 03 80 22 22 36).

Tapestries from displays at the wine museum and the church

214 C5
Tourist Information Office
✉ 1 rue de l'Hôtel-Dieu, 21200 ☎ 03 80 26 21 30; www.ot-beaune.fr
🕐 Mon–Sat 9:30–8, Sun 10–12:30, 2–6 Jun–Sep; Mon–Sat 10–6, Sun 10–12:30, 2–5, Oct–May

Musée du Vin
✉ rue d'Enfer, Hôtel des Ducs de Bourgogne
☎ 03 80 22 08 19
🕐 Daily 9:30–9:30, Apr–Nov; 9:30–12:30, 1:30–5 Dec–Mar

Hôtel-Dieu
✉ rue de l'Hôtel-Dieu
☎ 03 80 24 45 00
🕐 Daily 9–6:30, Mar to mid-Nov; 9–noon, 2–5:30 mid-Nov to Feb

BEAUNE: INSIDE INFO

Top tips There are 15 different **wine cellars**, or *caves*, to visit in the locale, each offering tastings. The tourist office can advise you where to start.
• The town fills up quickly for the annual grape harvest in September and October, so **book ahead** for a visit at this time.
• The **Beaune Pass**, available from the tourist office, gives reduced rates for all sorts of activities, from wine cellar tours and tastings to helicopter flights and rides on the petit train which transports visitors around the key sites.
• The Hôtel-Dieu owns 60ha (148 acres) of prime vineyards around the town, and on the third Sunday in November its **wines are auctioned** to raise funds. It's an event which attracts buyers from around the world.

One to miss Unless you're a dedicated gallery-bagger, skip the **Musée des Beaux-Arts** in the Porte Marie de Bourgogne and make the most of the viticulture instead.

At Your Leisure

6 Verdun

It's estimated that three quarters of a million soldiers died in the terrible fighting that took place along the banks of the River Meuse and around this peaceful little town in the middle of World War I. Today many of the battle sites are hidden under a blanket of woodland, but you can get a feel for the time by visiting the restored **Citadelle Souterraine** on avenue du 5ième RAP, an underground French command post (open daily). The village of **Fleury**, 6km northeast, was wiped out during the battle and now has a museum that explains and commemorates events (closed mid-Dec to Feb). Tour buses visit the main wartime sites daily between May and September – contact the tourist office for details.

➕ 220 B4
Tourist Information Office
✉ Maison du Tourisme, place de la Nation, BP 232 55106 ☎ 03 29 86 14 18; www.verdun-tourisme.com
🕐 Mon–Sat 8:30–7, Jul–Aug; Mon–Sat 8:30–6:30, May–Jun, Sep; Mon–Sat 9–noon, 2–6, Mar–Apr, Oct–Nov; Mon–Sat 9–noon, 2–5, Dec–Feb. Also Sun 9.30–5, Apr–Sep; 10–1 Nov–Feb

7 Metz

Metz (pronounced Mess) is an attractive old city on the Moselle river near the German border, and has changed hands between the two nations a few times in its history. It was most recently restored to France in 1918, after 47 years of German control – influence which can be seen in buildings such as the imposing railway station. Graceful bridges across the River Seille are built of the local dark yellow stone, known as *pierre de jaumont*. Look out for stained glass by Surrealist Marc Chagall (1887–1985) in the north transept and ambulatory of the 12th-century Gothic **Cathédrale St-**

Étienne. The building, on place d'Armes, is nicknamed the *Lanterne du Bon Dieu* (God's lantern) for its lofty interior and 6,500sq m (70,000 square feet) of windows. You'll find the main shopping area south of here, around place St-Louis. Metz is also known as a centre of excellence for classical music, with an annual summer festival and regular concerts.

Modern apartment blocks on the waterfront at Metz

➕ 221 D4
Tourist Information Office
✉ 2 place d'Armes, BP 80367, 57007 ☎ 03 87 55 53 76; http://tourisme. mairie-metz.fr 🕐 Mon–Sat 9–8:30, Sun 10–3, Jul–Aug; Mon–Sat 9–7, Sun 10–3, Mar–Jun, Sep–Oct; Mon–Sat 9–6:30, Sun 10–3, Nov–Feb

8 Nancy

Eighteenth-century urban planning on a grand scale by a deposed king of Poland made Nancy the attraction it is today. The man responsible was Stanislas Leszczynski, Duke of Lorraine, and the splendid buildings,

Vineyards surround Riquewihr

fountain and gilded gateway of the long central square which now bears his name are his greatest monument. Nancy was also prominent in the art nouveau movement, thanks largely to the efforts of locally born designer Émile Gallé, who founded a glass workshop here in 1874. You can admire his sumptuous works, including furniture, in the fabulous **Musée de l'École de Nancy**, housed in a delightful mansion. The Majorelle Villa (not open) and other buildings across the city also reveal the exuberant, organic influence of art nouveau, most notably in window surrounds and doorways.

221 D3
Tourist Information Office ✉ place Stanislas, BP 810, 54011 ☎ 03 83 35 22 41; www.ot-nancy.fr
🕐 Mon–Sat 9–7, Sun 10–5, Apr–Oct; Mon–Sat 9–6, Sun 10–1, Nov–May
Musée de l'École de Nancy ✉ 36 rue du Sergent Blandan ☎ 03 83 40 14 86 🕐 Wed–Sun 10:30–6

9 Riquewihr

Riquewihr, in the foothills of the Vosges mountains, surrounded by vineyards, is an essential stop on the 170km (105-mile) Route du Vin d'Alsace, which runs from Marlenheim south to Thann.

Traffic is banned from the cobbled streets at the heart of the town, which throng with visitors in summer, eager to sample the local wines in a beautiful setting of mellow stone and timbered buildings decked with scarlet geraniums. Medieval citizens threw up a wall to protect Riquewihr, and parts of this survive, along with two gate towers. One of these, the **Tour des Voleurs**, became a prison and now has a grisly reconstruction of a torture chamber (daily 10:15–12:30, 2–6:30, Apr–Oct).

Magnificent adornment in the central place Stanislas, Nancy

221 E2
Tourist Information Office
✉ 2 rue de la 1ière Armée, 68340
☎ 03 89 49 08 40; www.ribeauville-riquewihr.com 🕐 Mon–Sat 9:30–noon, 2–6 (also Sun 10–1, 2–5, May–Oct)

⑩ Château de Haute Kœnigsbourg

This much-visited castle, looming above the woodland west of Sélestat on a crag 757m (2,483 feet) high, has attracted controversy since its reconstruction in the early 20th century.

It's a debate fed by the ambiguity of the comment inscribed on a fire screen in the great hall by its restorer, Kaiser Willhelm II, on his last visit in 1918: "*Ich habe es nicht gewollt*" ("I didn't want this"). Did he mean World War I, which would see the château returned to French control, along with the region of Alsace, or the neatly executed but dubiously neo-Gothic reconstruction of his medieval castle? You'll have to make your own mind up when you see it.

➕ 221 E3 ✉ 67600 Orschwiller
☎ 03 88 82 50 60; www.haut-koenigs-bourg.net ⏱ Daily 9:30–6:30, Jun–Aug; 9:30–5:30, Apr–May, Sep; 9:45–5, Mar, Oct; 9:45–noon, 1–5, Nov–Feb
✋ Moderate

⑪ Colmar

In terms of visitor numbers, Colmar's **Musée d'Unterlinden**, in the street of the same name, ranks second only to the Louvre in the whole of France. The reason is the dramatic Issenheim altarpiece, the masterwork of Matthias Grünewald, which he painted for a nearby monastery between 1512 and 1516. Eight panels conceal vivid depictions of religious scenes, most famously the agony of Christ on the cross. The museum, in a former Dominican convent, has other treasures, including popular art from the local area.

The town itself, a key location on the Route du Vin d'Alsace, has a charming centre of narrow cobbled streets, timbered houses painted in warm colours, and cafés spilling on to pretty squares. The Krutenau district, with its small houses and pretty gardens set around the channels of the River Lauch, is known as **Petite Venise**.

Colmar's most famous son was the sculptor Frédéric Auguste Bartholdi, who created the Statue of Liberty for New York in 1886, and there's a small **museum** in his birthplace on rue des Marchands (Wed–Mon 10–noon, 2–6, Mar–Dec).

➕ 221 E2
Tourist Information Office
✉ 4 rue d'Unterlinden, 68000
☎ 03 89 20 68 92; www.ot-colmar.fr

A shuttered window in Colmar

🕒 Mon–Sat 9–7, Sun 9:30–2,
Jul–Aug; Mon–Sat 9–6, Sun 10–1,
Apr–Jun, Sep–Oct; Mon–Sat
9–noon, 2–6, Sun 10–1, Nov–Mar

Musée d'Unterlinden
✉ 1 rue d'Unterlinden, 68000
☎ 03 89 20 15 58 🕒 Daily 9–6,
Apr–Oct; Wed–Mon 9–noon, 2–5,
Nov–Mar 💶 Moderate

🔢 Besançon

This majestic city, capital of
Franche-Comté, grew up in a
loop of the River Doubs,
overlooked by the superb
17th-century Citadelle. Poet
Victor Hugo was born here
in 1802.

It was a major centre of
clock- and watchmaking,
and this is celebrated in the fascinating 19th-century **astronomical
clock** below the bell tower inside the
cathedral, which has 30,000 parts, 57
faces, and various automata that
come and go on the hour. Learn
more at the **Musée du Temps**, which
is in the splendid Renaissance Palais

The Gothic cathedral of St-Étienne rises
above the River Yonne at Auxerre

Granvelle on Grand Rue, designed
for Charles V's chancellor, Nicolas
Perrenot (open Wed–Sun from 1pm).

The views from the **Citadelle**
are spectacular. The fortress was
designed by the great military
engineer Sébastien le Prestre de
Vauban, and begun in 1668. There
are several attractions within its
extensive walls, including a zoo
and a museum dedicated to the
Résistance (open daily).

➕ 221 D1
Tourist Information Office ✉ 2
place de la 1ière Armée Française,
25000 ☎ 03 81 80 92 55; www.besan-
con-tourisme.com 🕒 Mon–Sat 9:30–7,
Sun 10–5, Jun–Sep; Mon–Sat 9:30–6,
Sun 10–12:30, Oct–May

🔢 Auxerre

Auxerre is a pleasant old Burgundian
town, built on a hillside above the
River Yonne. Explore the historic
quarter on foot, seeking out the
17th-century astronomical clock on
the **Tour de l'Horloge**, and the
Abbaye St-Germain – frescoes in
the crypt date back to the mid-9th

Besançon – the stunning view from
Vauban's Citadelle

century, and are the oldest in France. You can take a **river cruise** here, and Auxerre makes a good starting point for exploring the beautiful waterways of this region, notably the Canal du Nivernais to the south, and the Canal de Bourgogne to the southeast.

➕ 219 F2
Tourist Information Office
✉ 1–2 quai de la République, 89000
☎ 03 86 52 06 19; www.ot-auxerre.fr
🕐 Mon–Sat 9–1, 2–7, Sun 9:30–1, 3–6:30, Jun–Sep; Mon–Fri 9:30–12:30, 2–6, Sat 9:30–12:30, 2–6:30, Sun 10–1, Oct–May

🔟 Troyes

Troyes was a wealthy city in medieval times – a major centre for the manufacture of stained glass, and a Champagne capital to which merchants came from all over Europe for the great fairs. Today it's a sleepy place, its medieval heart largely intact, with narrow streets and rambling timbered buildings housing intriguing small museums, and no less than nine churches with outstanding stained-glass windows.

Don't miss the 17th-century *grisaille* shading work by master craftsman Linard Grontier in the windows of the **Église St-Martin-ès-Vigne** on avenue Marie de Champagne. Marie de Champagne, daughter of Louis VII, made Troyes a cultural centre in the mid-12th century. Chrétien de Troyes, poet of the great Arthurian romances of courtly love, was one of her *protégés*. The **modern art museum**, next to the cathedral, is another highlight, with works by Rodin, Soutine and Derain.

➕ 220 A2
Tourist Information Office
✉ 16 boulevard Carnot, BP 4082 10018
☎ 03 25 82 62 70; www.tourisme-troyes.com 🕐 Mon–Sat 9–12:30, 2–6:30

Top champagne from the Caves Mercier

🔟 Épernay

They've been making champagne in Épernay since 1743, and today it's home to some of the greatest labels in the history of bubbly. Vineyards surround the town, and the names of the *maisons de champagne* read like a top-quality restaurant listing, including De Castellane and Mercier. Moët et Chandon operate **guided tours** of their vast cellars, and you can sample it at their *dégustation* at 18 avenue de Champagne (open daily 9:30–11:30, 2–4:30, Apr–Nov; Mon–Fri, Dec–Mar).

➕ 219 F4
Tourist Information Office ✉ 7 avenue de Champagne, 51201
☎ 03 26 53 33 00
🕐 Mon–Sat 9:30–12:30, 1:30–7, Sun 11–4, mid-Apr to mid-Oct; Mon–Sat 9:30–12:30, 1:30–5:30, mid-Oct to mid-Apr

For Kids

• **Beaune:** Take a one-hour interactive tour of the historic Fallot mustard mill, complete with infrared lighting and 3-D animation (La Moutarderie Fallot, 31 faubourg Bretonnerie; tours Mon–Sat, 9:30 and 11 am, Mar to mid-Nov; moderate).
• **Besançon:** The cathedral has one of the best moving clocks of the region, with automata that take off on the hour (► 113).
• **Strasbourg:** Treat them to the fun of a Christmas market in December, when the city is transformed into a storybook wonderland of wooden chalets selling toys and gingerbread (tourist office, tel: 03 88 52 28 28).

THROUGH THE VOSGES ON THE ROUTE DES CRÊTES

Drive

This drive takes in some of the best scenery in the Parc Naturel Régional des Ballons des Vosges, an area of mountains and spectacular natural beauty near the German border, southwest of Strasbourg. Its start and end point is the lakeside town of Gérardmer, where the pine forests are popular with walkers, and it includes the famous Route des Crêtes.

1–2

Leave **Gérardmer** on the D417, towards Colmar. After 2km (1.2 miles) pass the Hôtel de la Pierre Charlemagne on the right, and a parking area on the left signed La Cercenée, just before a roundabout (traffic circle). Go all the way round the roundabout and back towards Gérardmer, to swing right into **La Cercenée** parking area. Cross the D417

DISTANCE 120km/75 miles **TIME** Allow a full day
START/END POINT Gérardmer ✚ 221 E2

at the pedestrian crossing to reach the **Saut des Cuves**, where the Vologne river rushes through an unfenced narrow, rocky gorge. You can view the cascade from the footbridge above. Return to the car park, where signboards give information about further walking routes in the area – with around 16,000km (9,940 miles) of mapped trails through the Forêt de Gérardmer, there's plenty of choice.

2–3

Turn right out of the car park, and immediately left alongside the Hôtel de la Pierre Charlemagne on to the C12 Route du Saut des Cuves, towards **Xonrupt-Longemer**. Pass through the village, joining the D67a towards Longemer.

3–4

The route passes **Lac de Longemer**, then the smaller **Lac de Retournemer**. Both are surrounded by meadows and pine forests, with the Schlucht and Hohneck mountains ahead. At the junction with the D34d, turn

left to rejoin the D417 at the **Col de la Schlucht**, a pass which links the Vosges to Alsace. Turn right off the D417 along the D430 towards the **Jardin d'Altitude du Haut-Chitelet**, which specialises in alpine plant species from across the globe (open in high season only). Stay on the D430, which now becomes the **Route des Crêtes**.

Above: Memorial to Les Diables Bleues fighters
Inset: A climber remembered on Grand Ballon

dedicated to the Diables Bleus (Blue Devils). Further on, 30,000 men lost their lives in the fighting at Le Vieil Armand. Continue along the D431 to **Cernay**, then follow the N66 along the Thur valley and through Willer-sur-Thur to **Bussang**, a high point of the Vosges. Its main claim to fame is its Théâtre du Peuple (People's Theatre), a summer theatre in a woodland setting which has been going strong since 1895. Continue in the same direction on the N66 and at **Le Thillot** take the D486 to return to **Gérardmer**.

TAKING A BREAK

There are lots of good picnic stops along the route – but expect to share them with other visitors in summer. You will find **cafés and restaurants** along the route to suit all pockets and tastes – try to pick one with good views.

When

This drive is spectacular at any time of year, and the Route des Crêtes is popular, so be prepared for heavy traffic through the summer months. In winter, there may be ice and snow at high points along the route, so check locally for information before you set out..

5–6

Just below the summit of the road, look out for a World War I **monument**

Climbing towards Hohneck

4–5

This winding, scenic road along the mountain tops (crête means crest) was constructed during World War I to link the Hohneck mountain area with the rounded peaks of the Grand Ballon to the south. It is this second feature that gives the Parc Naturel Régional its name. Pass Lac de Blanchemer to reach the winter sports resort of **Le Markstein**. Turn right on to the D431 towards Le Grand Ballon, at 1,424m (4,672 feet) the highest mountain in the region, with views to the Alps.

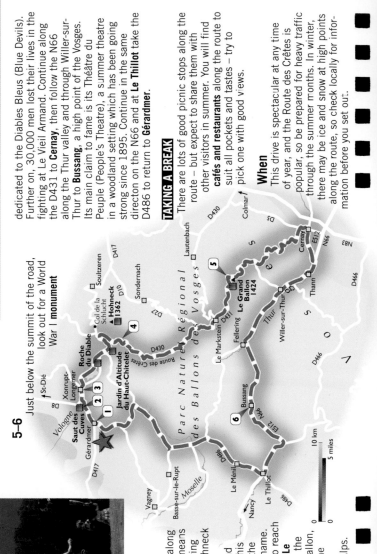

Where to... Stay

Prices
Expect to pay per night for a double room
€ up to €100 €€ €100–€200 €€€ over €200

Hôtel Breughel €
This hotel is conveniently close to the railway station in Lille, on a peaceful traffic-free street. It overlooks a beautiful Gothic church, and is named after the 16th-century Flemish artist, Pieter Breughel. The 65 bedrooms are light and airy, with a decorative style influenced by Breughel's paintings.

🚇 222 C2 ⊠ 5 parvis St-Maurice, 59000 Lille ☎ 03 20 06 06 69; www.hotelbreughel.com

Hôtel du Dragon €–€€
For a special place to stay in the heart of Strasbourg, try this 32-bedroom hotel, which is a pleasing blend of ancient and modern. It is housed in a building that dates from the 17th century, but inside you'll find the style is cool and contemporary, with grey-on-grey colour schemes and furniture designed by modern masters such as Mallet Stevens, Philippe Starck and Gaetano Pesce. For a touch of luxury, ask for a room with a king-size bed.

🚇 221 F3 ⊠ 2 rue de l'Écarlate, 67000 Strasbourg ☎ 03 88 35 79 80; www.dragon.fr

Villa Fleurie €
Relax in stylish comfort at this restored house in Beaune, where the genteel décor harks back to the 1900s. The place is full of period features, including fireplaces in all of the ten bedrooms (as well as modern essentials such as TV), and you can enjoy the sunny terrace and garden, too.

🚇 214 C5 ⊠ 19 place Colbert, 21200 Beaune ☎ 03 80 22 66 00; www.lavillafleurie.fr

Hôtel de la Cathédrale €
You can't exactly miss this attractive old hotel in the middle of Metz – right by the famous cathedral. It's in a historic town house and dates back to 1627, with interesting period furniture, paintings and objets d'art in the public areas. Some of the 20 bedrooms have wrought-iron bedsteads and beamed ceilings. Note that there is no restaurant.

🚇 221 D4 ⊠ 25 place de Chambre, 57000 Metz ☎ 03 87 75 00 02; www.hotelcathedrale-metz.fr

Hostellerie le Maréchal €–€€€
This lovely half-timbered, water-front hotel, with its floral window boxes, is a charming place to stay. It's in Colmar's "Little Venice" district, and has its own restaurant. The interior is appealing, with beamed ceilings, period furnishings and even canopied beds in most rooms. Power-showers and satellite TV come as standard in the 30 non-smoking bedrooms.

🚇 221 E2 ⊠ place des Six Montagnes Noires, 68000 Colmar ☎ 03 89 41 60 32; www.hotel-le-marechal.com

Le Clos Raymi €€
Tuscany, Provence and Champagne – no, not the views from the windows, but rather the names of just some of the themed bedrooms in this comfortable, small hotel in Épernay. It's set in a 19th-century mansion, with a 1930s interior. There are seven bedrooms, and on sunny mornings breakfast is served on the terrace.

🚇 219 F4 ⊠ 3 rue Joseph de Venoge, 51200 Épernay ☎ 03 26 51 00 58; www.closraymi-hotel.com

Where to...
Eat and Drink

Prices

Expect to pay per person for a meal, excluding drinks

€ up to €25   €€ €25–€50   €€€ over €50

À l'Huitrière €–€€

If you're looking for a very special dining experience in Lille, try this top-notch restaurant, set in a venerable house with an art deco frontage. The menu is classic seafood, and the wine list extensive. Inside it's all pale oak panelling and grand Aubusson tapestries, with dripping crystal chandeliers.

✚ 222 C2 ☒ 3 rue des Chats Bossus, 59800 Lille ☎ 03 20 55 43 41; ◉ Mon–Sat noon–2:30, 7:30–10, Sun noon–2:30

Alcide €€–€€€

Dine on *moules frites* (mussels and chips) and *potjevleesch* (cold cuts of meat in aspic) at this classic, timber-fronted brasserie near the centre of Lille. Inside, beneath a glass ceiling, the style is 1930s-retro, with comfortable bench seats.

✚ 222 C2 ☒ 5 rue des Débris St-Étienne, 59800 Lille ☎ 03 20 12 06 95 ◉ Mon–Sat noon–2:30, 7:30–11, Sun noon–2:30

Au Vigneron €€€

For a good introduction to the flavours of the region, try this champagne-themed restaurant in the heart of Reims. They even cook duck in champagne here – but

poached egg with Maroilles cheese is another favourite.

✚ 220 A4 ☒ place Paul Jamot, 51000 Reims ☎ 03 26 79 86 86 ◉ Mon–Fri noon–3, 7:30–10:30, Sat 7:30–10:30

Au Crocodile €€–€€€

This gourmet restaurant in Strasbourg owes its reputation to the inventive cooking of chef Émile Jung. Dishes such as lobster served with vermicelli and pink peppercorns with a citrus sauce give an idea of the richness of the flavour combinations. The setting is all antique furniture, wooden panelling and heavy drapes, and the restaurant takes its name from the stuffed crocodile in the dining room.

✚ 221 F3 ☒ 10 rue de l'Outre-France, 67060 Strasbourg ☎ 03 88 32 13 02 ◉ Tue–Sat noon–2:30, 7:30–10, closed three weeks in Jul and end Dec

Restaurant Stéphane Derbord €

This graceful modern restaurant in Dijon serves a menu loaded with

Burgundian specialities, from crayfish roasted with ginger, pineapple and red pepper compote, to black pudding in spicy breadcrumbs. Save space for desserts such as pear caramelized in honey with nut and raisin ice cream.

✚ 220 B1 ☒ 10 place Wilson, 21000 Dijon ☎ 03 80 67 74 64 ◉ Wed–Sat noon–1:15, 7:30–9:15, Mon–Tue 7:30–9:15; closed 3 weeks in Aug

La Grole €

Treat yourself to a hearty dinner of local favourites in this restaurant, marked outside by a statue of a cow – it specialises in food local to the Savoy region such as fondues, and meat grilled on a hot stone (*braserades*). And if you thought all fondues were the same, think again and save room for pudding – there's a Toblerone chocolate version!

✚ 221 D3 ☒ 47 rue des Ponts, 54000 Nancy ☎ 03 83 35 12 13 ◉ Mon–Fri 7 pm –10, Sat 7 pm–midnight

Where to...
Shop

There's lots of shopping choice for bargain hunters in this varied area of France – quite apart from all the local food delicacies you might expect to find spread across the region, this is the centre of the country's mail-order retail industry, and huge outlet stores sell designer clothes at discount prices.

Lille is famous for its shopping, and also has a number of interesting markets. **Le Cèdre Rouge** is a great place for craftwork and home furnishings from across the globe, including French porcelain and Italian terracotta (Parvis de la Treille 3 place Gilleson, tel: 03 20 51 96 96, www.lecedrerouge.com, open Mon 2–7, Tue–Sat 10:30–7).

The tiny **N de B Haute Mode** sells a range of unique, high-quality accessories from hats and gloves to bags, at affordable prices (6 rue Jean-Jaques Rousseau, tel: 03 20 42 19 79, open Tue 2–7, Wed–Sat 10:30–noon, 2–7), while **Charles at Charlus** is a good source of contemporary leather goods (4 rue Basse, tel: 03 20 51 01 01, open Mon 2:30–7, Tue–Sat 10:30–7).

The **Marché aux Livres et aux Fleurs** combines books and flowers in the attractive setting of the courtyard of a 17th-century former stock exchange (Tue–Sun 1–7, Métro: Rihour). The **Marché de Wazemmes**, held in the surroundings of a church, is good for local fruit and vegetables, with antiques and North African items thrown in for good measure (place de la Nouvelle-Aventure, open Sun, Tue and Thu 7 am–2 pm, Métro: Wazemmes). For the biggest second-hand market in the country, time your visit to coincide with the **Braderie de Lille** 24-hour rummage sale (first Sat–Sun in Sep). Around 200km (125 miles) of walkways are lined with stalls selling everything you could possibly imagine, as the entire city joins in with the fun.

Strasbourg is famous for its quaint **Christmas markets**, held throughout December, with wooden booths selling home-made toys and gingerbread. Its weekly market, the **Marché des Producteurs**, attracts growers and buyers from all over Alsace (place du Marché-aux-Poissons, Sat 7–1). Among the city's other shopping treats, sample the outstanding confectionery and cakes at **Pâtisserie Confiserie Kubler** – the Verger d'Alsace cake, with apple and cinnamon mousse inside, is fabulous.

In Beaune, look out for special Burgundian cheeses at **Le Tast'Fromages** (23 rue Carnot, tel: 03 80 24 73 51, open Mon–Sat 8:30–12:30, 2:30–7:30, Sun 8:30–12:30). Around 120 varieties of cheese are sold here, including the local Époisses au Marc de Bourgogne and Amour de Nuits-St-Georges.

Cité Europe is a giant shopping mall 4km (2.5 miles) outside Calais popular with UK visitors (1001 boulevard du Kent, tel: 03 21 46 47 48, www.cite-europe.com, open Mon–Thu 10–8, Fri 10–9, Sat 10–9). It has a hypermarket, wine merchants, clothes and shoe shops, and a range of eating places.

CHAMPAGNE

This is the champagne region of France. Tour the vast cellars before a tasting session to help you select the best at **Champagne Taittinger** (9 place St-Nicaise, Reims, tel: 03 26 85 84 33, www.taittinger.com, open Mon–Fri 9:30–noon, 2–4:30, Sat–Sun 9–11, 2–5, Mar–Nov, tour €6). **Maxim's**, at 17 rue des Crénaux, offer an alternative tour, showcasing their vintage Brut rosé (tel: 03 26 82 70 67; www.champagnemartel.com, daily 10–7).

Where to...
Be Entertained

There's a buzzing nightlife in the main cities of this part of France – Lille, Reims, Strasbourg – while in the smaller towns you'll find cafés that double as bars in the evenings. Look out for summer festivals – one of the best is **Les Flâneries Musicales d'Été**, held in venues all across Reims in July and August. It celebrates classical music and blues with around 100 concerts, in a (largely free) festival started by the great violinist Yehudi Menuhin. Lille also has a great collection of festivals through June, including the **Parade of Giants**.

CINEMA

Le Metropole is a modern cinema in Lille, screening a variety of retrospectives, with films shown in their original languages and followed by discussions (26 rue des Ponts de Comines, tel: 0892 680 073/303).

BARS

If you're passing through Calais, call in at **Les Pirates**, a bar that may be firmly landlocked in the city centre but with a fun, piratical themed interior (130 boulevard Jacquard, tel: 03 21 97 93 39, open to 2 am Fri–Sat, 1 am Sun–Thu).

If you're in Reims but a night of champagne drinking is not to your taste, head for the bar at **L'Escale**, where more than 200 varieties of beer are on tap (132 rue de Vesle, Reims, tel: 03 26 88 17 85, open Fri–Sat 4 pm–1:15 am, Sun–Thu 4 pm–midnight).

It seems that no French city is complete today without its own lively version of the Irish theme pub. The effect may be surreal, but for one of the best, check out the Wednesday quiz nights and live music at the **Irish Times** pub in Strasbourg (19 rue Sainte-Barbe, tel: 03 88 32 04 02), complete with fireplace and traditional long bar.

A different national theme is found at Lille's **Le Kremlin** bar (51 rue Jean-Jaques Rousseau, tel: 03 20 51 85 79, open Mon–Sat 6 pm–1 am). As the name suggests, it's a Russian bar, with 40 different vodkas on offer, under the watchful eye of a bust of Lenin.

For a different flavour again, the walls of **Zen Café** in Metz are adorned with paintings inspired by Japanese manga cartoons (4 rue du Change, tel: 03 87 36 56 75, open Mon–Sat 8 pm–2 am, Sun 3–8 pm). The bar has a live DJ and house music at weekends.

NIGHTCLUBS

For a great night out in Beaune, try **L'Opera Night** (rue de Beaumarché, Palais des Congrès, tel: 03 80 24 10 11, www.operanight.fr, open Fri–Sun 10:30 pm–5 am, free entry Sun). Despite the name, it has nothing to do with opera – it's a nightclub complex, with a huge dance floor, music from the 1980s and '90s, a cocktail bar, and the smarter L'Armstrong bar.

In Reims, **Le Tigre** is the rock venue to head for (2 bis avenue Georges Clemenceau, tel: 03 26 82 64 00, open nightly 5 pm–5 am). It's primarily a concert hall, but there's a good-sized dance floor, and guitars hanging from the walls set the scene.

Strasbourg's home of underground culture is a former dairy, **La Laiterie** (13 rue Hohwald, tel: 03 88 23 72 37, open Tue–Sat 7:30 pm–11:30 pm). Check out the bar, theatre and concert hall, where live rock and pop concerts are held.

The Loire

Getting Your Bearings 122 – 123
In Three Days 124 – 125
Don't Miss 126 – 131
At Your Leisure 132 – 135
Where to... 136 – 138

Getting Your Bearings

The Loire is a wide, shallow river that threads slowly westwards through northern France to emerge at the sea beyond Nantes. Its valley and tributaries encompass the ancient provinces of Anjou, Touraine, Orleanais and Berry, making it the historic heart of the country. An end to centuries of struggle against invading Enlish forces came in the mid-15th century, making way for a building boom on a scale of grandeur that is unique in France.

The majority of the magnificent Renaissance châteaux or palaces for which this area is so well known lie along the stretch of river between Angers in the west and Orléans in the east. They range from fairytale turretted piles to more intimate stately homes which are still inhabited, and any visit to the area should try to include a mixture of both.

There is fast autoroute access to the main cities, including centrally placed Tours. For exploring at leisure, the most scenic minor roads are to the south of the river.

Previous page: The château
of Azay-le-Rideau

Left: Doorway at Azay-le-Rideau

★ **Don't Miss**

1 Château de Chambord ➤ 126
2 Château Royal de Blois ➤ 128
3 Château de Chenonceau ➤ 129
4 Château d'Azay-le-Rideau ➤ 130

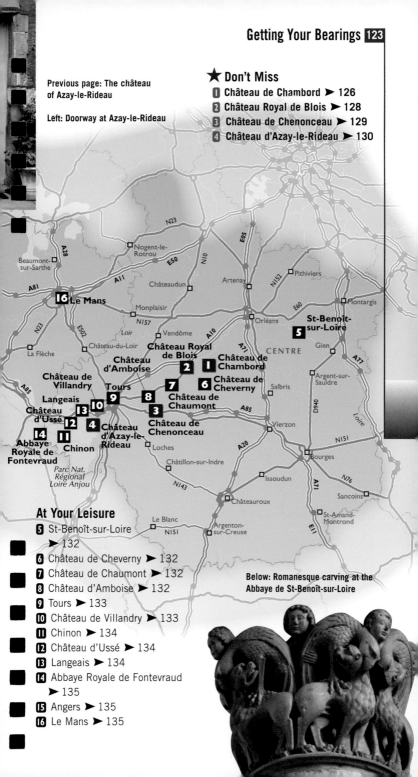

N23

A28

Nogent-le-Rotrou

E50 N10

Beaumont-sur-Sarthe

A81 A11

Châteaudun

Artenay

N152 Pithiviers

E05

Le Mans **16**

Monplaisir

N157

E05 Montargis

E50

Orléans

N23

Loir Vendôme

A10

E502

Château-du-Loir

La Flèche

**Château Royal
de Blois**

Château
d'Amboise

2 **1** **Château de
Chambord**

CENTRE

Gien

A71

St-Benoît-
sur-Loire

5

Château de Villandry

Tours **9**

Langeais

Château d'Ussé **13** **10**

12 **4**

11 Chinon

14

**Abbaye
Royale de
Fontevraud**

7

8 **Château de
Chaumont**

3 **Château de
Chenonceau**

**Château
d'Azay-le-
Rideau**

Loches

Châtillon-sur-Indre

6 **Château de
Cheverny**

Salbris

A85

Vierzon

A20

Argent-sur-
Sauldre

D940

Loire

N151

Bourges

A71

N76

Issoudun

Sancoins

Parc Nat.
Régional
Loire Anjou

N143

Châteauroux

A71

Le Blanc

N151

Argenton-
sur-Creuse

E11

St-Amand-
Montrond

At Your Leisure

5 St-Benoît-sur-Loire
➤ 132
6 Château de Cheverny ➤ 132
7 Château de Chaumont ➤ 132
8 Château d'Amboise ➤ 132
9 Tours ➤ 133
10 Château de Villandry ➤ 133
11 Chinon ➤ 134
12 Château d'Ussé ➤ 134
13 Langeais ➤ 134
14 Abbaye Royale de Fontevraud
➤ 135
15 Angers ➤ 135
16 Le Mans ➤ 135

Below: Romanesque carving at the
Abbaye de St-Benoît-sur-Loire

None of the distances on this tour are particularly great, but with so many magnificent mansions and castles to see, it's easy to get château-ed out – so combine some of the best with visits to Le Mans and other places.

The Loire in Three Days

Day One

Morning
Start with the biggest and one of the most splendid of the royal châteaux, François I's **1 Château de Chambord** (► 126–127). If you're there early you may be lucky enough to spot some of the park's famous **wildlife** (► 127). **Take a picnic** to eat in the grounds, or try the **restaurant** of the château for lunch (► 127).

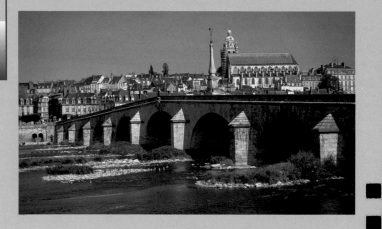

Afternoon
Head the short distance south to see the more intimate **6 Château de Cheverny** (► 132), a privately owned mansion, and still lived in by its owners. Then make your way northwest to the town of **Blois**, and **Le Bouchon Lyonnais** for supper (above, ► 128).

Evening
Stay on in Blois and visit the **2 Château Royal de Blois** (► 128) for a spectacular *son-et-lumière* performance.

Day Two

Morning

Visit the romantic and beautiful **3 Château de Chenonceau** (➤ 129), and take a short **trip on the river** if there's time, before moving on to the contrastingly grim **8 Château d'Amboise** (below, ➤ 132–133). Find a **café** in the small town for lunch.

Afternoon

Spend the afternoon relaxing in **9 Tours** (➤ 133), with some **shopping** thrown in for good measure, or head north on the N138/E502 to **16 Le Mans** (➤ 135) for a sight of gleaming **racing cars** in the museum there.

Evening

Stay on in either **Tours** or **Le Mans** for the **nightlife** (➤ 138).

Day Three

Morning

Spend a morning discovering the delights of picturesque **4 Château d'Azay-le-Rideau** (➤ 130–131), and visit the ancient **Église St-Symphorien** (➤ 131) in the nearby village. Try the cave-built **Les Grottes** (➤ 137) restaurant in **Azay-le-Rideau** for lunch.

Afternoon

Continue west along the Loire valley to the charming "Sleeping Beauty's Castle", **12 Château d'Ussé** (➤ 134), or while away the afternoon n the extensive gardens of **10 Château de Villandry** (right, ➤ 133).

Evening

Take your pick of excellent **restaurants** in the area (➤ 137).

▢ Château de Chambord

The biggest and architecturally one of the most splendid of the Loire châteaux, Chambord is at the top of many visitors' lists of favourites. Its vital statistics – which include 440 rooms and a chimney for every day of the year – defy its purpose as an up-market royal hunting lodge: this was regal ostentation on a grand scale. The interior, stripped of most of its artefacts during the Revolution, is rather bare, but this successfully shows off some architectural oddities which make a visit worthwhile. The surrounding 5,440 ha (13,440-acre) park is a setting for special events throughout the summer.

Above: A forest of turrets and chimneys adorns the château

Centre: The double stair-case

Above right: A roof detail

Building the Dream

François I commissioned the château in 1519, on a patch of marshy ground near the River Loire. He later demanded that the river be diverted to surround his palace, but had to make do with a moat instead, fed by a small tributary. Initial construction of the château took 12 years. His main architects were Jacques Sordeau and his nephew Pierre Neveu, and Jacques Coqueau.

However, the most famous name associated with the building of Chambord is that of Leonardo da Vinci (1452–1519), who François brought to live at nearby Amboise. The great master is widely credited with the

Château de Chambord

design of the extraordinary Grand Escalier du Logis, an open-sided double spiral staircase by which people could ascend and descend at the same time without meeting each other, leading up, via the king's bedroom, to a lantern tower. It's the most complex and intriguing of 14 large and 60 small staircases in the building.

The roofscape of Chambord is its best-loved feature, a forest of turrets and towers, chimneys and columns. Balconies up here allowed the royal party a bird's-eye view of the hunting below.

Successive monarchs added to Chambord, most significantly the theatrical King's Bedroom of 1748, lined with panelling from Versailles. Long before that, royalty had lost interest, and Chambord was granted to a succession of owners until finally coming under state control in 1932.

TAKING A BREAK

A small **restaurant at the château** serves excellent food at reasonable prices. There are also plenty of places to picnic in the grounds.

➕ 218 C1 ✉ Château et Domaine National de Chambord, Maison des Réfractaires, 41250
☎ 02 54 50 40 00; www.chambord.org 🕐 Daily 9–6:15, Apr–Sep; 9–5:15 Oct–Mar 💶 Moderate, under 17 free, free to all 1st Sun of month Oct–Mar

François I
- 1494 Born in Cognac.
- 1515 Succeeded his uncle, Louis XII, to the throne of France.
- 1519 Lost out in the election for Holy Roman Emperor to Charles I/V of Spain, who became a life-long enemy. Started building the château at Chambord.
- 1520 Met with Henry VIII of England at the Field of the Cloth of Gold, in Picardy, an event named after the lavish tents of the French.
- 1525 Captured in battle against Charles V and ransomed the following year at a cost of Artois, Burgundy, Flanders and various Italian territories.
- 1547 Died and succeeded by his second son, Henri II.

CHÂTEAU DE CHAMBORD: INSIDE INFO

Top tips If you want to get in **for free**, time your visit for the first Sunday in the month, when all access charges are waived.
- Guided **tours in English** are available daily throughout July and August.
- The park, once a royal hunting forest, is still good for seeing deer, wild boar and other wildlife. Be there at **dawn or dusk** for the best chance of spotting them.

Don't miss In the **king's study** a window has been scratched with a message, using a diamond. It is believed that François himself wrote "*Souvent femme varie, bien fol est qui s'y fie*", which translates as "Women are fickle and it's a fool who trusts them."

2 Château Royal de Blois

The magnificence of this royal palace hides an unrivalled tale of bloody intrigue, while its contrasting architecture reflects changes in fashion across the centuries. The earliest parts of the structure, built around a central courtyard, date from the 13th century. One outstanding feature is the open-sided spiral staircase, part of a decorative Italianate wing added by François I, and reminiscent of his work at Chambord (►126–127).

Tours of the château take in the royal bedchamber where a foul murder took place in 1588 at the command of Henri II. The unfortunate victim was Henri, Duc de Guise, a serious political rival to the king's power in France.

As you explore the château and its surroundings, hang on to your entry ticket – it also gives entry to the **Musée des Beaux-Arts**, the Gaston d'Orléans wing, St-Calais chapel, the gem-cutters museum and the St-Saturnin churchyard on the opposite bank of the river. The Gaston d'Orléans wing was a later addition in the more reserved classical style, complete with high-pitched roof, by master architect François Mansard (1598–1666).

For a different view of the château and its history, attend a *son et lumière* show in the courtyard. They're held every evening from the end of April through to mid-September, with commentary in English on Wednesdays.

TAKING A BREAK

A good value option serving local dishes of the region is **Au Bouchon Lyonnais** (25 rue des Violettes, Blois, tel: 02 54 74 12 87).

Above: The distinctive spiral stair
Below: Louis XII

➕ 218 C1
✉ place du Château, 41000 Blois ☎ 02 54 90 33 33; www. loiredeschateaux .com ⊙ Daily 9–6, mid-Mar to Sep; 9–noon, 2–5:30, Oct to mid-Mar
♿ Moderate

3 Château de Chenonceau

With a three-storey gallery built out over the River Cher, Chenonceau is one of the most beautiful and romantic of the Loire châteaux, and it comes as no great surprise that its history is caught up with the lives of the strong women of the age. Tours reveal a richly furnished interior, as well as the kitchens and wine cellar, and there's plenty to see in the park, including the formal walled garden, a maze, and a floral workshop.

Catherine de Briçonnet built the main structure in the early 16th century, and it was later given by Henri II to his charismatic mistress, Diane de Poitiers (1499–1566). She left her mark in the first bridge over the river, and the parterre garden, but was thrown out on Henri's death by his jealous widow, Catherine de Médicis. Catherine's contribution was to build the gallery above the bridge, and lay out the park, before passing it on her death to her daughter-in-law, Louise of Lorraine. Restoration in the mid-19th century was done by Madame de Pelouze.

For a water-borne view of the château, take a **boat trip on the river** from Chisseaux. Contact La Bélandre, tel: 02 47 23 98 64, operates May–Oct.

TAKING A BREAK

There's a choice of **two restaurant**s in the outbuildings, open mid-Mar to Nov.

Catherine de Médicis's formal gardens at the château

➕ 218 C1
✉ 37150 Chenonceaux
☎ 02 47 23 90 07;
www.chenonceaux.com
🕐 Daily 9–7, mid-Mar to mid-Sep; 9–6.30 mid- to end Sep; 9–6 early to mid-Oct and early to mid-Mar; 9–5:30 , mid- to end Oct and mid- to end Feb; 9–5 early to mid-Nov and early to mid-Feb; 9–4:30 mid-Nov to Jan
🎫 Moderate

Chimneypiece in Diane de Poitier's chamber

4 Château d'Azay-le-Rideau

The small, white, L-shaped château of Azay-le-Rideau sits on an island in the River Indre. Its sumptuous Renaissance interior includes furniture dating from the 16th century, and paintings and tapestries that reflect gracious living for the wealthiest people at the time when these châteaux were built.

Above and inset: The château is surrounded by moats and gardens

Italian and Gothic influences can be seen in a seamless blend of opulence, as you explore the salons, the great hall, the library and the dining room. The grand staircase has straight flights, considered an innovation in an age when spiral was the norm. A salamander, the royal symbol of François I, is carved above the main entrance, but this compliment to the king was not enough to save the château from a royal manipulation that saw its creator disgraced and exiled.

A Bloody Revenge

In 1418, an entire garrison of 350 men was hanged here, and the village and fortress razed. It happened during the period of the Hundred Years' War, as French and English factions sought control of France. Azay-le-Rideau belonged to the Duke of Burgundy, but when the Dauphin – the future Charles VII – passed through the area he was insulted by the garrison. Charles promptly laid siege to fortress and village, and exacted his bloody revenge.

Royal Connections

There was a castle on the site here until 1418, when it was wiped out by the future Charles VII, and it was exactly 100 years before Marcelin Berthelot, courtier to both Louis XI and Charles VIII, laid the plans for his new mansion.

The architects were Étienne Rousseau, Pierre Maupoint and Jacquet Thoreau. Berthelot's son Gilles, treasurer to François I, is credited with completing the job in 1524, but in fact it was Gilles's wife, the formidable Philippa Lesbahy, who supervised all the building and design work.

A Building Interrupted

Two of the proposed four sides of the château were complete when disaster struck: the king, feeling threatened by his most powerful ministers, engineered a financial scandal and Gilles Berthelot was forced to flee. All his possessions were confiscated, and he died in exile in Lorraine, in 1530, having never actually lived in the beautiful château he had created.

TAKING A BREAK

Explore the restaurant **Les Grottes**, built into the solid rock, in the village of Azay-le-Rideau (➤ 137).

➕ 218 B1   ✉ 37190 Azay-le-Rideau
☎ 02 47 45 42 04; www.monum.fr ◷ Daily 9:30–7, Jul–Aug; 9:30–6 Apr–Jun, Sep; 10–12:30, 2–5:30 Oct–Mar
📷 Moderate, under 18 free

CHÂTEAU D'AZAY-LE-RIDEAU: INSIDE INFO

Top tip Check locally for details of evening **son-et-lumière** shows in summer.

Hidden gem The village of Azay-le-Rideau has a second, less showy treasure, which is worth seeking out. It's the old, weathered **Église St-Symphorien**, parts of which date back to the 10th century. Look for the carvings of rows of saints around the doorway.

At Your Leisure

5 St-Benoît-sur-Loire

In a landscape dominated by fine châteaux, the village of St-Benoît-sur-Loire provides a different perspective: its claim to fame is its **abbey church**, said to be one of the best Romanesque buildings in France. It was raised as the Abbaye de Fleury between c1067 and 1218, but pilgrims had been coming here since AD 675 for the shrine of the Italian St Benedict. Known as the founder of Western monasticism, Benedict (c480–547) had been buried at Monte Cassino, near Naples, and his relics were presumably stolen and brought here.

The building is sublime, accessed via the tall stone archways of the belfry porch. Inside, look for the carved choir screen presented by Cardinal Richelieu in 1635, and the mosaic floor imported from Italy. The resident Benedictine monks offer guided tours between the daily services.

➕ 219 D2
Tourist Information Office ✉ 44 rue Orléanaise, 45730 ☎ 02 38 35 79 00

6 Château de Cheverny

Cheverny lies southeast of Blois, and is worth a visit as one of the most interesting privately owned châteaux in the region. The handsome exterior

A dramatic Gobelin tapestry depicting the Abduction of Helen, at Cheverny

is regular and classical in style, the interior sumptuously decorated to reflect the first half of the 17th century, in the flamboyant style of Louis XIII, complete with tapestries and grand paintings. Despite all of this, it still manages to feel like somebody's home rather than a museum. You can explore the extensive grounds in summer via electric buggy.

➕ 218 C1 ✉ 41700, Cheverny ☎ 02 54 79 96 29; www.chateau-cheverny.fr ⏰ Daily 9:15–6:45, Jul–Aug; 9:15–6:15, Apr–Jun, Sep; 9–5, Oct–Mar 💰 Moderate

7 Château de Chaumont

When Henri II died in 1559, his widow Catherine de Médicis evicted his powerful and charismatic mistress, Diane de Poitiers, from Chenonceau and banished her to this lesser château, where she might live out her days in seclusion. It's a massive, rather bleak castle, with huge pepper-pot corner and gateway towers, in a strategic location favoured by the counts of Blois since the 10th century.

The grounds are the setting for a spectacular annual **garden festival** (mid-Jun to mid-Oct), when around 25 original gardens are created to a selected theme by some of France's top garden designers.

➕ 218 C1 ✉ 41150, Chaumont-sur-Loire ☎ 02 54 51 26 26; www.chaumont-jardins.com ⏰ Daily 9:30–6:30 mid-May to mid-Sep; 10:30–5:30, mid-Sep to mid-May 💰 Moderate

8 Château d'Amboise

Amboise is one of the royal châteaux of the Loire, built by Charles VIII (1470–98) in an elaborate Italianate style that set new trends in its day. It has a mixed history. In 1560 it was the focus of the bloody backlash against the Amboise Conspiracy, when 1,300 Protestants who had plotted to kidnap the young François II were hanged from the battlements. After that, royalty abandoned it, and only fragments of the structure survive today. The highlights are the little Gothic chapel of St-Hubert on the ramparts, and the broad spiral ramp inside the great drum tower.

Medieval timber-framed houses on place Plumereau, in the heart of Tours

Amboise's château looms above the town

The attractive town of Amboise, with its narrow streets, clusters around the château. Leonardo da Vinci (1452–1519) came to live on the outskirts of the town during the last four years of his life, with a pension from François I, and models created from his drawings are displayed in a **museum** here.

➕ 218 C1 ✉ 37400, Amboise
☎ 02 47 57 00 98; www.chateau-amboise.com ⏰ Daily 9–6:30, mid-Mar to Jun; 9–7, Jul–Aug; 9–6 Sep–Oct; 9–noon, 2–4:45, Nov–Feb; 9–noon, 1:30–5:30, 1–15 Mar 🎟 Moderate

🟥9 Tours

Tours is a busy city at the centre of the Loire area, with an appealing old town and lots of opportunities for high-class shopping. The best streets for this are rue des Halles and rue Nationale. Great antiques shops line rue Colbert, and you'll find restaurants and art galleries along here, too. There are street markets galore, including the **flower market** on Boulevard Béranger, held on Wednesday and Saturday. The **Musée des Beaux-Arts** by the Cathédrale St-Gatien is worth a look, too, for its works by Mantegna, Rubens and Rembrandt (open Wed–Mon 9–12:45, 2–6).

➕ 218 B1
Tourist Information Office ✉ 78–82 rue Bernard Palissy, BP 4201, 37042 Tours Cedex 1 ☎ 02 47 70 37 37; www.ligeris.com ⏰ Mon–Sat 8:30–7, Sun 10–12:30, 2:30–5, mid-Apr to mid-Oct; Mon–Sat 9–12:30, 1:30–6, Sun 10–1, mid-Oct to mid-Apr

🟥10 Château de Villandry

Villandry is best-known for its 6ha (15 acres) of formal gardens, restored to their 16th-century glory by Joachim de Carvallo in the 20th century. They are laid out on three levels, with a water garden at the highest. A decorative garden in the middle has beds outlined by box hedges and punctuated with clipped bushes of yew, while at the lowest level, directly in front of the château itself, is the potager – a supreme example of a formal kitchen garden, where fruit trees and vegetables are set in rectangular beds according to the colour of their foliage. Jean le Breton built the château and garden in 1532. Inside, look out for paintings by Goya and Velázquez.

➕ 218 B1 ✉ 37510 ☎ 02 47 50 02 09; www.chateauvillandry.com ⏰ Daily 9–6, May–Sep; 9–dusk, Oct to mid-Nov, mid-Feb to Apr; gardens open daily, all year 🎟 Moderate

🔟 Chinon

The château on the high rocks at Chinon, on a bend of the River Vienne, was no Renaissance palace but rather an imposing medieval stronghold. Today it is a ruin, still dominating the old town at its feet, with its narrow medieval streets and crazy timbered houses, and wine cellars, or *caves*, which undermine the cliffs below. There are in fact two castles on the site, including Fort St-George, built by Henry II of England, who died here in 1559.

The most significant event in Chinon's history came in 1429, when Joan of Arc came here to convince the Dauphin that she could retake Orléans from the English. The event is celebrated by a **museum** in the old clock tower of the château (open daily).

➕ 212 B5
Tourist Information Office ✉ place Hofheim, 37500, BP 141 ☎ 02 47 93 17 85; www.chinon.com ⏰ Daily 10–7, May–Sep; Mon–Sat 10–noon, 2–6, Oct–Apr

🔢 Château d'Ussé

The most romantic and beautiful of

Costumes are displayed in the sumptuous Chambre du Roi at Château d'Ussé

Paddling in the river shallows at Chinon

the Loire châteaux, multi-turreted Ussé lies on the Indre, surrounded by the dark forest of Chinon. It is said to have inspired Charles Perrault to write the fairytale of *Sleeping Beauty* in 1697, and as a result is widely known as the Château de la Belle au Bois Dormant.

It was started in the late 15th century, and originally had four sides around the central courtyard – remodelling in the 17th century removed one to make the most of the views. The stunning formal gardens were designed by André Le Nôtre. The château is still in private hands, and access to the 18th-century interior, with its elegant furniture and costume displays, is by guided tour.

➕ 212 B5 ✉ 37420 ☎ 02 47 95 54 05; www.tourisme.fr/usse ⏰ Daily 9:30–6:30, Apr–Sep; 10–noon, 2–5:30, mid-Feb to Mar, Oct to mid-Nov
♿ Expensive

🔢 Langeais

Approaching Langeais from the south, a suspension bridge over the Loire sweeps you into the village, which lies on the eastern edge of the Parc Naturel Régional Loire Anjou. Troglodyte dwellings are built into the rocks, and there's extensive parkland around the château to explore.

The castle dates from 1465 and was intended as a fortress to ward off the threat of invasion from Brittany at a time when Louis XI held court in Tours. Louis's son Charles VIII neutralised the threat in 1491 by marrying Anne of Brittany here. Behind the rather grim exterior is a richly furnished Renaissance interior.

➕ 212 B5
Château de Langeais ✉ Fondation

Jacques Siegfried, 37130 ☎ 02 47 96 72 60 🕐 Daily 9:30–6:30, Apr to mid-Jul, mid-Aug to mid-Oct; 9:30–8, mid-Jul to mid-Aug; 10–5:30, mid-Oct to Mar 💰 Moderate

14 Abbaye Royale de Fontevraud

Much of this great 11th-century abbey fell into decay after it was abandoned during the Revolution, and it served as a prison between 1804 and 1965. Restoration is on-going, and one of its principal points of interest is the set of tombs in the church: it's the last resting place of Henry II of England, his wife Eleanor of Aquitaine and their Crusader son, Richard the Lionheart.

Royal tombs at Fontevraud

🔳 212 B5 ✉ BP 24, 49590 Fontevraud-l'Abbaye ☎ 02 41 51 71 41; www.abbaye-fontevraud.com 🕐 Daily 9–6:30, Jun–Sep; 10–5:30, Oct–May 💰 Moderate, under 18 free

15 Angers

Angers is a good-sized town on the River Maine, with an old quarter, the Doutre, that is pleasant to wander through. The **château**, built in the 15th century to fend off the Bretons, is boldly striped with the local black-coloured stone. Here you can see the surviving fragments of a remarkable tapestry, commissioned by the Duc d'Anjou in 1375 to hang in the local cathedral. The tapestry pieces illus-trate scenes from the writings of St John the Divine. More modern tapes-

For Kids

• **Port St-Père**: Planète Sauvage is a brilliant drive-through safari-park between Nantes and Pornic (44170, tel: 02 40 04 82 82, open daily Apr–Oct).

• **Blois**: Toys ancient and modern are displayed at Le Paradis des Enfants in the centre of town (2 rue des Trois-Clefs, tel: 02 54 78 09 68).

try can be seen at the **Musée de la Tapisserie Contemporaine**, at 4 boulevard Arago (tel 02 41 24 18 43).

🔳 218 A1 **Tourist Information Office** ✉ 7 place Kennedy, 49051 ☎ 02 41 23 50 00; www.angers-tourisme.com 🕐 Mon–Sat 9–7, Sun 10–6, May–Sep; Mon 2–6, Tue–Sat 9–6, Sun 10–1, Oct–Apr

16 Le Mans

Visit this busy industrial town in June for all the excitement of the 24-hour motor race. If you can't make it, then the next best thing is the **Musée Automobile de la Sarthe**, in rue de Laigné (open daily 10–7, Jun–Sep; 10–6 Oct–Dec, Mar–May; Sat–Sun only Jan–Feb). Here you can admire 11 previous race winners, plus around 140 other vehicles, all polished and gleaming.

🔳 218 B2 **Tourist Information Office** ✉ Hôtel des Ursulines, rue de l'Étoile, 72000 ☎ 02 43 28 17 22; www.ville-lemans.fr

A 1965 Ferrari in the museum, Le Mans

🕐 Mon–Sat 9–6, Sun 10–12:30, 2–5, Jun–Sep; Mon–Fri 9–6, Sat 9–noon, 2–6, Sun 10–noon, Oct–May

Where to... Stay

Prices
Expect to pay per night for a double room
€ under €100   €€ €100–€200   €€€ over €200

Mercure Centre €–€€

This medium-sized hotel is conveniently set within walking distance of the old town of Blois. Huge windows make the most of the river views, and the styling is contemporary, with TV and air-conditioning as standard. Facilities include an indoor pool, Jacuzzi and an exercise room.

➕ 218 C1 ⊠ 28 quai St-Jean, 41000 Blois ☎ 02 54 56 66 66; www.mercure.com

Hôtel du Bon-Laboureur €–€€

A grand old 18th-century inn with an excellent restaurant, this hotel makes a good base for exploring the area around Chenonceau. Rooms are relatively small, but each is well equipped with TV and kitchenette. Air-conditioning is available in many. The restaurant is popular in its own right, so reserve early. There is also an outdoor pool.

➕ 218 C1 ⊠ 6 rue de Dr Bretonneau, 37150 Chenonceaux ☎ 02 47 23 90 02; www.bon-laboureur.com ☯ Closed mid-Nov and Jan

La Roseraie €

Another excellent choice in Chenonceaux, La Roseraie has the more intimate feel of a boutique hotel, with just 17 rooms. Bedrooms are small but well-equipped, and there's an outdoor swimming pool. An excellent restaurant is attached, complete with terrace for alfresco summer dining.

➕ 218 C1 ⊠ 7 rue de Dr Bretonneau, 37150 Chenonceaux ☎ 02 47 23 90 09; www.charmingroseraie.com ☯ Open Mar to mid-Nov

Jean Bardet's Château Belmont €€–€€€

For a stately treat in Tours, book into Château Belmont, a gracious 17th-century mansion on a hilltop. It is surrounded by luxuriant flower gardens created out of the old vineyard, which also supply the hotels restaurant with the freshest of vegetables (book ahead). The 16 bedrooms are elegant and simple, with views over the gardens and the outdoor (heated) swimming pool, and air-conditioning is available.

➕ 218 B1 ⊠ rue Groison, 37000 Tours ☎ 02 47 41 41 11; www.jeanbardet.com

Le Prieuré €€–€€€

This former priory at Chênehutteles-Tuffeaux, 7km (4.5 miles) northwest of Saumur, is great for families. The setting is a wooded hillside above the river Loire, with an outdoor pool, tennis courts and a lawn for bowling. Parts of the building itself date back to the 12th century, and all rooms enjoy views of the river.

➕ 218 A1 ⊠ 49350 Chênehutteles-Tuffeaux ☎ 02 41 67 90 14; www.prieure.com ☯ Closed Feb

Hôtel Lion d'Or €–€€

Romorantin-Lanthenay is south of Orleans, away from many of the main sites of the Loire, but it's worth the diversion if you're looking for somewhere special, with an excellent restaurant. The hotel is in a Renaissance mansion, surrounded by immaculate gardens.

➕ 219 D1 ⊠ 69 rue Clemenceau, 41200 Romorantin-Lanthenay ☎ 02 54 94 15 15; www.hotel-liondor.fr ☯ Closed mid-Feb and late Nov

Where to...
Eat and Drink

Prices

Expect to pay per night for a meal, excluding drinks:
€ up to €25   €€ €25–€50   €€€ over €50

Hotel Grand St-Michel
€€–€€€

Enjoy views of the Château de Chambord from the dining room and terrace of this restaurant, in a building that once served as the château's hunting pack. The food is unfussy, with a regional bias – try the duck breast in a green peppercorn sauce, or the local pâté. This place is especially popular on Sundays and holidays, so be prepared to book ahead.

➕ 218 C1 ☒ 103 place St-Michel, 41250 Chambord ☎ 02 54 20 31 31 ❿ Daily noon–2, 7–8:30, mid-Dec to mid-Nov

Les Grottes €€–€€€

If you thought restaurants carved out of solid rock only happened in Flintstone cartoons, think again – this charming eaterie at Azay-le-Rideau is built into two caverns carved straight from the cliff. Sample regional specialities such as duck with apple, or sausage with scrambled egg. There are lots of local wines on the list.

➕ 218 B1 ☒ 23 rue Pineau, 37190 Azay-le-Rideau ☎ 02 47 45 21 04 ❿ Fri–Wed 12:15–1:45, 7:15–8:45, May–Aug; Fri–Tue 12:15–1:45, 7:15–8:45, Sep–Dec, Feb–Apr; closed Jan and first week Jul

Licorne €€€

A starter such as prawn and basil ravioli in morel sauce should whet your appetite in this popular restaurant in Fontevraud, with a Louis XIV-styled interior. Other temptations might include sweet treats such as warm chocolate tart with a pear and lemon-butter sauce. Advance booking recommended.

➕ 212 B5 ☒ Allée Sainte-Catherine, 49590 Fontevraud-l'Abbaye ☎ 02 41 51 72 49 ❿ Tue–Sat 12:15–1:30, 7:15–9, Sun 12:15–1:30, Apr–Nov; Thu–Sat 12:15–130, 7:15–9, Wed, Sun 2:15–1:30, early Dec, Feb–Mar

Rascasse €€–€€€

This is a great place for a break and a restorative lunch of hearty traditional fare in art deco surroundings. Try the regional speciality of les diableries (shredded meat and sausage), but make sure to save room for a bugattise – a chocolate-covered bonbon local to the area.

➕ 218 B2 ☒ 6 rue de la Mission, 72000 Le Mans ☎ 02 43 84 45 91 ❿ Tue–Thu, Sat–Sun noon–2, and Tue–Sat 7:30–9:30; closed Aug

Grand St-Benoît €€–€€€

This restaurant overlooks a 12th-century church. Inside, exposed oak beams reveal its age, but the furniture is contemporary. The menu is seasonal, with carefully prepared regional dishes.

➕ 219 D2 ☒ 7 place St-André, 45730 St-Benoît-sur-Loire ☎ C2 38 35 11 92 ❿ Tue–Fri 12:15–1:45, 7:15–8:45, Sat 7:15–8:45, Sun 12:15–1:45; closed end Aug–early Sep and late Dec–late Jan

Auberge de Porc Vallières
€–€€

A former pub on the banks of the Loire, once the haunt of fishermen, now offers a hearty menu of regional specialities; you'll find that herb-stuffed cabbage complements the meat dishes.

➕ 218 C1 ☒ 37230 Vallières ☎ 02 47 42 24 04

Where to...
Shop

There are plenty of shopping opportunities in the area, including unusual gift ideas at the châteaux.

For a little souvenir of history, call in at **Tapisserie Langlois** in Blois (route du Château, tel: 02 54 78 04 43, open daily). Here, some of the best tapestries from the local châteaux are painstakingly reproduced; prices range from €180 to €3,000. One of the best château gift shops is at **Cheverny**, where you can buy anything from comic books to a replica suit of armour (Cour-Cheverny, tel: 02 54 79 96 29, open daily). And if you're looking for real, top quality antique art treasures, try **Christian Dumartin**'s shop in the elegant setting of the Manoir de Beauvais, Chinon (Ligre,

tel: 02 47 98 36 63, open Tue–Fri 9–noon, 2–7, but check ahead).

The Loire region, like much of France, has good local markets. One of the best is the **Marché d'Orléans**, which sets up in different parts of the city on different days. Look for it on Tuesdays on Blossière (7 am–2 pm) and Dauphoine (7–noon), on Thursdays in place Dunois (3 pm–7:30 pm), and on Saturdays at Charpenterie Quai du Roi (6 am–12.30 pm). **Tours** has a daily market, with a dazzling array of *charcuterie*, local fruit and vegetables, and good local crafts, seen at its best on Sundays (place des Halles, 7 am–2 pm).

For top-range designer shopping, head for **rue Crebillon** in Nantes, and the boutiques of the **passage Pommeraye** arcade. If rustic craftwork is more to your taste, don't miss the **Cooperative de la Vannerie** at Azay-le-Rideau, where local artisans have got together to sell their wares, from baskets to wooden benches.

Where to...
Be Entertained

At night, some of the châteaux have *son et lumière* (sound and light) shows depicting the history of the buildings. The most spectacular of these is at **Puy du Fou**, where at weekends a cast of hundreds takes part in historical re-enactments (Jun to mid–Sep, tel: 02 51 64 11 11, expensive).

CINEMA

The **Gaumont Angers Multiplex**, in the St-Serge district of Angers, close to the university, shows new movies, with around half in English (avenue des Droits de l'Homme, tel: 0892 696 696, www.gaumont.fr). Nantes holds the **Three Continents Film Festival** in late November, with movies from Asia, Latin America and Africa (tel: 02 40 69 74 14; www.3continents.com).

MUSIC AND DANCE

Lasers blazing into the night sky announce the Loire's biggest dance venue, **Le Metro**, at Beaulieu-sur-Layon, south of Angers, with a capacity of 3,000 (tel: 02 41 78 30 97, open Thu–Sat 11 pm–dawn).

For a more intimate experience, try **La Péniche Excelsior** club in Le Mans, set on a barge on the River Sarthe (tel: 02 43 80 35 06, open generally from 10 pm). **Le Pyms**, in Tours, is a club that favours up-to-the-minute music, and is popular with a younger crowd (170 avenue de Grammont, tel: 02 47 66 22 22, open Tue–Sun 10:30 pm–4 am).

Southeast France

Getting Your Bearings 140 – 141
In Four Days 142 – 143
Don't Miss 144 – 156
At Your Leisure 157 – 164
Drive 165 – 167
Where to... 168 – 172

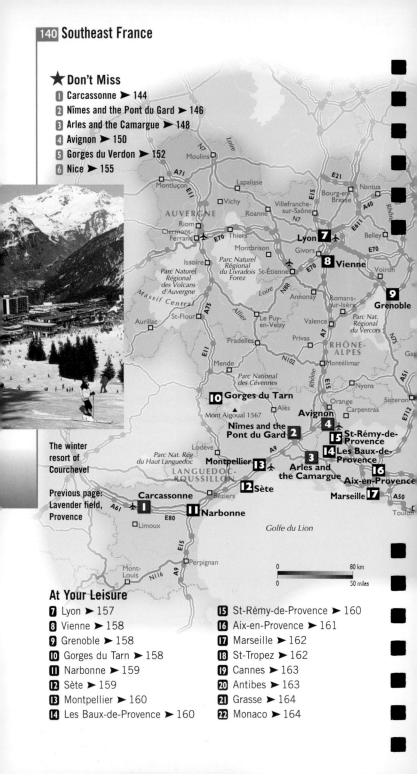

★**Don't Miss**

1 Carcassonne ➤ 144
2 Nîmes and the Pont du Gard ➤ 146
3 Arles and the Camargue ➤ 148
4 Avignon ➤ 150
5 Gorges du Verdon ➤ 152
6 Nice ➤ 155

The winter
resort of
Courchevel

Previous page:
Lavender field,
Provence

At Your Leisure

7 Lyon ➤ 157
8 Vienne ➤ 158
9 Grenoble ➤ 158
10 Gorges du Tarn ➤ 158
11 Narbonne ➤ 159
12 Sète ➤ 159
13 Montpellier ➤ 160
14 Les Baux-de-Provence ➤ 160
15 St-Rémy-de-Provence ➤ 160
16 Aix-en-Provence ➤ 161
17 Marseille ➤ 162
18 St-Tropez ➤ 162
19 Cannes ➤ 163
20 Antibes ➤ 163
21 Grasse ➤ 164
22 Monaco ➤ 164

Getting Your Bearings

France's Mediterranean coastline is well known as the playground of the rich and famous. In fact, most of the chic resorts are to be found east of the cultural melting-pot of Marseille, stretching up to the tiny principality of Monaco. West of the city is a low-lying, sandy shore, with quieter villages and historic towns, and the wildlife-rich lagoons of the Camargue region.

Chamonix-
Mont-Blanc

N90

Val d'Isère

Modane

E70

Parc
Nat.
des
Ecrins

Briançon

Parc Nat.
Régional
du Queyras

N94

PROVENCE-
ALPES-
COTE D'AZUR

Digne-
les-Bains

Parc National
du Mercantour

Tende

**Gorges du
Verdon**

5

N85

Nice

6 22 MONACO

Grasse

Draguignan

A8

21

19 20 Antibes

Cannes

E80

Fréjus

Côte d'Azur

N98

18

St-Tropez

Hyères

Îles d'Hyères

A fortress castle dominates the skyline at Carcassonne

Inland there's a great diversity of landscapes to discover, from the sometimes rugged hills and rolling farmland of Provence to the east, the wild high country of the Causses around the spectacular Gorges du Tarn in the west, and the dry, harsher landscapes of the Cévennes in the middle. The fertile valley of the Rhône stretches northwards to the major hub of Lyon. On the eastern edge, the borders are with Switzerland and Italy, a mountainous country popular for winter sports.

The A7/E15 is the main driving route from the north, and the A9/E15 and A8 are the autoroutes along the coast – all can become jammed on white-hot holiday weekends. If you can take your time and spread your journey out, there's a more appealing network of minor roads to explore, and recent improvements to some of the narrowest sections of the A75, between Clermont Ferrand and Montpellier, make that another good option.

Looking down over Monaco

There's lots to see in the southeast, from Roman remains to stunning natural landscapes to the brash resorts of the Riviera – combine the best of all worlds in this short tour, and allow an extra day to include the scenic drive from Menton (➤ 165–167).

Southeast France in Four Days

Day One

Morning
Explore the fascinating **medieval fortress** at **1** **Carcassonne** (➤ 144–145), and wander through the ancient streets of this captivating city before lunching in style on local specialities at **Le Languedoc** restaurant (➤ 145).

Afternoon
Head east towards the Mediterranean shore on the A61/E80 *autoroute*, or the quieter inland roads, pausing at peaceful **11** **Narbonne** (➤ 159) for a stroll by the water. Continue east on the N112 coast road via the attractive old harbour at **12** **Sète** (➤ 159).

Evening
Catch some **open-air theatre** outside the town (➤ 172), or make for the bright lights of **13** **Montpellier** (➤ 160), with its restaurants and lively student-based nightlife.

Day Two

Morning
Visit **2** **Nîmes and the Pont du Gard** (above, ➤ 146–147) for some of the best **Roman relics** in the area. Pick out a **café in Nîmes**, or dine at the shady **restaurant** by the aqueduct, to avoid the midday heat.

Afternoon
Drive southeast to **3** **Arles and the Camargue** (➤ 148–149), for another stunning **Roman amphitheatre**. Have a cooling drink in a café here before continuing south into the marshlands of the **Camargue** delta, and the wildlife of the **Étang de Vaccarès** (right, ➤ 149).

Evening

Make your way northeast of Arles to the remote village of **14 Les Baux-de-Provence** (➤ 160), to watch the sunset.

Day Three

Morning

Start the day with an exploration of **4 Avignon** (➤ 150–151), including the **Palais des Papes** and a quick dance on the **old bridge** (➤ 151). There's lots of choices of places to eat, or grab a **freshly filled baguette** and get on the road again.

Afternoon

Head east on the N100, then the D907 and D6 to **Moustiers-Ste-Marie** (right) and the start of the dramatic **5 Gorges du Verdon** (➤ 152–154). At the eastern end link up with the N85 (Route Napoléon) southeast, and head into **21 Grasse** (➤ 164), centre of France's perfume industry, for the refreshment of all your senses.

Day Four

Morning

Take the N7 coast road east along the Riviera via popular **19 Cannes** (➤ 163) and less showy **20 Antibes** (➤ 163) to the city of **6 Nice** (below, ➤ 155–156). Be seen to stroll along the **Promenade des Anglais**, and lunch on fresh seafood, with views of the harbour, at **L'Âne Rouge** (➤ 156).

Afternoon

Cool off in the air-conditioned interiors of one or two of the best **museums and art galleries** (➤ 156).

Evening

Go a little further east to **22 Monaco** (➤ 164), for an extravagant night out at **Monte Carlo's famous casino** (➤ 172) – but don't break the bank!

❶ Carcassonne

Carcassonne is a fascinating city in two distinct parts. On the east bank of the River Aude lies the Cité, the largest medieval fortress in Europe, restored in the 19th century to spectacular glory. On the west bank lies the Bourg, or Ville Basse, a settlement founded in 1260 to a strict grid pattern, which owes its fortune to the arrival of the Canal du Midi in the 17th century. Together they make Carcassonne an intriguing and rewarding town to explore.

The 3km (2 miles) of **battlemented double ramparts** that surround the Cité are one of the most striking features. They are studded with more than 50 defensive towers and turrets, and are remarkably complete. Originally there were just two ways in and out: the western Porte d'Aude and the eastern Porte Narbonnaise. People still live within the defences, and there are lots of shops and restaurants to explore in the narrow streets around **place Marcou**.

The lower town centres on **place Carnot**, and was once also walled and moated. The town's battlements were pulled down and the ditches filled in after the Revolution, to be replaced with leafy boulevards. Its prosperity was built on textiles and wine, both trades aided by its strategic place on the canal. Stroll around the pedestrianised streets to admire the 17th- and 18th-century town houses and good boutiques. The **market** (Tuesday, Thursday and Saturday mornings) has

Right: Exploring the narrow medieval streets around the Cité

Below: The restored Cité fortress

Below right: Tours give access to the ramparts

The Missing Link

The **Canal du Midi** is one of the engineering wonders of the Ancien Régime, and still very much in use today by pleasure craft. The visionary force behind its construction, started in 1666, was Pierre-Paul Riquet. He dreamed of a waterway that would give access to shipping between the Atlantic and Mediterranean coasts of France, without the dangers and expense of sailing around Spain. The River Garonne was navigable to Toulouse – all that was needed was the eastern link through Carcassonne and Béziers to Sète, which took 15 years to build. Riquet died a month before its completion, but his legacy brought great prosperity to the towns and villages along the route.

been held here since medieval times, and is another strong link in the town's history.

TAKING A BREAK

Treat yourself to a sustaining dish of the classic *cassoulet* (meat and bean casserole), perhaps rounded off with a Grand Marnier ice-cream, at the up-market **Le Languedoc** restaurant at 32 allée d'Iéna (tel: 04 68 25 22 17).

🔢 208 A2
Tourist Information Office
✉ 28 rue de Verdun ☎ 04 68 10 24 30; www.carcassonne-tourisme.com
🕐 Daily 9–7, Jul–Aug; Mon–Sat 9–6, Sun 9–1, Sep–Jun

CARCASSONNE: INSIDE INFO

Top tips Access to the walls of the Cité is by **guided tour only** – enquire at the tourist office for details.
• Look out for **jousting tournaments** in the Cité in summer, which evoke an age of chivalry long gone. They're occasionally held in the grassy slips of the *lices hautes*, between the inner and outer ramparts.

For Kids The **Im@ginarium** is an interactive multimedia show in the Cité which helps to bring the Middle Ages and especially the Crusader knights to life (3–5 rue St-Jean-la-Cité, tel: 04 68 47 78 78).

2 Nîmes and the Pont du Gard

The Roman town of Nîmes and the spectacular aqueduct that was built to bring water to its citizens combine to form one of the great sights of France. They are 20km (12.5 miles) apart, so you can choose which to see first (but see the tip, below).

Around Nîmes

The buildings of the city's old quarter are moderately interesting, but what makes this a "must see" site is **Les Arènes**, the 2,000-year-old amphitheatre. It's the best preserved Roman amphitheatre in the world, and its still in regular use for bullfights and other events. As a concession to modern requirements, an inflatable roof can be added in winter time. There are three tiers of stone seats inside, designed to seat around 20,000 spectators – be warned, there's no safety rail on the top tier.

Nîmes's Roman temple, the **Maison Carrée**, is less spectacular in scale, but still amazingly well preserved. There are some exquisite small mosaics in the interior. The whole structure dates from the 1st century BC. The temple is next door to the contemporary art gallery, more widely known as the **Carrée d'Art**. It's a light and spacious modern building designed by English architect Sir Norman Foster in 1984, and displays a regular collection of modern art and temporary exhibitions.

La Garrigue

The low-growing, scrubby **vegetation** found around the Pont du Gard is called *la garrigue*. In these tough, dry conditions, the plants that thrive are often tough and dry themselves, like box and holm oak, or with spiny leaves, such as thistles and gorse. Growing among these are the aromatic herbs that create the scents and flavours of Provence – thyme, marjoram, rosemary, sage and lavender.

The Pont du Gard

This huge, honey-coloured marvel strides across the River Gardon in three imposing tiers. Examine it closely from the bridge immediately beside it and you'll see there's no hint of mortar holding it up, just the skill of the Roman

engineers who constructed it around 19 BC, using stone blocks that weigh 6 tonnes. Projecting stones were built into the design, to hold scaffolding in place for repairs. The water channel is the top tier, part of an ambitious but successful scheme to transport water from the spring near Uzès 50km (31 miles) to Nîmes, where it could be used for bathing and fountains, as well as drinking. Learn more about the context of its building and 19th-century restoration in the excellent exhibition centre, on the left bank.

Did you know?

Nîmes is the birthplace of a hard-wearing cotton fabric that has become the essential ingredient of everybody's favourite leisure-wear around the world. The clothing is jeans, and the fabric, of course, is *serge de Nîmes*, better known as **denim**.

Above: Nîmes's remarkable Roman arena

Below left: The Pont du Gard aqueduct

TAKING A BREAK

Call in for a light meal and a glass of wine at the art-filled **Vintage Café** in Nîmes, located at the back of a tiny square with a fountain, between the arena and the Maison Carée (7 rue de Bernis, tel: 04 66 21 04 45).

⊞ 209 D4
Tourist Information Office
✉ 6 rue Auguste, 30000 ☎ 04 66 58 38 00; www.ot-nimes.fr
🕐 Mon–Fri 8:30–7, Sat 9–7, Sun 10–5, Oct–Easter; Mon–Fri 8:30–7, Sat 9–7, Sun 10–6, Easter–Sep; Mon–Wed and Fri 8:30–8, Thu 8:30–9,

Sat 9–7, Sun 10–6 Jul–Aug

Les Arènes
✉ place des Arènes
☎ 04 66 76 72 77
🕐 Daily 9–7, mid-March to mid-Oct, 10–5, mid-Oct to mid-Mar 🎟 Inexpensive

Maison Carrée
✉ place de la

Comédie ☎ 04 66 36 29 76 🕐 Daily 10–7, summer; 10–5 rest of year 🎟 Free

Musée d'Art Contemporain (Carrée d'Art)
✉ place de la Maison Carré
☎ 04 66 76 35 35
🕐 Tue–Sun 10–6
🎟 Inexpensive

Pont du Gard
⊞ 209 D4
✉ Exhibition Centre, Pont du Gard, 30210
☎ 04 66 37 51 10
🕐 Site open 7 am–1 am all year; exhibition hall open daily 9:30–7, Easter–Sep; 10–6 Oct–Easter
🎟 Exhibition hall: inexpensive

NÎMES AND THE PONT DU GARD: INSIDE INFO

Top tips In midsummer the **heat can be blistering**, so it pays to plan your visit around a shady lunch stop in Nîmes, visiting the Pont du Gard either early in the morning or later in the afternoon, when the sun is not so fierce.

• For a great **overview of Nîmes**, head straight for the Magne tower, in the Jardin de la Fontaine.

• At the Pont du Gard, the **car park fee** (inexpensive) also pays for access to the aqueduct. Entry to the exhibition centre costs €€€€, and there's also the option of an informative 25-minute video. Ludo is a discovery zone for kids.

3 Arles and the Camargue

Roman Arles is the gateway to the mysterious and romantic natural wilderness of the Camargue, a marshy flatland famous for its exotic wildlife, its semi-wild white horses, its little black bulls bred for fighting and its annual gypsy festival. Thousands of pink flamingos come to feed in the shallow waters here, and evaporating sea water leaves vast crystalline saltpans. Roads are few, so prepare to extend your exploration on foot or – better – by guided boat trip.

Salon de Thé

Arles

This small town is one of the most appealing of Provence, with Roman public buildings – including a well-preserved 20,000-seat **amphitheatre** – rubbing shoulders with medieval houses and churches in the centre. It makes a good base for exploring the area. There are various excellent and worthy museums of antiquities in and around the town, but the most unusual and fun of all is the local folk museum, the **Musée Arlatan**. A folk culture festival is held here in July.

In 1888 the painter Vincent Van Gogh (1853–90) left Paris and came to Arles, where he fell under the spell of the Provençal light and landscapes. He lived in a modest cottage known as the "yellow house" (destroyed by bombing in 1944), but at this productive time he painted masterpieces including the famous *Sunflowers* series. The end came the following year when, after a row with his friend Paul Gauguin over the founding of an artists' colony at Arles, and cutting off part of his own left ear, Van Gogh was committed to hospital.

The Camargue

Comparatively few roads penetrate this low-lying marsh, the delta of the Rhône, and its protected status means that visitor access is to some extent contained. The nature reserve centres on the shallow **Étang de Vaccarès**, and there's a superb visitor facility at **La Capelière**, with marked nature trails and information about the birds and plants of the area. South of here, the salt marshes give way to an expanse of sand dunes and ponds. It's great for bird-watching: look out for flamingos, avocets and egrets feeding in the shallows, bitterns and herons in the reedbeds, and ducks, geese and waders on the shore.

TAKING A BREAK

When you've been exploring the arenas in Arles, recover in the rustic **La Mamma** restaurant near by (20 rue de l'Amphithéâtre, tel 04 90 96 11 60). It serves tasty but inexpensive Italian and regional cuisine, including pizzas and sautéed beef with olives.

Above: Inside the Arena

Left: Rooftop view of Arles from the Arena

✚ 209 E3 **Tourist Information Office** ✉ esplanade Charles de Gaulle, boulevard des Lices, 13200 ☎ 04 90 18 41 20; www.tourisme.ville-arles.fr 🕐 Mon–Fri 10–6:45, Sat–Sun 9–6:45	**Musée Arlatan** ✉ rue de la République ☎ 04 90 93 58 11 🕐 Daily 9:30–1, 2–6:30, Jun–Aug; 9:30–12:30, 2–6, Sep; Tue–Sun 9:30–12:30, 2–6 Apr–May; Tue–Sun 9:30–12:30, 2–5, Oct–Mar	**Réserve Nationale de Camargue** ✚ 209 E3 ✉ Centre d'Information, La Capelière, 13200 Arles ☎ 04 90 97 00 97; www.camargue.reserves-naturels.org

ARLES AND THE CAMARGUE: INSIDE INFO

Top tips You are likely to **see much more** on a boat trip, horse ride or cycle tour than you will from a car. The village of **Saintes-Maries-de-la-Mer** is a good base for activities; contact the tourist office at 5 avenue Van Gogh, 13460, tel: 04 90 97 82 55, www.saintesmariesdelamer.com, open daily.

• The handsome, fortified 12th-century church in Saintes-Maries-de-la-Mer is the focus of the annual two-day **gypsy fair**, held on 24 to 25 May to celebrate the feast days of Marie Jacob, sister of the Virgin Mary, and Marie Salome, mother of the apostles James and John. Sarah, maid to both Maries, and the gypsies' patron saint, is buried within the church.

One to miss If you're expecting to see paintings by Van Gogh in Arles's **Fondation Van Gogh**, near the amphitheatre, then you'll be disappointed. However, the gallery has some interesting art by other modern painters, including Francis Bacon, which takes its inspiration from Van Gogh's works.

4 Avignon

The grandeur of Avignon's medieval walled city, dominated by a huge papal palace, makes it an intriguing place to visit. And for humble contrast, there's the remains of a venerable bridge that everybody knows a song about…

**Right: An exuberant fountain
Below:The Palais des Papes**

Avignon was thrust on to the world stage in 1309, when Pope Clement V decided to move here from Rome. For almost 70 years the town became the heart of the Christian world, and the enduring legacy of this exciting period, when culture and scholarship flourished, is the magnificent fortified palace, the **Palais des Papes**. When the popes eventually returned to Rome in 1403 they took many of their treasures with them, and there is a bleak emptiness about it. Hints of past luxury can be seen in the frescoed walls and ceiling of the papal bedchamber, and the Gobelin tapestries of the banqueting hall.

Around the town, you'll find the best shopping along rue de la République, while the cafés of the place de l'Horloge offer the chance to relax with a coffee and watch the world go by. There are several museums to explore, and an essential stop is the **Pont St Bénézet** – the Pont d'Avignon immortalised in song. It was originally a wooden structure, built in 1177 by the young shepherd St Bénézet, and was rebuilt in stone after a siege in 1226. It was constantly buffeted by the strong flow of the Rhône, and in the mid-17th century, most was washed away. Now just four picturesque arches remain.

TAKING A BREAK

Enjoy tea and cakes or
perhaps a light lunch at
le Simple Simon, a
decorative English-style tea
room and restaurant in the
heart of the old town (26 rue
Petite-Fusterie, tel: 04 90
86 62 70).

Left:
Mechanical
timepiece in
the place de
l'Horloge

Sur le Pont d'Avignon

The cheerful **children's song**
about dancing on the bridge
dates back to the 15th
century, but its composer is
unknown. It came to wider
attention in 1853, when
Adolphe Adam (better remembered for his ballet, *Giselle*)
included it in an operetta, *Le
Sourd ou l'Auberge Pleine*.
The song proved so popular
that it became the focus of its

own operetta in 1876. Crooner Jean Sablon recorded a famous swing version of
the song in 1939, and it is said that BBC radio played it 14 times in one day as
a coded message before the D-Day landings. Recorded hundreds of times in
different ways, it has even inspired classical piano variations. Today it is used
widely around the world to teach children the French language.

🔲 209 E4
Tourist Information Office
✉ 41 cours Jean-Jaurès, 80400 ☎ 04 32 74
32 74; www.ot-avignon.fr 🕐 Mon–Sat 9–6,
Sun 10–5, Apr–Oct; Mon–Fri 9–6, Sat 9–5,
Sun 10–noon, Nov–Mar

Palais des Papes
✉ 6 rue Pente Rapide – Charles Ansidéi,
BP 149 cedex 1, 84008 ☎ 04 90 27 50 00;
www.palais-des-papes.com 🕐 Daily 9–9,
Aug; 9–8, Jul, Sep; 9–7, Apr–Jun, Oct;
9:30–5:45 Nov–Mar

AVIGNON: INSIDE INFO

Top tip The **Avignon Passport**, available from
the tourist office, gives reduced price entry
to the main sights.

Hidden gem The **Fondation Angladon
Dubrujeaud**, on rue Laboureur, is a privately-
owned art gallery with some treasures of
20th-century art, including works by Picasso
and Cézanne (tel: 04 90 82 29 03, open
Wed–Sun 1–6; also Tue, May–Nov).

5 Gorges du Verdon

France's version of the Grand Canyon is the deepest and most dramatic river gorge in mainland Europe: an unmissable 21km (13 miles) of steep cliffs and precipitous vegetation punctuated by stupendous viewpoints. At the bottom run the clear green waters of the river which gives the chasm its name, and which run out into the artificial Lac de Ste-Croix, created in 1970.

The gorge was formed over millions of years by the River Verdon, and is one of the natural wonders of the world. Today it seems incredible that it was only surveyed for the first time in 1905, by the great speleologist Édouard-Alfred Martel. Yet even now, geology dictates that the roads are few and modest in scale as the canyon narrows to 198m (650 feet) across, and the steepness of the limestone cliffs at each side, up to 700m (2,296 feet) high, makes them accessible only to experienced climbers. The southern route from Moustiers-Sainte-Marie, the **Corniche Sublime** (D71), carved out in the 1940s, gives the best views, with the **Balcons de Mescla** viewpoint the highlight. Loop north via Trigance to return along the northern side and the **Route des Crêtes**.

Left: The Verdon River threads through the gorge

Right and inset: Adrenalin sports in the canyon

Exploring in the Gorges

The river powers a hydro-electric plant, and is dammed below Moustiers, offering good opportunities for experienced canoeists. Short walks lead from many of the view-points, such as the zig-zag path from the Point Sublime, on the north side. Hardy walkers can tackle the challenging **Sentier Martel footpath**, which runs along the valley floor between Rougon and Meyreste and takes at least one day.

Édouard-Alfred Martel

Martel (1859–1938) is known worldwide as the father of speleology – the science of cave exploration. From an early age, and despite training as a lawyer, Martel began a pioneering exploration of the underground caverns in the limestone landscape of the Causses. His three-day exploration of the Gorges du Verdon, previously believed impenetrable, was undertaken with two companions. Martel's journey was driven partly by curiosity, and partly by the need for research into water supplies, and in the 1950s the government considered blocking the whole valley for a reservoir, settling instead for the more limited Lac de Ste-Croix.

TAKING A BREAK

There are plenty of cafés to choose from in
the cobbled squares of **Moustiers-Ste-Marie**,
though parking may be scarce in high
summer. There are also lots of good
belvédères, or viewpoints, where you can stop
for a picnic and enjoy the panoramas.

Above and left:
Old houses
cling to the
rocks at
Moustiers-Ste-
Marie

🞧 210 A4
Tourist Information Office
✉ Hôtel-Dieu, rue de la
Bourgade, Moustiers-Sainte-
Marie, 04360 (western edge
of canyon) ☎ 04 92 74 67
84; www.ville-moustiers-
sainte-marie.fr 🕐 Daily
10–12:30, 2–6:30 summer;
2–4:30 winter

**Musée de la Préhistoire
des Gorges du Verdon**
✉ route de Montmeyan,
04500 Quinson ☎ 04 92 74
09 59; www.museeprehis-
toire.com 🕐 Daily 10–8
Jul–Aug; Wed–Mon 10–6,
Feb–Jun, Sep to mid-Dec
🎫 Moderate

GORGES DU VERDON: INSIDE INFO

Top tips The roads which run along each side of the canyon are **narrow and
winding**, and in places only just wide enough for two cars to pass – so take
extra care if you are in a wider vehicle or towing.

• The **Sentier Martel footpath** along the river has collapsed tunnels and is
subject to sudden changes in water level. It is best walked in the safety of
a group or with an experienced guide.

• If you don't feel like driving along the whole canyon, then **a short stretch of
the Corniche Sublime** will give you a good taster of this natural phenomenon.

• **Faïence** is the local decorative earthenware pottery, and you'll see it on sale
in villages around the Gorges, but especially on the streets and in the little
shops of Moustiers-Ste-Marie.

Don't miss The stunning modern, boat-shaped **Musée de la Préhistoire
des Gorges du Verdon**, designed by English architect Sir Norman Foster, is at
Quinson, just west of Lac de Ste-Croix. It opened in 2001, and with its
re-created cave, interactive displays and neolithic tools and other items
found in the area, it's a fabulous museum dedicated to the people who
inhabited the Gorges area around 400,000 years ago.

⑥ Nice

Nice, one of the biggest cities along the Mediterranean coast and the capital of the Riviera, fairly buzzes with life.
There's an old Italian corner to discover, plus some of the top art galleries of the region, and if you're here in the two weeks before Lent, you're bound to get swept up by the colourful frenzy of the Mardi-Gras carnival.

Nice's history has been influenced by successive owners, including the Ligurians, the Greeks and the Romans, and only became part of France when the Italians (who called it Nizza) handed it over in 1860. In the 19th century it became a chic winter resort, numbering Queen Victoria among its illustrious visitors.

Many splendid *belle-époque* buildings line the broad, noisy promenade des Anglais along the seafront, including the magnificent domed **Hotel Negresco**. The Paillon promenade divides the new town from the Italianate jumble of the old quarter, where you'll find interesting little shops and cafés and churches. The Cimiez hill was the centre of the Roman settlement, and you can explore a small oval **amphitheatre** here and a **museum** of excavated remains.

There are 19 different galleries and museums to discover in Nice – the panel on the next page is a quick guide to the best of them.

Top: The curve of the beach is backed by the promenade des Anglais

Inset: Small boats wait, tethered, in the marina

TAKING A BREAK

Dine on fabulous fresh seafood with a Mediterranean twist at the moderately-priced **L'Âne Rouge**, overlooking the harbour (7 quai des Deuz-Emmanuel, tel: 04 93 8949 63).

Top Galleries at a Glance

Musée d'Art Moderne et d'Art Contemporain
✉ place Yves Kline
☎ 04 93 62 61 62;
www.mamac-nice.org
🕐 Wed–Mon 10–6
♿ Inexpensive, free Sun

This intriguing modern structure of four towers linked by bowed girders and glass holds a great collection of avant-garde and pop-art dating from the 1960s. Highlights include Andy Warhol's Campbell's Soup Can.

Musée Henri Matisse
✉ 164 avenue des

Arènes de Cimiez
☎ 04 93 81 08 08;
www.musee-matisse-nice.org 🕐 Wed–Mon 10–6
♿ Inexpensive

Matisse (1869–1954), who spearheaded the Fauvist movement in the early 20th century, moved to Nice in 1917, and is buried in the cemetery near by. This gallery, in a 17th-century villa in the gardens at Cimiez, contains the artist's breathtaking collection of his own sinuous sketches and brightly coloured gouache paintings.

Musée Marc Chagall/Musée du Message Biblique
✉ avenue de Dr Ménard, Boulevard du Cimiez ☎ 04 93 53 87 20
🕐 Wed–Mon 10–5
♿ Moderate

A museum specially designed to hold the French Surrealist artist's biblical works, with fabulous stained-glass panels, mosaics and paintings.

Musée des Beaux-Arts
✉ 33 avenue des Baumettes ☎ 04 92 15 28 28
🕐 Tue–Sun 10–6
♿ Inexpensive

In a private mansion dating from 1876, near the western end of the beach, with paintings and sculpture, mainly 17th to 19th-century. Highlights include works by Fragonard, Degas, Rodin and Dufy.

Musée national Message Biblique Marc Chagall

✚ 210 C3
Tourist Information Office
✉ 5 promenade des Anglais, 06000
☎ 0892 707 407; www.nicetourism.com
🕐 Mon–Sat 9–8, Sun 9–6, summer; Mon–Sat 9–6, winter

NICE: INSIDE INFO

Top tips The **Carte Passe-Musées**, available from the tourist office, gives unlimited access to many of the galleries and museums over seven days for just €6.
• Admission to the municipal galleries is **free to all** on the first and third Sundays of every month.

Hidden gems Two of the lesser-known museums, but well worth seeking out, are the **Asian Arts Museum**, at 405 Promenade des Anglais, and the **Anatole Jakovsky International Museum of Modern Art**, on avenue de Fabron, which houses naïve art from all over the world.

One to miss If you have to miss out on one of the galleries, skip the **Musée d'Art et d'Histoire**, on rue de France, which is limited to the story of Nice and only open at weekends.

At Your Leisure

7 Lyon

France's third most populous city, Lyon is a gastronomic centre *par excellence*, and boasts a history that once saw it as the capital of the Roman Gallic empire.

Its centre lies along the narrow wedge, or Presqu'île, sandwiched between the rivers Saône and Rhône, with modern suburbs sprawling to the east. To the west lies the old Renaissance quarter known as **Vieux Lyon**, and this is a good place to start any exploration. The main streets – rue St-Jean and rue de Boeuf – run parallel with the Saône, and are characterised by the tall houses which rest on a warren of *traboules* – vaulted walkways and arcades filled with boutiques, galleries and cafés. For the quintessential Lyon experience, stop off at a *bouchon* bistro for a snack and watch the world go by. The **Cathédrale St-Jean** is also in this area, a remarkable building with four low, sturdy towers that marks the transition between Romanesque and Gothic architecture.

To catch up with the city's Roman history, take the funicular from near the cathedral up the Fourvière hill, where the landmark **Basilique Notre Dame de Fourvière** was constructed in the 19th century on the site of the original forum. Just south of here, the underground **Roman museum** has intriguing remains, including a rare mosaic depicting a circus.

There are more great museums to explore around the centre, including a world-class art gallery, the **Musée des Beaux-Arts**, and various smaller museums dedicated to the silk industry, on which much of the city's wealth was founded. Four métro lines make it easy to get around.

➕ 214 C3

Tourist Information Office ✉ place Bellecour, 69002 ☎ 04 72 77 69 69; www.lyon-france.com ⏰ Mon–Sat 9–7,

The Gothic entrance to the cathedral

Sun 9–6, mid-Apr to mid-Oct; Mon–Sat 10–6, Sun 10–5:30, mid-Oct to mid-Apr

Cathédrale St-Jean ✉ place St-Jean ⏰ Daily 8–noon, 2–7:30

Musée de la Civilisation Gallo-Romaine ✉ 17 rue Cléberg ☎ 04 72 38 81 90 ⏰ Tue–Sun 10–6 💶 Inexpensive, free on Thu

Musée des Beaux-Arts ✉ 20 place des Terreaux ☎ 04 72 10 17 40 ⏰ Sat–Mon, Wed–Thu 10–6, Fri 10:30–6; alternate galleries closed at lunchtime 💶 Inexpensive

8 Vienne

This ancient town lies around 20km (12.5 miles) south of Lyon, on the Rhône, offering a vivid picture of a major Roman settlement, built when the Roman empire was at the height of its powers. A *petit train* links the main sites in summer. The best remains are at the **Musée et Sites Archéologique de St-Romain-en-Gaul**, where you can wander among the outlines of houses, streets, public baths and workshops, and admire the mosaics. The huge, stepped, semicircular amphitheatre, or **Théâtre Romain**, on rue du Cirque, was built in AD 50 and thoroughly restored in the 20th century, and is a venue for summer concerts. Vienne flourished again as an ecclesiastical centre in the 12th century, but declined as Lyon, expanded.

➕ 214 C2
Tourist Information Office ✉ cours Brilliet, 38200 ☎ 04 74 53 80 30; www.vienne-tourisme.com ⊙ Mon–Sat 9–noon, 1:30–6, Sun 10–noon, 2–5

Musée et Sites Archéologique de St-Romain-en-Gaul ✉ route D502 ☎ 04 74 53 74 01 ⊙ Tue–Sun 10–6, Mar–Oct; 10–5, Nov–Feb 🎟 Inexpensive

9 Grenoble

Grenoble is a vibrant high-tech city built on a flat plain in the shadow of the Alps. The best way to see it is from the **cable-car** which goes from the centre of the old-town quarter, high over the River Isère and up to the 16th-century Fort de la Bastille (moderate, closed Jan). Its proximity to the mountains makes it an obvious year-round sporting destination for walkers, skiers, climbers and adrenaline enthusiasts, but Grenoble is also keen to promote its connections to the arts. It's proud of its links with the novelist Stendhal, who was born here in 1783, and has several excellent art museums, of which the **Musée de Grenoble** has the best collection, and the **Centre National d'Art Contemporain** the more eccentric.

➕ 215 D2
Tourist Information Office ✉ 14 rue de la République, 38019 ☎ 04 76 42 41 41 ⊙ Mon–Sat 9–6:30 all year; also Sun 10–1, 2–5, May–Sep; Sun 10–1 Oct–Apr

Musée de Grenoble ✉ 5 place de Lavalette ☎ 04 76 63 44 44; www.museedegrenoble.fr ⊙ Wed–Mon 10–6 🎟 Inexpensive

Le Magasin – Centre National d'Art Contemporain ✉ 155 cours Berriat ☎ 04 76 21 95 84 ⊙ Tue–Sun noon–7 🎟 Inexpensive, under 10 free

10 Gorges du Tarn

The precipitous and winding limestone chasm along the River Tarn is

Ancient villages cluster along the Tarn

one of the great beauty-spots of France. It is threaded through by the D907b, which strings together tiny medieval villages from Ispagnac in the northeast to Le Rozier in the southwest, including Ste-Énimie, St-Chély and Peyreleau.

Throughout its 50km (31 miles) length the gorge is never more than 500m (1,640 feet) wide, sometimes narrowing to just 30m (98 feet), and driving through is a challenge in summer for the sheer volume of slow-moving vehicles, and in winter for the Col de Perjuret, which can be blocked off by heavy snow. Kayaking is one way to avoid the traffic, and boats are available for rent at several points along the route. Above the canyon stretch the limestone plateaus of the **Causses**, grazed by sheep and goats.

➕ 208 B4
Tourist Information Office
✉ Gorges du Tarn, Causse, Dourbie, 12640 Rivière sur Tarn ☎ 05 65 59 74 28

🔟 Narbonne

An appealing small town with Roman origins, linked to the Canal du Midi, Narbonne was once a hub

of activity and is now thankfully bypassed by the E15/A9 coast road. Leave your car by the Canal de la Robine and walk along the shady waterside to explore the town. Little lanes with shops and boutiques radiate from quai Dillon, on the canal's right bank, while the town hall dominates the main square on the left bank. The passage de l'Ancre leads through from here to the town's museums and the Gothic, pinnacled cathedral of **St-Just-et-St-Pasteur**.

➕ 208 B2

Tourist Information Office ✉ place Salengro, 11100 ☎ 04 68 65 15 60
🕐 Mon–Sat 8–7, Sun 9:30–12:30, mid-Jun to mid-Sep; Mon–Sat 8:30–noon, 2–6, mid-Sep to mid-Jun

🔢 Sète

The 17th-century fishing port of Sète, on the northwest fringe of the

Canal-side moorings at Sète

Golfe du Lion, is sandwiched between the Mediterranean sea and the Thau lagoon, and marks the eastern end of the Canal du Midi. Italianate buildings add an air of distinction to the old harbour area, its tall buildings painted in warm pastel shades, and there's a 12km (7.5-mile) sandy beach to enjoy. Poet Paul Valéry (1871–1945) was born here, and lends his name to the local history museum. An annual highlight is the **water jousting festival**, when "knights" balance on raked platforms on the back of rowing boats and try to knock each other into the water with wooden poles.

➕ 208 C3
Tourist Information Office ✉ 60 Grand rue Mario Roustan, 34200 ☎ 04

Montpellier's broad place de la Comédie

67 74 71 71; www.ot-sete.fr ⊙ Mon–
Fri 9:30–6; Sat–Sun 10–noon, 2–5

🔢 Montpellier

White buildings, modern architecture, wide squares, open green parks
and broad walkways are some of the
distinctive features of this lively
Mediterranean city. Its 120km
(75 miles) of cycle routes make it a
pleasure to explore, and bicycles and
mopeds can easily be rented, with
the bonus of secure parking at more
than 1,000 points across the city. It's
a city of 24-hour entertainment and
buzzing arts festivals, which makes
it very popular with younger people.

Place de la Comédie, in the old
town, is the centre of the action,
with the rue du Peyrou offering some
of the best historical architecture
and a triumphal arch. The **Musée
Fabre** (currently closed) is one of
the biggest art galleries in France,
and well worth a visit for its touring
exhibitions, as well as permanent
collections of Flemish and Dutch art
from the 16th to 17th centuries,
neo-classical works, and paintings
by 19th-century romantic artists
including Delacroix, Carot and
Sisley.

➕ 208 C3
Tourist Information Office ✉ place
de la Comédie, 30 allée Jean de Lattre
de Tassigny, 34000 ☎ 04 67 60 60 60;
www.ot-montpellier.fr ⊙ Mon–Fri 9–7,
Sat 10–6, Sun 10–1, 2–5

Vill' à Vélo (cycle rental) ✉ rue
Maguelone ☎ 04 67 22 87 82
Musée Fabre (reopens 2006) ✉ 39
boulevard Bonne Nouvelle, 34200
☎ 04 67 14 33 00

🔢 Les Baux-de-Provence

For the classic views of this ruined
pinnacle fortress, be there at dawn
or sunset if you can, when the low
light turns the walls to gold. The
panorama from the top across the
surrounding Alpilles hills and to the
plain below is stunning at any time,
and shows what an excellent
defensive position this was for the
powerful and often brutal lords of
Baux in the 12th to 15th centuries.

Beneath the walls of the citadel
lies a small village, its pretty streets
lined with appealing arts and crafts
shops and places to eat. It can get
very busy here in the height of
summer, and when parking areas fill
up the access road may be closed. In
the 19th century Les Baux gave its
name to the red, clay-like mineral

The historic village of Les Baux

bauxite, found locally and used in
the manufacture of aluminium.
➕ 209 E3
Tourist Information Office
✉ Maison du Roi, 13520 ☎ 04 90 54
34 39; www.lesbauxdeprovence.com
⊙ Mon– Fri 9–7, Sat–Sun 10–12:30,
2–6, Apr– Sep; Mon–Fri 9–12:30, 2–6,
Oct–Mar

15 St-Rémy-de-Provence

Vincent Van Gogh sought asylum at the beautiful old monastery of St Paul-de-Mausole, just south of St-Rémy in 1889, after cutting off part of his own ear. The relief was temporary – the great painter died after shooting himself the following July – but his stay is commemorated with a display of letters and other items at the gallery in the town that bears his name. Artists are still drawn here by

Glanum is a Roman site in the foorhills of the mountains south of St-Rémy

the shady squares and fountains, narrow old streets and relaxed atmosphere of this attractive town, a centre of the local wine-making industry. Astrologer and prophet Nostradamus was born in rue Hoche in 1503.

➕ 209 E4
Tourist Information Office ✉ place Jean-Jaurès, 13210 ☎ 04 90 92 05 22 🕐 Mon–Sat 9–12:30, 2–7, Sun 10–noon, 3–6, Jun–Sep; Mon–Sat 9–noon, 2–6, Oct–May
Centre d'Art Présence Van Gogh ✉ Hôtel Estrine, 8 rue Estrine ☎ 04 90 92 34 72 🕐 Tue–Sun 10:30–12:30, 2:30–6:30, Apr–Dec 💲 Inexpensive

16 Aix-en-Provence

There are more than 100 fountains in this gracious town, including one on the broad and bustling Cours Mirabeau which comes straight from the ground at a temperature of 36°C

(96°F). The boulevard, with shady plane trees down the centre, is the heart of **Vieil Aix**, and a great place to pause for a coffee in one of the many cafés, watch the world go past and admire the grand 17th- and 18th-century mansions on the opposite side. Between here and the **Cathédrale St-Sauveur** are some of the most interesting shops, selling antiques, *haute couture* and colourful Provençal handicrafts.

The cathedral has some good tapestries and medieval art, but the artist celebrated in the town is Paul Cézanne, who was born in 1839 at 28 rue de l'Opéra. His most famous series of paintings depicts the landscapes around Montagne Ste-Victoire, which lies to the east of Aix. You can view his preserved studio on rue Cézanne, but for a view of some of his paintings the better option is the **Musée Granet**, which has 18 in its collections.

➕ 209 F3
Tourist Information Office
✉ 2 place Général de Gaulle, 13100

A cherub on swan's back, part of a fountain in the old part of Aix

☎ 04 42 16 11 61; www.aixenprovence-tourism.com 🕐 Mon–Sat 8:30–8, Apr–Jun, Sep; 8:30–9, Jul–Aug; 8:30–7, Oct–Mar; Sun 10–1, 2–6 all year
Musée Granet (reopens 2006)
✉ place St-Jean de Malte, quartier Mazarin ☎ 04 42 38 14 70

17 Marseille

The trading port of Marseille, a city of around 1 million people, has a reputation as a melting pot of cultures, with a significant population of North African immigrants.

Start any visit at the **Vieux Port** (Old Port), where thousands of boats jostle for space in the rectangular basin. To the north is the colourful le Panier district, heavily damaged during World War II but scattered with interesting historic buildings. It leads up to the art gallery and archaeology museum, **La Vieille Charité**, in a 17th-century former hospice, and the bold, striped 19th-century **Cathédrale de la Major**.

To the east the main shopping streets are off the artery of la Canebière, and you'll also find the fascinating **Musée de l'Histoire de Marseille** here. Restaurants are plentiful in the area south of the Vieux Port, the **Quartier de l'Arsenal**, and this is where you should go to taste the local fish soup, *bouillabaisse*.

If you have time, the 15-minute boat ride to the **Château d'If** is worth it for the views over the city, and the thrill of the fortress there, linked to novelist Alexandre Dumas's 19th-century tale, *The Count of Monte Cristo*.

✚ 209 F3
Tourist Information Office ✉ 4 la Canebière, 13001 ☎ 04 91 13 89 00; www.marseille-tourisme.com
🕔 Mon–Sat 9–7, Sun 10–5

La Vieille Charité ✉ place de Corette ☎ 04 91 14 58 80 🕔 Tue–Sun 11–6, Jul–Sep; 10–5, Oct–Jun
🎟 Inexpensive

Musée de l'Histoire de Marseille ✉ cours Belsunce, Centre Bourse ☎ 04 91 90 42 22 🕔 Mon–Sat noon–7
🎟 Inexpensive, under 5 free

18 St-Tropez

St-Tropez is famous for fun, sun and celebrity glitz, its quay packed with expensive yachts, its narrow streets with visitors enjoying the glamour

Luxury yachts and cruisers line the pontoons at St-Tropez

and the *chic*. Despite all this surface luxury, what drew the rich and famous here in the first place can still be found in glimpses of the lovely old fishing village, seen in the **Vieille Ville**, with its small-scale, charming old houses.

The easiest way to get into the town, avoiding the worst of the traffic, is to park at Port Grimaud and catch the passenger ferry across the bay.

✚ 210 B3
Tourist Information Office ✉ quai Jean-Jaurès (main part of harbour front) ☎ 04 94 97 45 21; www.saint-tropez.st
🕔 Daily 9:30–8:30, Jul–Aug; 9:30–12:30, 2–7, Apr–Jun, Sep–Oct; 9:30–12:30, 2–6, Nov–Mar

appealing parts of the town are in the old quarter, where Italianate buildings are crowded into the remains of a 17th-century defensive wall designed by the great military engineer Vauban.

The chief reason to visit Antibes is the **Musée Picasso**. Paintings, drawings, ceramics and sculptures, mostly dating to the three months in 1946 that Picasso spent here, are housed in a severe medieval fortress that once belonged to the Grimaldis of Monaco.

✚ 210 C3
Tourist Information Office
✉ 11 place Général de Gaulle, 06600
☎ 04 92 90 53 00 🕐 Daily 9–7, Jul–Aug; Mon–Fri 9–12:30, 1:30–6, Sat 9–noon, 2–6, Sep–Jun

Musée Picasso ✉ Château Grimaldi
☎ 04 92 90 54 20 🕐 Tue–Sun 10–6, Jun–Sep; 10–noon, 2–6, Oct, Dec–May
💰 Moderate

🄳 Cannes

Classy Cannes is unusual among Riviera resorts: it has a long sandy beach. Unfortunately, access to many parts is limited by private and hotel ownership, but there's a public beach at the western end of the town's great seafront promenade, **la Croisette**. Floodlit by night and lined with expensive shops, this is the place to see and be seen, or perhaps try your own hands in the concrete prints of the stars, set in the pavement outside the Palais des Festivals. There's more shopping along the rue d'Antibes.

The town is busy at any time of the year, but the social highlight is undoubtedly in May, when Cannes transforms into Hollywood-on-Sea for the prestigious film festival.

✚ 210 B3
Tourist Information Office
✉ Palais des Festivals, 1 boulevard de la Croisette, 06403
☎ 04 93 39 24 53; www.cannes.fr; www.cannes-festival.fr
🕐 Daily 9–8, Jul–Aug; 9–7, Sep–Jun

🄴 Antibes

Less showy than its neighbour Cannes, Antibes still attracts its share of luxury yachts. The most

Above: Summer on the beach at Antibes
Left: Café life in Cannes

Fountain in the flower market, Grasse

21 Grasse

Lavender fields are one of the memorable sights of Provence, and the flowers they produce are a key ingredient in the modern perfume industry. Molinard, Galimard and Fragonard are the great perfumeries located in Grasse, the so-called Perfume Capital of the World, which supplies perfumes to all the biggest names, including Chanel and Dior. All three offer factory tours. Roses and jasmine, flowers essential to the industry, are celebrated with their own **festivals** in May and August. The **cathedral**, on place Godeau, is worth a quick look inside for the three early paintings by Rubens, dating from 1601.

✚ 210 B3
Tourist Information Office
✉ Palais de Congrès, 22 cours Honoré Cresp, 06130 ☎ 04 93 36 66 66; www.grasse-riviera.com ⊙ Mon–Sat 9–7, Sun 9–1, 2–6, Jul–Sep; Mon–Sat 9–12:30, 2–6, Oct–Jun

22 Monaco

The Grimaldi dynasty's principality of Monaco covers just 2sq km (0.8 square mile) of ground, and is known as the glitzy tax refuge of the super-rich. Since its origins as a medieval fortress it has become a highly charged and spotlessly clean city, expanding upwards via skyscrapers and outwards on to artificial rocky platforms. Its unique status is due to its protection by Napoléon, who gets his own museum in the royal **Palais du Prince**. Witness the changing of the palace guard, daily at 11:55. Members of the Grimaldi family, including movie star Princess Grace (1929–82), are buried in the nearby **cathedral**.

East of here is Monte Carlo, where the famous **Casino** raises a steady revenue (➤ 172).

✚ 210 C4
Tourist Information Office
✉ 2a boulevard des Moulins, 98000 ☎ 377/92 16 61 16; www.visitmonaco.com ⊙ Mon–Sat 9–7, Sun 10–noon

---

For Kids
• **Gorges du Verdon**: Try the thrills and spills of white-water rafting or canoeing down the river from Aboard Rafting at Castellane (8, place de l'Église, tel: 04 92 83 76 11, open Apr–Oct).
• **Mougins**, north of Cannes: At Buggy Cross three tracks offer racing on quad bikes, karts or mini-motorcycles, and there are even vehicles for over-4s (by the Automobile Museum, tel: 04 93 69 02 74, open Wed and Sat–Sun).

High-rise apartments and luxury craft around an exclusive marina in Monaco

EXPLORING INLAND FROM THE CÔTE D'AZUR

Drive

This circular route into the countryside which lies behind the principality of Monaco contrasts some of the prettiest – and busiest – villages and towns of the Riviera with the peace and natural beauty of the Parc National du Mercantour.

DISTANCE 150km/93 miles **TIME** Allow a full day for this drive, and be aware that the roads inland from the coast are often winding and slow.
START/END POINT Menton ✚ 210 C4

1–2

Start from **Menton**, a pretty, and curiously Italian town on the French side of the border. There's a **museum** by the waterfront to the poet, playwright and film director Jean Cocteau (1889–1963), which is worth a quick look if you have time. Pick up the road in the town centre signed **Autoroute (Nice, Italia) and Sospel**. Follow signs for Sospel on the winding **D2566**, passing under the A8 and through Castillon-Neuf. At **Sospel** go over the railway crossing and turn left, following signs for Moulinet and Col de Turini. The bridge at Sospel, with its central tower, was rebuilt in the 20th century after the 11th-century original was blown up during World War II.

2–3

Bear left at a bend on to the **D2204**. The road climbs to Col St-Jean, with great views back down to Sospel. Go over **Col de Braus**

Left: Menton is close to the Italian border
Right: Houses back on to the River Bevera at Sospel

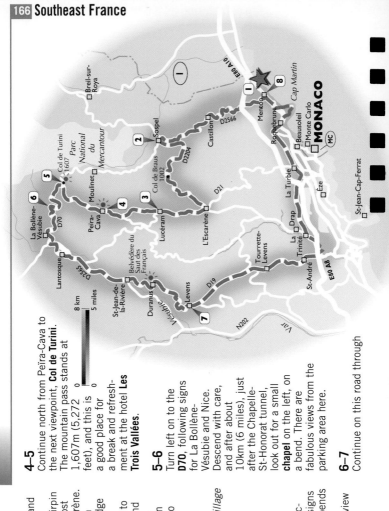

Place de la République, Levens

3–4

Go through Lucéram, and at the next junction, on a steep hill, bear left, following signs for Turini. There are many more hairpin bends to negotiate before you reach the superb viewpoint of **Peïra-Cava**. To the east, the view is of the Parc National du Mercantour.

(1,002m) and descend through hairpin bends almost into L'Escarène. Just after a railway bridge turn right, signposted to Lucéram and Peïra-Cava. Continue on this road, to reach the attractively jumbled medieval *village perché* (perched village) of **Lucéram**.

4–5

Continue north from Peïra-Cava to the next viewpoint, **Col de Turini**. The mountain pass stands at 1,607m (5,272 feet), and this is a good place for a break and refreshment at the hotel **Les Trois Vallées**.

5–6

Turn left on to the **D70**, following signs for La Bollène-Vésubie and Nice. Descend with care, and after about 10km (6 miles), just after the Chapelle-St-Honorat tunnel, look out for a small **chapel** on the left, on a bend. There are fabulous views from the parking area here.

6–7

Continue on this road through

La Bollène-Vésubie and at a T-junction (intersection) turn left on to the **D2565**, signed for Nice and St-Martin-Vésubie (Vésubie is the name of the river which runs through here). This brings you to the valley floor. Follow signs for Lantosque and Nice, going straight on at first, then left along the main road. After 1km (0.6 mile) divert right to go through **Lantosque** village, then rejoin the main road. Continue southwards through **St-Jean-de-la-Rivière**. About 1km (0.6 mile) beyond St-Jean fork left on to the **D19**, signed Nice par Levens. This road becomes narrower as it ascends the valley. Go through a tunnel just before Duranus and look for a viewpoint on the right. The **Saut des Français**, it looks out from sheer cliffs. Stay on the road into **Levens**, an appealing old town with two 18th-century chapels standing on two sides of the square, and a grand gateway – the remnant of a castle that has long-since disappeared.

7–8

Leave Levens on the **D19**, following signs for Nice, and passing Tourette-Levens. Soon after St-André the road passes under the A8. Turn left at traffic lights here, signed to Sospel. Cross a river and go straight over another set

The Trophée des Alpes looms above La Turbie

of traffic lights, passing under the A8 again. Take the next right turn, signed Route de Turin, cross the river and a level (grade) crossing, then turn left at traffic lights, signed La Trinité and Drap. At the roundabout (traffic circle) take the road signed for La Turbie and Laghet, and follow the **D2204a** up a winding valley to **Laghet**. There a hairpin bend takes the road sharply right.

Pass under the A8 once more, anc turn left at the next junction, an autoroute slic road, following signs to Menton. Turn left at the next junction, signed for La Turbie and Monaco, and stay on this road to the ancient Roman village of **La Turbie**. Its outstanding monument is the Trophée des Alpes, a triumphal arch built by Augustus Caesar around 6BC. After La Turbie, bear left past a hotel, signed Roquebrune and Menton, and turn right at traffic lights at the bottom of the hill, signed Nice and Beausoleil. At the next lights turn left, signed to Cap Martin. As it leaves the heart of the village the road veers sharp left – go straight ahead here, s gned for Mayerling and Cap Martin, to reach t e sea. Follow the coast road back to **Menton**.

TAKING A BREAK

Les Trois Vallées hotel-restaurant stands at the high point of this tour, at the Col de Turini (tel: 04 93 04 23 23). There is also a choice of bars and restaurants in **Sospel**.

Musée Jean-Cocteau

⊠ Le Bastion, Port de Menton, quai Napoléon III, 06500 Menton ☎ 04 93 57 72 30 ⊘ Wed–Mon 10–12, 2–6 🎟 Inexpensive, child under 18 free

Where to... Stay

Prices
Expect to pay per night for a double room
€ under €100   €€ €100–€200   €€€ over €200

Hôtel de la Cité €€€

Hotels don't come much more sumptuous than this one in Carcassonne, and it's no surprise to learn that Queen Elizabeth II has stayed here. It's in the old part of the city, and one of the few places to retain its garden. There are 50 rooms and 11 themed suites, decorated in styles that vary from Provençal comfort to neo-Gothic grandeur. Every service and amenity is discreetly available, including an outdoor pool.

➕ 208 A2 ⊠ place de l'Église, 11000, Carcassonne ☎ 04 68 71 98 71; www.hoteldelacite.orient-express. com ⊕ Closed Dec to mid-Jan

Hôtel Imperator Concorde €€€

There's more than a touch of extravagance in this beautiful hotel, which overlooks Jardin de la Fontaine and place Picasso in the heart of Nîmes. Its roadside setting is made up for by the wonderful gardens. There are 62 spacious rooms, well-designed and comfortable, with air-conditioning. Sip a cocktail before dinner with the ghosts of Ava Gardner and Ernest Hemingway, who both stayed here in the past. Breakfast is not included in the room price.

➕ 209 D4 ⊠ quai de la Fontaine, 30000 Nîmes ☎ 04 66 21 90 30; www.hotel-imperator.com

Hôtel Calendal €

A two-star hotel located close to the arenas in Arles, the Calendal makes a comfortable and inexpensive base for exploring the town and the wider area. There are 38 air-conditioned bedrooms, with views to the arenas or over a garden courtyard. Inside, you'll find the tiled floors and wrought iron typical of Provence. Breakfast can be eaten in the garden under the palm trees.

➕ 209 E3 ⊠ 5 rue Porte-de-Laure, 13200 Arles ☎ 04 90 96 11 89; www.lecalendal.com ⊕ Closed Jan

Le Mas des Amandiers €

This small, peaceful Logis hotel is the perfect get-away, lying amid orchards and farmland 12km (8 miles) south of Avignon and with easy access to Les Baux and Arles. The 28 rooms are simply furnished in Provençal style, and facilities include an excellent restaurant and an outdoor pool. The welcome is particularly friendly.

➕ 209 E4 ⊠ Route d'Avignon, 13690 Graveson ☎ 04 90 95 81 76; www.hotel-des-amandiers.com

Hôtel Negresco €€€

Prominently located on the famous promenade des Anglais, the black dome of the Negresco is a much-loved Nice landmark dating back to 1912. Inside, it's a luxurious palace to art, with works covering all periods from the Renaissance to the 21st century. Everything is on a grand scale, and guests staying in the 145 rooms or 24 suites have access to the hotel's own private stretch of Mediterranean beach.

➕ 210 C3 ⊠ 37 promenade des Anglais, 06000 Nice ☎ 04 93 16 64 00; www.hotel-negresco-nice.com

Hostellerie de Cacharel €€

Style and simplicity are the watchwords at this comfortable hostellerie, set in the middle of a nature reserve in the Camargue, complete with its own stables.

Where to...
Eat and Drink

Le Bouchon et l'Assiette €–€€

Set in a lovely old building beside the Fontaine gardens, this apparently exclusive restaurant offers great value prixe-fixe menus which make it well worth seeking out. The style in the dining room may be simple, but the cooking is richly flavoured and beautifully presented – try the *foie gras*, served grilled with peppers and grape caramel.

➕ 209 D4 ⊠ 5 rue de Sauve, 3000 Nîmes ☎ 04 66 62 02 93
⊙ Thu–Mon noon–1:30, 7:30–10; closed 1–15 Jan and 3 weeks Aug

Christian Étienne €€

The food does not come cheap at this Avignon restaurant, but the quality is excellent and the setting superb. It's housed in a 14th-century palace, complete with painted ceilings and frescoes, and with a priceless view out from the terrace over the fabulous Palais des Papes. Truffles are a significant feature of the menu, and the black truffle omelette is not to be missed.

➕ 209 E4 ⊠ 10 rue de Mons, 84000 Avignon ☎ 04 90 86 16 50 ⊙ Tue–Sat noon–1:15, 7:30–9:15

Flamingos feed in the surrounding ponds and marshes, and there's an appealing terraced restaurant on site, or you can easily walk the short distance to sample the local eateries. The hotel facilities also include a reading lounge, a cocktail bar and a gym, and air-conditioning is standard.

➕ 214 C3 ⊠ 26 boulevard des Belges, 69006 Lyon ☎ 04 72 82 18 00; www.warwickhotels.com

Le Mas d'Aigret €–€€

If you want to see the dawn rise over Les Baux, then you'll need to stay in the village, and this unusual hotel carved into the rocky hillside is a great place to be, with wonderful views. There are 16 air-conditioned bedrooms, simply but tastefully furnished, with cool, white-painted furniture and pretty floral bedcovers. Facilities at this three-star hotel include a lounge, a bar and an outdoor swimming pool.

➕ 209 E3 ⊠ 13520 Les Baux-de-Provence ☎ 04 90 54 20 00; www.masdaigret.com

---

there's an appealing terraced restaurant on site, or you can easily walk the short distance to sample the local eateries. There's no restaurant either, but a dinner platter can be ordered in advance. The white-painted building is typical of the area, with beamed ceilings, big fireplaces and tiled floors, and furnishings in the 16 bedrooms are stylish and comfortable. There's also an outdoor swimming pool – great in the sticky heat of summer.

➕ 209 D3 ⊠ route de Cacharel, 13460 Saintes-Maries-de-la-Mer ☎ 04 90 97 95 44; www.hotel-cacharel.com

La Reine Astrid €€–€€€

For a touch of luxury in Lyon, head for this four-star hotel in a residential district, close to the Parc Tête d'Or. There are 90 suites (including 25 non-smoking), with one or two bedrooms each, richly furnished in shades of deep blue, red and gold. Suites are also equipped with a kitchen, and

L'Âne Rouge €€

Seafood is the flavour of every day in this elegant restaurant with a terrace overlooking the harbour. High-backed chairs offer every comfort inside as you dine, perhaps, on succulent scallops roasted with chorizo, tomatoes and thyme.

✚ 210 C3 ☒ 7 quai des Deux-Emmanuel, 06300 Nice ☎ 04 93 89 49 63 ⊚ Mon–Tue and Fri–Sun noon–2:30, 7:30–10, Thu 7:30–10

La Brasserie des Brotteaux €€–€€€

This splendid old brasserie in Lyon has been serving customers since 1913. Inside you'll find antique decorations, bright tiles, and lots of polished glass and mirrors. Eat outside in fine weather, or retreat into the air-conditioning if it's just too hot. There's a choice of prix-fixe menus and salads, and even Aberdeen Angus beef.

✚ 214 C3 ☒ 1 place Jules Ferry, 69006 Lyon ☎ 04 72 74 03 98 ⊚ Mon–Sat 7:30 am–10:30 pm

La Cours des Miracles €€

You'll find an unusual mixture of circus and restaurant at this Grenoble restaurant, located opposite Parc Paul Mistral. It is run by business partners Thierry Chiaberto and Jean Jerome Bouron, one of whom developed a circus school, while the other runs the restaurant. The two come together in front of the diners, and there's also a magic show on Tuesday evenings and Saturday lunchtimes. The restaurant menu is international, and there's a children's menu, too.

✚ 215 D2 ☒ 7 bis place Paul Vallier, 38000 Grenoble ☎ 04 38 37 00 10 ⊚ Tue–Thu noon–2, 7:30–10, Fri–Sat noon–2, 7:30–11; closed 8–26 Aug

Les Bains €–€€€

As the name tells you, this smart, stylish restaurant is in Montpellier's former public bathhouse. The menu reflects modern Mediterranean

cooking, with an emphasis on seafood, and the €24 prix-fixe menu, with a choice for each of three courses, offers especially good value. There's a terrace for al fresco dining, and you can also take afternoon tea here.

✚ 208 C3 ☒ 6 rue Richelieu, 34000 Montpellier ☎ 04 67 60 70 87 ⊚ Mon 7:30 pm–10:30 pm, Tue–Sat noon–10.30

Chez Fonfon €€€

Escape the touristy areas of the old port in Marseille, and come instead to the fishing port, now a conservation area, to taste bouillabaisse, the quintessential fish soup for which the city is famous. Chez Fonfon is a family-run place on the waterfront, well known to the local people for more than 50 years. Inside the styling is cool, elegant Mediterranean, with green basket-weave chairs and a tiled floor, and bright splashes of colour are provided by Provencal fabrics. A bottle of house wine with your

meal costs around €15.

✚ 209 F3 ☒ 140 rue du Vallon des Auffes, 13007 Marseille ☎ 04 91 52 14 38 ⊚ Mon 7:30–10, Tue–Sat noon–2, 7:30–10

Le Louis XV €€€

If you're feeling in extravagant mode, there's only one place to dine out in Monaco – this very special restaurant in the magnificent Hôtel de Paris. The hotel was built in 1864, and the plush Louis XV styling of the dining room is the perfect backdrop for food cooked by one of France's top chefs, Alain Ducasse. The menu, which varies according to the season and reflects themes such as hunting or the farm, does not disappoint. The house wine starts at €90 a bottle.

✚ 210 C4 ☒ Hôtel de Paris, place du Casino, 98000 Monaco ☎ 337 92 16 29 76 ⊚ Thu–Mon noon–2, 7:30–9:30; Wed 7:30–9:30, Jul–Aug; closed 3 weeks Dec and 2 weeks Mar

Where to... Shop

There's no shortage of great shopping in this affluent part of France, with boutiques and big names in the towns and cities. Look out for the giant shopping mall on the edge of Grenoble, **Grand'Place**, with around 140 shops and restaurants (tel: 04 76 09 55 45, open Mon–Sat 9:30–8). Lyon has the **Part Dieu Shopping Centre**, with branches of **Galeries Lafayette** and **Carrefour** supermarket (17 rue de Dr Bouchut, tel: 04 72 60 60 62, open Mon–Sat 9:30–7:30).

FASHION AND SCENT

Fashionistas head for Cannes, and the likes of **Jacques Loup**, which stocks the latest designs and hottest labels in shoes, clothes and accessories (21 rue d'Antibes,

tel: 04 93 39 28 35, open Mon–Sat 9:30–8). St-Tropez also has a reputation for glamour.

Look out for individual, family-run shops in the various towns of the region. These include **Bijoux Dumont** in Arles, where Provençal jewellery in gold, silver and semi-precious stones is made (3 rue du Palais, tel: 04 90 96 05 66, open Tue–Sat 9–noon, 2:30–7). Seek out the hand-made Roman-style sandals at **Rondini** in St-Tropez, as worn by Picasso (16 rue Clémenceau, tel: 04 94 97 19 55, open daily 9:30–noon, 3–7). **Chapelier Mouret**, in Avignon, is a great hat shop (20 rue des Marchands, tel: 04 90 85 39 38, open Tue–Sat 9:30–12:30, 2–7).

Grasse is the centre of the perfume industry – check out the factory and shop of **Fragonard**

there, a prestigious perfumerie dating back to the 18th century (20 boulevard Fragonard, tel: 04 93 36 44 65, open daily 9–6).

FOOD AND DRINK

Provence is known for its sweet treats. The best place to buy the diamond-shaped marzipan sweets called *calissons* is **Confiserie Entrecasteaux** at Aix-en-Provence, where they've been made to the same family recipe for over four generations (2 rue Entrecasteaux, tel: 04 42 27 15 02, open Mon–Sat 8–noon, 2–7).

Olive oil is also widely produced, and you can buy oil and related products such as soap at Nice's **Moulin à Huile Alziari** (4 rue St-François-de-Paule, tel: 04 93 85 76 92, open Tue–Sat 8:30–7).

Lyon has two great markets. The covered **Les Halles** has food and flowers (102 cours Lafayette, tel: 04 78 62 39 32), while the **Marché de la Croix Rousse**, held on the

boulevard of the same name, also includes fabric, household goods, crafts and clothing on a Tuesday (tel: 08 25 08 15 15, open Tue–Sun 7–1). Grenoble has several markets, including the **Marché place aux Herbes** for food (Tue–Sun 6–1), **Marché Victor Hugo** on place Victor Hugo for manufactured goods (Mon–Sat 10–8), and **Marché de l'Abbaye** on place de la Commune for food and crafts (Tue–Sun 6–1).

ARTS AND CRAFTS

At **Atelier St-Michel** in Moustiers-Sainte-Marie, *faïence* porcelain is seen at its best (tel: 04 92 74 67 46, daily 10–7), and check out the craft glassware at **l'Artisan du Crystal** in the middle of Eze (place du Général-de-Gaulle, tel: 04 93 41 16 74, open daily 9–7). Nice has an evening arts and crafts market, perfect for a post-supper stroll (**Marché Saleya d'Artisanat d'Art**, open Tue–Sun 6 pm–midnight, Jun–Sep).

Where to...
Be Entertained

MUSIC AND THEATRE

Nîmes's **Roman amphitheatre** hosts a range of events from concerts to bull fights (les Arènes, tel: 04 66 76 72 77). The **Roman amphitheatre** in Lyon is the spectacular setting for concerts, dance, theatre and cinema in summer – bring a cushion to sit on (6 rue de l'Antiquaille, tel: 04 72 32 00 00, open mid-Jun to mid-Aug). An **old fort** on the coast road 2km outside Sète has been transformed into an open-air theatre, with performances mainly in French (route de la Corniche, tel: 04 67 74 98 86).

A more traditional venue for classical music and opera is **l'Opéra Nationale de Lyon** (place de la Comédie, tel:04 72 00 45 45), while Montpellier has the grandiose **l'Opéra Comédie** (11 boulevard Victor Hugo, tel: 04 67 60 19 99). Experimental theatre is on offer at Avignon's **Big Bang Théâtre**, open year-round (18 rue Guillaume-Puy, tel: 04 90 27 12 71).

For jazz, the intimate **Pelle-Mêle** in Marseille is hard to beat (8 place aux Huiles, tel: 04 91 54 85 26, open Tue–Sat 6 pm–3 am, closed Jul–Aug). Grenoble also has a jazz club, **La Soupe aux Choux**, north of the river, which caters for all tastes from modern to trad (7 route de Lyon, tel: 04 76 87 05 67, open Tue–Sat 8:30 pm–1 am, closed Aug).

Cannes' modern **Palais des Festivals et des Congrès** hosts the annual film festival in May, but is also a year-round venue for international concerts, ballet, theatre and exhibitions (1 boulevard de la Croisette, tel: 04 93 39 01'01).

CINEMA

There are no less than 11 auditoriums to choose from at Marseille's **Les Trois Palmes** (2 boulevard Léon-Bancal, tel: 04 91 87 91 87). **Le Club** in Grenoble is a six-screen cinema which often shows movies in their original language (9 bis rue de Phalonstère, tel: 04 76 46 13 38). Lyon has the **UGC Astoria** and **UGC Comoédia**, both of which show many films in their original language (Astoria, 31 cours Vitton; Comoédia, 13 avenue Berthelot, both tel: 0892 70 00 00).

BARS, CLUBS, CASINOS

The popular band, the Gypsy Kings used to hang out at the café of **La Movida** in Nîmes – it's a tapas bar, noted for its live flamenco music (2 place de la Placette, tel: 04 66 67 80 90, Mon–Sat 7 pm–2 am, closed 3 weeks Aug). If you're looking for authentic Marseille, try the **Bar de la Marine**, facing the old harbour (15 quai de Rive-Neuve, tel: 04 91 54 95 42, open daily 7 am–2 am).

La Siesta at Antibes offers every sort of night-time entertainment, from a casino to several dance floors (route du Bord de Mer, tel: 04 93 33 31 31, daily 11 pm–5 am, mid-Jun to mid-Sep, Fri–Sat mid-Sep to mid-Jun).

The **Casino de Monte-Carlo** is probably the most famous in the world, and has featured in James Bond movies (place du Casino, tel: 377 92 16 20 00). If you're still feeling lucky, head for the bright lights of Cannes and **Casino Croisette** (1 esplanade Lucien Barrière, tel: 04 92 98 78 00, open daily 10 am–5 am, games room from 8 pm), or simply chill out and people-watch from the terrace of **Le Festival bar** (52 la Croisette, tel: 04 93 38 04 81, open daily 9 am–midnight).

Southwest France

Getting Your Bearings 174 – 175
In Four Days 176 – 177
Don't Miss 178 – 182
At Your Leisure 183 – 186
Walk 187 – 188
Where to... 189 – 192

Getting Your Bearings

Pine forest, dunes and long sandy beaches characterise the Atlantic coastline of France. What it lacks in fashionable cachet it makes up for in wide open spaces, and in the watersports offered along its inland lakes which make it such a great family holiday destination.

Top: Door knocker, Pau
Above: La Rochelle
Below: Mist in the Dordogne valley

The coastal flatlands, more rugged to the north of the Gironde estuary, more predictable to the south, stretch down to the Pyrénées. This mountain chain forms a natural boundary between France and Spain, and is covered with pasture and forest at this western end. Mineral and thermal springs in the mountains' shadow, their potential first spotted by the Romans, have left a legacy of small resorts and spa towns, with the faded queen of them all, Biarritz, drawing a new young crowd to its surfing beaches today. The N117 is the main route for access across the south.

Inland, to the southeast of Périgueux lies the lush green countryside of the Dordogne, threaded with a slow-moving river and dotted with ancient villages.

The major cities of the region are the busy wine capital, Bordeaux, and modern, high-tech Toulouse, linked by fast autoroute.

Previous page: Roadside sculpture near Pau

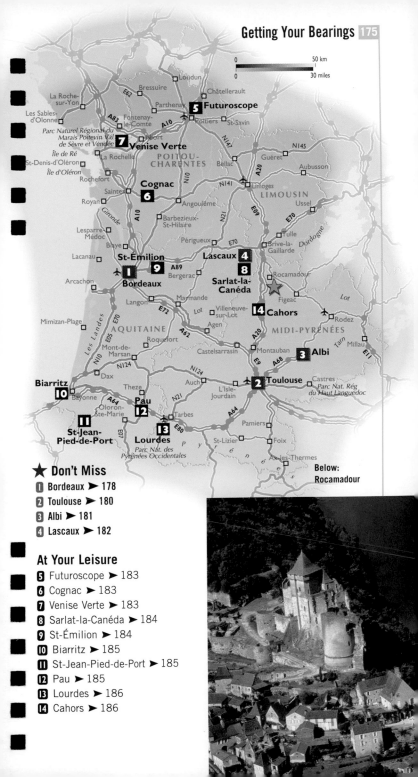

Map labels:

Loudun
La Roche-sur-Yon
Bressuire
Châtellerault
Parthenay
5 **Futuroscope**
Les Sables-d'Olonne
Fontenay-le-Comte
Poitiers
St-Savin
Parc Naturel Régional du Marais Poitevin Val de Sèvre et Vendée
7
Niort
Venise Verte
N145
Île de Ré
La Rochelle
POITOU-CHARENTES
Bellac
Guéret
Aubusson
St-Denis-d'Oléron
Île d'Oléron
Rochefort
LIMOUSIN
Saintes
Limoges
Ussel
Cognac
6
Angoulême
Royan
Gironde
Barbezieux-St-Hilaire
Brive-la-Gaillarde
Tulle
Dordogne
Lesparre-Médoc
Périgueux
Blaye
Lascaux **4**
Lacanau
St-Émilion
9
8
Rocamadour
Bergerac
Sarlat-la-Canéda
Arcachon
Bordeaux
1
Figeac
Lot
Langon
Marmande
Villeneuve-sur-Lot
14 **Cahors**
Mimizan-Plage
Les Landes
AQUITAINE
Agen
Rodez
MIDI-PYRÉNÉES
Roquefort
Montauban
Millau
Mont-de-Marsan
Castelsarrasin
3 **Albi**
Tarn
Dax
Biarritz
10
Theze
Auch
Toulouse
2
Castres
Parc Nat. Rég du Haut Languedoc
Bayonne
Pau
12
L'Isle-Jourdain
Tarbes
St-Jean-Pied-de-Port
11
Lourdes
13
Pamiers
Oloron-Ste-Marie
Parc Nat. des Pyrénées Occidentales
St-Lizier
Foix
Ax-les-Thermes
Pyrénées

0 50 km
0 30 miles

★ Don't Miss

1 Bordeaux ➤ 178
2 Toulouse ➤ 180
3 Albi ➤ 181
4 Lascaux ➤ 182

At Your Leisure

5 Futuroscope ➤ 183
6 Cognac ➤ 183
7 Venise Verte ➤ 183
8 Sarlat-la-Canéda ➤ 184
9 St-Émilion ➤ 184
10 Biarritz ➤ 185
11 St-Jean-Pied-de-Port ➤ 185
12 Pau ➤ 185
13 Lourdes ➤ 186
14 Cahors ➤ 186

Below:
Rocamadour

A whistle-stop tour starts in the flatlands of the Atlantic coast, runs east through the foothills of the Pyrénées and loops north again via the modern city of Toulouse and through beautiful region of the Dordogne.

Southwest France in Four Days

Day One

Morning
Enjoy a morning exploring the wine city of **1 Bordeaux** (➤ 178–179), and stock up on a few bottles to take with you. Climb the **Tour Pey-Berland** (➤ 178) for the views, and take your time over a bistro lunch at **Le Café des Arts** (➤ 179).

Afternoon
Head south through the pine forests of Les Landes to the holiday resort of **10 Biarritz** (above, ➤ 185), where you can relax on the **beaches**, or perhaps sample the pleasures of the **Musée du Chocolat**.

Evening
Unwind in a café or bar, or perhaps treat yourself to a night out at the **ballet** (➤ 192).

Day Two

Morning
Take the minor roads south inland into the foothills of the mountains and visit pretty **11 St-Jean-Pied-de-Port** (➤ 185), close to the Spanish border. Continue on small roads across country to the phenomena that is the modern pilgrimage town of **13 Lourdes** (left, ➤ 186),

and break there for a **café lunch**.

Afternoon
Join the A64/E80 for a fast-track journey east and north to the high-tech city of **2 Toulouse** (➤ 180), and a visit to the **Cité de l'Espace** space centre.

Evening
There's plenty of **nightlife** to choose from in the city, from wine bars to an arts cinema (➤ 192).

Day Three

Morning
Take the A68 east and follow the trail of artist Toulouse Lautrec at the old town of **3 Albi** (above, ➤ 181), before heading north on minor roads to ancient **14 Cahors** (➤ 186), where the historic railway, **Quercyrail**, may prove a serious distraction.

Afternoon

Spend the afternoon and evening exploring the golden-stone town of **8 Sarlat-la-Canéda** (➤ 184), sampling the local delicacies of duck, *foie-gras* and walnuts in the local restaurants.

Day Four

Morning
Make sure you've booked ahead to visit the famous recreated **prehistoric caves** at **4 Lascaux** (➤ 182), with their vivid paintings faithfully reproduced. Lunch at the nearby **Restaurant la Vieille Auberge** (➤ 182).

Afternoon
Enjoy a **walk** at **Rocamadour** (right, ➤ 187–188), a stunningly beautiful, historic village built against a sheer cliff.

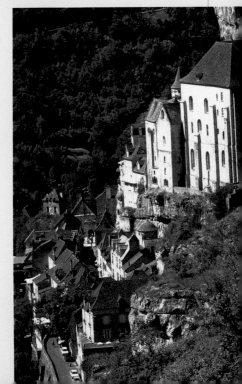

❶ Bordeaux

This great city and port on the River Garonne is the capital of the world's biggest wine-producing area. A lively hub, with its own university, it has magnificent architecture and splendid open spaces, with attractions that include a 1,000-year-old church, a remarkable Palladian theatre and a rich variety of museums and galleries.

The Romans may not have been the first to settle here (there is evidence that Celtic tribes were here 300 years before), but they were the first to make a serious impact – and the vine cultivation that they introduced set the city on a course of prosperity that has never faltered.

Bordeaux's wealth over the centuries can be seen in its expansive layout, with wide boulevards and open squares. The biggest of these is the **esplanade des Quinconces**, a vast tree-lined space by the river, established in the early 19th century on the site of a former château.

For good shopping in the city, head straight for **rue Sainte Catherine** and **cours Georges Clemenceau**.

Bordeaux Highlights

The medieval old town stretches west and south from place de la Bourse, on the riverbank. The twin spires of the **Cathédrale St-André** are an unmistakable city landmark to the southwest. Parts date back to the 10th century, and medieval sculptures adorn the huge space of the interior. Eleanor of Aquitaine, ex-wife of Louis VII and a powerful force in her own right, married the future Henry II of England here in 1152.

The bell tower next to the cathedral is the **Tour Pey-Berland**, 50m (165 feet) high and topped with the figure of

The Reluctant Mayor

In the esplanade des Quinconces, look out for a statue of **Michel Eyquem de Montaigne** (1533–92), the great essayist. He was celebrated in his day as an original thinker, which may have been a reflection on his experimental upbringing – until the age of six, he was encouraged to speak nothing but Latin. Having previously served as a city councillor, against his own wishes he was elected Mayor of Bordeaux in 1581, and served successfully for four years in all.

**Above: Alles de Tourny
Left: Fountain detail**

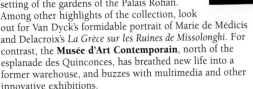

Notre-Dame-d'Aquitaine; the climb to the top is worth it for the views.

The tourist office shares the place de la Comédie with one of the city's most remarkable buildings, the **Grand Théâtre**. Dating from 1773, it was designed by Victor Louis (who restored the cathedral at Chartres, ► 66) in Greek Palladian style as a temple to the arts, with a façade incorporating 12 Corinthian columns and statues of the Muses. The magnificent gilded interior was restored in 1991, and the acoustics are excellent – catch a concert there if you can.

Bordeaux's compact **Musée des Beaux-Arts** is just west of the cathedral, in the peaceful setting of the gardens of the Palais Rohan. Among other highlights of the collection, look out for Van Dyck's formidable portrait of Marie de Médicis and Delacroix's *La Grèce sur les Ruines de Missolonghi*. For contrast, the **Musée d'Art Contemporain**, north of the esplanade des Quinconces, has breathed new life into a former warehouse, and buzzes with multimedia and other innovative exhibitions.

Above: The 15th-century bell-tower of Grosse Cloche

Top left: A vine ready for harvesting

TAKING A BREAK

Le Café des Arts, at 138 cours Victor-Hugo, is a lively place for a meal or a snack at any time of day, with bistro offerings such as salads, omelettes and scallops (tel 05 56 91 07 89).

➕ 212 A1

Tourist Information Office
✉ 12 cours 30 Juillet ☎ 05 56 00 66 00; www.bordeaux-tourisme.com
🕐 Mon–Sat 9–7, Sun 9:30–6:30, May–Jun, Sep;

Mon–Sat 9–7:30, Sun 9:30–6:30, Jul–Aug; Mon–Sat 9–6:30, Sun 9:45–4:40, Oct–Apr

Cathédrale St-André
✉ place Puy-Berland ☎ 05 56 52 68 10 🕐 Mon 10–11:30, 2–6:30, Tue–Sat 7:30–11:30,

2–6, all year, and Sun 8–12:30, 2–5:30 summer only

Grand Théâtre
✉ place de la Comédie ☎ 05 56 00 85 95

Musée des Beaux-Arts
✉ 20 Cours d'Albert

☎ 05 56 10 20 56
🕐 Wed–Mon 11–6
💷 Inexpensive

Musée d'Art Contemporain
✉ 7 rue Ferrière ☎ 05 56 00 81 50
🕐 Tue–Sun 11–6, also Wed 11–8
💷 Moderate

---

2 Toulouse

Toulouse, a major city on the banks of the Garonne, is a centre for high-tech industry with the largest aeronautical site in Europe – Airbus Industrie – and an adventure park themed around space exploration. The latter, the Cité de l'Espace, lies north of the centre and includes a planetarium and a full-sized Ariane rocket.

The city itself beats with a much older heart. It grew up at a key point on the pilgrimage route to Compostela in Spain, and the vast 11th-century **Basilique St-Sernin**, the biggest Romanesque church in France, dates back to that heady period. Note its distinctive pink, pillared spire. The construction of the Canal du Midi in the 18th century (▶ 145) brought further wealth to Toulouse, and the splendid **town hall**, on the place du Capitole, is one of the best examples of architecture from this period. Relax in one of the cafés here, or explore the boutique shopping streets just to the south.

Top: On place du Capitole
Above: The Pont Neuf
Below: The Basilique St-Sernin

The **Château d'Eau** at the southern end of the Pont Neuf is no Renaissance palace, but rather a redundant water tower from 1923 that has been converted to hold a photography museum and gallery (open Tue–Sun 1–7, inexpensive). Note the Toulouse en Liberté pass, available from the tourist office, which gives free entry to some museums and discounts at other attractions – good value if you plan to explore in detail.

TAKING A BREAK

Dine on local specialities and seafood in the stylish **Grand Café de l'Opéra**, the brasserie of a sumptuous hotel, at 1 place du Capitole (tel: 05 61 21 37 03; closed Aug).

✚ 207 F3
Tourist Information Office
✉ Donjon du Capitole
☎ 05 61 11 02 22; www.ot-toulouse.fr
🕒 Mon–Sat 9–7, Sun 9–1, 2–5:30,

May–Sep; Mon–Fri 9–6, Sat 9–12:30, 2–6, Sun 10–12:30, 2–5, Oct–Apr

Cité de l'Espace
✉ avenue Jean Gouard ☎ 0820 377

223; www.cite-espace.com 🕒 Daily 9–7 summer, 9:30–5 winter 💶 Expensive

Basilique St-Sernin
✉ place St-Sernin
🕒 Daily 8:45–6

3 Albi

This large brick-built town has two prominent claims to fame: a remarkable Gothic cathedral and a major museum to its most famous son, the painter Toulouse-Lautrec. There's good shopping around the central square, place du Vigan, and attractive formal gardens overlook the River Tarn.

The forbidding **Cathédrale Sainte-Cécile** dates from the 13th century, a time of bloody warfare between Catholics and Cathars. With its tall, narrow windows like arrow-slits, it is easy to see how the building once doubled as a fortress. The austerity of the exterior gives way to sumptuous Renaissance decoration on the interior, with elaborate frescoes over the ceiling and a vast, detailed 15th-century mural of the Last Judgement. The magnificent organ is claimed to be the biggest in France.

Albi is a gracious pink-brick town on the River Tarn

Homage is paid to Henri de Toulouse-Lautrec (1864–1901) in a **museum** in the former archbishop's palace, which also houses the tourist office. Toulouse-Lautrec was born into a wealthy aristocratic family, and suffered from various crippling genetic disorders from a young age. In 1884 he settled in Montmartre in Paris, where his stylish posters and paintings of the extraordinary, colourful characters all around him – barmaids, prostitutes, cabaret stars and race-goers – were to make him famous. Around 600 of his works are held here.

TAKING A BREAK
You'll find plenty of bars and cafés to choose from on the main square of Albi, **place du Vigan**.

+ 208 A4

Tourist Information Office
⊠ Palais de la Berbie, place Sainte-Cécile ☎ 05 63 49 48 80; www.tourisme.fr/albi
🕐 Mon–Sat 9–7, Sun 10–12:30, 2:30–6:30, Jul–Sep; Mon–Sat 9–12:30, 2–6, Sun

10–12:30, 2:30–6:30, Oct–Jun

Cathédrale Sainte-Cécile
⊠ place Sainte-Cécile
🕐 Daily 9–6:30, Jun–Sep; 9–noon, 2–6:30, Oct–May

Musée Toulouse-Lautrec
⊠ Palais de la Berbie, place

Sainte-Cécile ☎ 05 63 49 48 70; www.musee-toulouse-lautrec.com
🕐 Daily 10–noon, 2–6, Apr–May; 9–noon, 2–6, Jun, Sep; 9–6, Jul–Aug; Wed–Mon 10–noon, 2–5, Oct–Feb; 10–noon, 2–5:30, Mar
🎟 Inexpensive

4 Lascaux

A remarkable series of prehistoric paintings was discovered by accident at Lascaux, just south of Montignac, in the mid-20th century. While the originals have been sealed up again to preserve them from the destruction of micro-organisms in the air, the paintings have been carefully re-created for visitors at nearby Lascaux II, and seeing them gives an insight into the concerns and skills of our early ancestors. Advance booking is essential.

Vivid bison, horses and deer in shades of ochre, brown and charcoal gallop across the uneven face of the stone, to stunning effect. The original artists mixed pigments such as kaolin and haematite to achieve different colours, and you can learn more about their techniques – replicated faithfully for the reconstruction – in the accompanying display. The purpose of the paintings remains obscure: was this simply artistic expression, or a series of messages or records about hunting in the area, or perhaps linked to some religious ceremony? We'll never know, but the impact of the images is remarkably fresh and immediate after around 17,000 years.

Bulls and horses run free on the stone walls of Lascaux II

TAKING A BREAK

At the village of St-Genies, midway between Sarlat and Montignac, is the **Restaurant la Vieille Auberge**, where you can dine on excellent local food (le Bourg, tel: 05 53 28 90 38). Established in the late 19th century, it's still run by the great-great granddaughter of the original owner, and doubles as an art gallery.

✚ 212 C1

✉ Lascaux II, Montignac (enquiries via Semitour Périgord, BP 1024 Périgueux)

☎ 05 53 51 95 03; www.perigord.tm.fr ⊘ Daily 9–7, Jul–Aug; 9–6 Apr–Jun, Sep; 10–12:30, 2–5:30, Oct–Nov, Feb–Mar 💷 Expensive

At Your Leisure

The Kinemax "rock crystals", Futuroscope

5 Futuroscope

A high-tech leisure park with eye-catching architecture, Futuroscope is a main attraction 11km (7 miles) north of Poitiers. Wonder at the giant, mirrored crystals apparently growing at an angle from the earth, and the huge sphere hovering above sheets of glass. These and more bizarre structures hold a variety of stylish and fun exhibits, from an auditorium of co-ordinated moving seats in front of semicircular 3-D screens, to a 360-degree panorama to take your breath away. In the surrounding grounds you'll come across interactive water fountains and a lake which children can cross – on tricycles.

➕ 212 B4 ✉ Parc Futuroscope, BP 2000, 86130 Jaunay-Clan ☎ 05 49 49 11 12; www.futuroscope.com ⏰ Daily 10–dusk, Apr–Aug; 10–6, Sep to mid-Nov (hours may vary) 💷 Expensive

6 Cognac

This prosperous little town between Saintes and Angoulême is the centre of the worldwide cognac industry. Get into the spirit of the place by visiting one of the great **cognac houses**, where the brandy is distilled from the local grapes – Martell, Hennessy and Rémy Martin are some of the names to conjure with; the tourist office can supply details. Half-timbered buildings and stately Renaissance mansions rub shoulders in the old quarter, and you'll find the chic shops and restaurants around the central **place François I**.

➕ 212 A2
Tourist Information Office
✉ 16 rue du XIV Juillet
☎ 05 45 82 10 71; www.tourism-cognac.com ⏰ Mon–Sat 9–7, Sun 10–4, Jul–Aug; Mon–Sat 9:30–5:30, May–Jun, Sep; Mon–Sat 10–5, Oct–Apr

Some of the great names in cognac open their doors to visitors

7 Venise Verte

Also known as the **Marais Poitevin**, this marshy area lies on the western coast north of La Rochelle. Inland it is riddled with man-made waterways, and accessible only by boat. By the coast it is drier and more arid, with expansive salt pans. It's great to explore on foot, by bicycle or from the water – hire a punt (*une plate*) in **Coulon**. Eels are a local delicacy.

➕ 211 F3
Tourist Information Office
✉ 31 rue Gabriel Audier, 79510 Coulon
☎ 05 49 35 99 29; www.marais-poitevin.fr ⏰ Daily 10–1, 2–5:30, Apr–Jun, Sep; 10–1, 2–6, Jul–Aug; Tue–Sat 10–noon, 2–5:30, Oct–Mar

Enjoying the summer sun in Sarlat

8 Sarlat-la-Canéda

The lovely old town of Sarlat, with its honey-coloured stone, makes an excellent base for exploring the delights of the Dordogne region. You can sample its gastronomic pleasures, including *foie gras*, chestnuts, truffles and walnuts, in the many restaurants and small eateries, and wander at leisure through the streets of tall, distinguished-looking Renaissance town houses (known as *hôtels*) at its heart. They date mostly from the period 1450 to 1500, and their characteristic steep roofs are designed to support the heavy stone tiles. Don't miss the much-photographed **Maison d'Étienne de la Boétie**, birthplace of the 16th-century philosopher and poet, with its high gables and ornamental chimney stacks.

The **Saturday market** is a treat for the eye as well as the palate, and the **Halle Paysanne des Produits Fins au Terroir**, on rue Cahors, stocks the best of local produce.

✚ 213 D1
Tourist Information Office
✉ rue Tourny ☎ 05 53 31 45 45; www.ot-sarlat-perigord.fr ⏰ Mon–Sat 9–7, Sun 10–noon, 2–6, Apr–Oct; Mon–Sat 9–noon, 2–6, Nov–Mar

9 St-Émilion

St-Émilion has everything a prestigious and historic wine-producing village should have: steep and narrow cobbled streets threading between handsome old stone houses, shady squares with good restaurants, side-streets with stylish little shops, and all surrounded by neatly combed fields of top-quality vines. The old town was not designed for cars, so it's best to park outside the medieval walls and explore on foot.

One of the strangest sights here is the **Église Monolithe**, an underground church which was carved out of the rock between the 8th and 12th

A rooftop panorama at St-Émilion reveals the crowded houses of the old town

centuries. It's opposite the tourist office on place des Créneaux, and visits are by guided tour only. The tours also take in the catacombs, and the grotto where Aemilianus, a Breton hermit who gives the town its name, came to live during the 8th century.

September marks the start of the grape harvest, and St-Émilion celebrates with a festival, the **Ban des Vendanges**. Events include wine tastings and a procession through the town to the Tour du Roi, a tower from which a trumpet is blown to start the picking.

✚ 212 A1
Tourist Information Office
✉ place des Créneaux ☎ 05 57 55 28 28; www.saint-emilion-tourisme.com ⏰ Daily 9:30–8, Jul–Aug; 9:30–7, mid- to end Jun and early to mid-Sep; 9:30–12:30, 1:45–6:30, Apr to mid-Jun and mid-Sep to Oct; 9:30–12:30, 1:45–6, Nov–Mar

🔟 Biarritz

This faded beauty of a seaside resort was the holiday choice of the cream of European royalty in the late 19th century, and its casino and nightlife gave it a cachet with the smart set in the 20th century that lingers on. Now it's also popular with families, who come to enjoy the glorious sands, and with surfers, who make the most of the seemingly endless roll of the Atlantic breakers (catch the July surf festival, the biggest in Europe). The magnificent old Hôtel du Palais still queens it over the **Grande Plage**, the most fashionable of the three beaches. **Le Port-Vieux**, the smaller beach at the southern end, is where the whaling boats once sailed from. To the north, a light-house watches over all.

Back from the shore, you'll find elegant streets with chic shops and good restaurants. The aquarium, the **Musée de la Mer**, is well worth a

Enjoying the view over the Grande Plage at the resort of Biarritz

visit – there's also a shark pool and seals. Another popular attraction is the **chocolate museum**, which includes tastings.

➕ 206 A3
Tourist Information Office
✉ square d'Ixelles ☎ 05 59 22 37 10;
www.ville-biarritz.fr ☀ Daily 8–8,
Jul–Aug; Mon–Sat 9–6, Sun 10–5,
Sep–Jun

Musée de la Mer
✉ Plateau Atalaye, Rocher de la Vièrge
☎ 05 59 22 75 40 ☀ Daily 9:30–7,

Jun, Sep; 9:30–midnight, Jul–Aug;
9:30–12:30, 2–6, Oct–May; closed 1–15
Jan; feeding times 10:30 and 5
💷 Moderate

Musée du Chocolat
✉ 14 avenue Beau Rivage ☎ 05 59
41 54 64 ☀ Daily 10–noon, 2:30–7,
Jul–Aug; Mon–Sat 10–noon, 2:30–6, rest
of year 💷 Moderate

🔟 St-Jean-Pied-de-Port

Set in the rolling green heart of the Basque country, this appealing old town was once a gathering point for pilgrims on the route to Compostela, as they prepared to cross the Ronceveaux pass (*port*) into Spain. In Basque, its name is Donibane Garazi. The clustered medieval buildings of pinkish sand-stone are encircled by **fortified walls**, and there is a separate **Citadelle**, designed by the engineer Vauban in 1685. The River Nive runs through the centre, spanned by an elegant old bridge beside the restored church of Notre-Dame-du-Pont.

➕ 206 A2
Tourist Information Office
✉ place du Marché ☎ 05 59 37 03
57; www.pyrenees-basques.com
☀ Daily May–Sep; Mon–Sat Oct–Apr

🔟 Pau

It is said that Pau owes part of its success as a spa resort to the soldiers of the Duke of Wellington, who were given a warm welcome here in 1814 and decided to stay. Word soon spread back to England about the pleasantness of the mild winter climate and the opportunities for fox-hunting and other sports, and the town established its reputation as a comfortable retreat. Palm trees, cacti and bamboo lend the town an exotic air today, and there are spec-tacular views south to the mountains from the boulevard des Pyrénées. The much restored **château** was the birthplace of Henri IV in 1553.

➕ 206 C3
Tourist Information Office ✉ place
Royale ☎ 05 59 27 27 08; www.pau.fr
☀ Mon–Sat 9–6, Sun 9:30–1

Shrine to the Virgin, Lourdes

🔟 Lourdes

The pilgrimage town of Lourdes is well known worldwide, and attracts more than five million visitors every year who seek healing at the shrine of St Bernadette, the girl who saw visions in 1858. There are many sites for prayer, from the vast spaces of the underground basilica (up to 20,000 people) to intimate little churches. The tourist office has a map with full details, including service times.

➕ 206 C2
Tourist Information Office
✉ place Peyramale ☎ 05 62 42 77 40; www.lourdes-france.com
🕐 Mon–Sat 9–6:30, Sun 10–noon, May–Jun, Sep; Mon–Sat 9–7, Sun 10–6, Jul–Aug; Mon–Sat 9–noon, 2–5:30, Nov–Feb; Mon–Sat 9–noon, 2–6, Mar–Apr, Oct

🔢 Cahors

Cahors is built on a bend of the River Lot, and here you'll find one of its best-loved features, the **Pont Valentré**. This ancient stone bridge, with its three tall defensive towers, is a medieval gem fortified in the 14th century to fend off English invaders in the Hundred Years' War. Boulevard Gambetta is the main street through the town, splitting it into two parts – old and new.

A scenic restored railway, **Quercyrail**, runs from the town station 71km (44 miles) along the Lot valley to Capdenac – advance reservations are essential.

➕ 207 F5
Tourist Information Office ✉ place François Mitterand ☎ 05 65 53 20 65; www.tourisme-lot.com 🕐 Mon–Fri 9–12:30, 1:30–6:30, Sat 9–12:30, 1:30–6, Apr–Jun, Sep–Oct; Mon–Sat

The old bridge over the Lot at Cahors

9–6:30, Sun 10–12:30, Jul–Aug; Mon–Sat 9–12:30, 1:30–6 Nov–Mar

Quercyrail ✉ place de la Gare ☎ 05 63 40 11 93/05 65 23 94 72 (bookings) 🕐 Trains daily Jul–Aug; Sat–Sun, Apr–Jun, Sep–Oct
💰 Expensive

For Kids

• **Futuroscope**, near Poitiers: ➤ 183.
• **Biarritz**: Musée de la Mer ➤ 185. There's also a large, well-run aquarium at **La Rochelle** (Bassin des Grands Yachts, tel 05 46 34 00 00, open daily, expensive).
• **Bordeaux**: Bring your skates and take part in the regular in-line skating night, in the downtown pedestrian area (first Sun of the month, free).
• **Near Tarbes**, north of Lourdes: The Ferme Équestre du Bosc Clar is a family-run stables which can arrange special rides for children, along with lessons and trekking (8 Cami Deu Bosc Clar, 65800 Chis, tel 05 62 36 27 36, open Tue–Sun).

ROCAMADOUR

Walk

Rocamadour is one of the top tourist sites of the Dordogne – a lovely old village pressed against the cliffs with a castle perched dramatically at the top.

1–2

From the **top car park**, go through the coin-operated barrier (€2.50 per person) to explore the **ramparts** of the castle. There are fabulous views over the village. Walk down the steeply winding **Chemin de Croix**, with the Stations of the Cross marked at each bend. Rocamadour was originally settled by a hermit, Amadour, and after his preserved body was discovered in the 12th century, the rock became a centre of pilgrimage. Pass through a tunnel under the basilica to reach the **Cité Religieuse**.

2–3

There are seven chapels to explore here, but the most important one is to the left of the basilica, the **Chapelle de Notre-Dame**. Inside is a small carving of the Madonna,

DISTANCE 1km (0.6 mile) **TIME** 1.5 hours
START/END POINT Upper car park (free), by the château ⊞ 207 F5

blackened by candle soot over the centuries. Also here is the Musée d'Art Sacré Francis Poulenc, with an interesting collection of religious artefacts. It commemorates composer Francis Poulenc (1899–1963), who had a vision when he visited here in 1936, and dedicated a series of

Rocamadour is built up against the cliff-face

litanies to the Black Virgin of Rocamadour. Walk down the 223 steps of the **Grand Escalier**, to explore the village at the bottom of the rock.

3–4

Turn left along the **main street**, which is lined with souvenir shops. Pass the tourist office (tel: 05 65 33 22 00, www.rocamadour.com), next to the Hôtel de Ville. Just before one of the original town gates, the Porte Salmon, turn right down a lane, and go down a flight of steps. This brings you out at the **lower car park**, by the river. From here, take the lift and funicular through the rock (inexpensive, under 8 free), and back up to the **top car park**.

4–5

For an 8km (5-mile) extension from the lower car park, follow the **dragonfly signposts**, crossing the River Alzou by the stone bridge, and taking the lane to the left. After 150m (165 yards), a little path on your right leads to the **Fontaine de la Fillole**. Climb the hill among hazel and oak trees, and once on the plateau, continue past the farm of **Fouysselaze**, on your right.

5–6

When the path meets the **tarmac road**, turn right and follow this past the farm entrance and a wall on the right. Skirt a large hollow

An old stone-roofed house in the village

on the right, the Cloup de Magès. On your left is a **dolmen**, around 4,000 years old. Leave the road and take the **GR46 footpath** to Rocamadour. Cross the D32 and follow a sign for the Fontaine de Berthiol. Cross the Alzou by the little bridge near the Moulin de Roquefraîche, go straight over a small cross-roads, and enter the village via **Porte Basse.** Go through Porte Hugon to return to the **lower car park.**

TAKING A BREAK

There are plenty of **bars and restaurants** to choose from in the lower part of the town.

Other Ways to See Rocamadour

At night the town is illuminated, and there is a 30-minute **guided tour**. Contact the tourist office for more detailed information (tel: 05 65 33 22 00, inexpensive).

Between Easter and September the **Petit Train** (Little Train) carries visitors between the lower parking areas and the shops and restaurants (inexpensive). There is also a funicular **lift**, which operates between the Cité Religieuse and the top car park (inexpensive, under 8 free). Frequencies vary according to the season.

Where to… Stay

Prices
Expect to pay per night for a double room
€ under €50   €€ €50–€100   €€€ over €100

Hotel de France €

This budget hotel is well placed on the edge of the traffic-free centre of Bordeaux. Its 20 air-conditioned rooms each have a private bathroom, and while the comforts are basic, it's clean and convenient, and a practical base for a short stay.
🔁 212 A1 ☒ 7 rue Franklin, 33000 Bordeaux ☎ 05 56 48 24 11

Hôtel St-James €€–€€€

Drive southeast of Bordeaux for around 15 minutes to find the attractive village of Bouliac. This modern hotel, part of the Relais & Château group, has an attached bistro – Le Café de l'Espérance – that's worth a stop in its own right,

plus two further restaurants. There are 15 air-conditioned rooms and 3 suites to choose from, furnished with top-quality audio systems, electric blinds, and views over the outdoor pool to Bordeaux itself.
🔁 212 A1 ☒ 3 place Camille-Hostein, 33270 Bouliac ☎ 05 57 97 06 00; www.saintjames-bouliac.com

Hôtel des Beaux-Arts €€

The views to the river and the Pont Neuf alone make the Hôtel des Beaux-Arts in the heart of Toulouse worth a visit. The building dates from the 18th century, but the three-star facilities are up-to-date, with satellite TV and mini-bars. There are 19 air-conditioned rooms,

and the nearby Dix-Neuf restaurant is part of the same owner-group.
🔁 207 F3 ☒ 1 place du Pont Neuf, 31000 Toulouse ☎ 05 34 45 42 42; www.hotelsdesbeauxarts.com

Le Domaine Rochebois €€–€€€

Vitrac is 8km (5 miles) south of Sarlat-la-Canéda, and this medium-sized hotel at the heart of the Dordogne region makes a good base from which to explore. The building is neo-classical in style, and the views from the 34 air-conditioned bedrooms are of the surrounding gardens and the Dordogne Valley. Four stars mean there are lots of great facilities, including an outdoor pool, tennis court and billiards.
🔁 213 D1 ☒ route de Montfort, 24200 Vitrac ☎ 05 53 31 52 52; www.rochebois.com ⊘ Closed Nov–Mar

Hôtel le Postillon €€

Its friendly atmosphere and very reasonable prices mean that this

popular hotel is always busy, so book ahead. It's family-run, with 28 air-conditioned bedrooms – ask for one with a balcony overlooking the courtyard, filled with flowers in summer. There is no restaurant, but there are plenty of cafés and restaurants to choose from close by.
🔁 206 C3 ☒ place de Verdun, 10 cours Camou, 64000 Pau ☎ 05 59 72 83 00; www.hotel-le-postillon.fr

Chambres d'Hôte, Mme Vives €

If you want to visit Lourdes but get away from the bustle of the place, then this tranquil house 5km (3 miles) north of the town offers the perfect escape. It has just six modern bedrooms, but most enjoy inspiring views to the Pyrenees. Unusually, the room price includes both breakfast and dinner, and meals are taken in the rustic dining room.
🔁 206 C2 ☒ 28 route de Bartres, 65100 Loubajac ☎ 05 62 94 44 17 ⊘ Closed Nov to mid-Feb

Where to...
Eat and Drink

Prices

Expect to pay per person for a meal, excluding drinks

€ under €25 €€ €25-€50 €€€ over €50

Le Franchouillard €€

Sample different regional specialities on a regularly changing menu, *France à la carte* menu, at this popular restaurant in the pedestrianised heart of Bordeaux. The clientele include students and young people who come for the fun atmosphere and reasonable prices. Be prepared for the highlight of the evening, at around 11:30 pm, when music sheets are handed out and everybody joins in to sing along with classic French songs.

✚ 212 A1 ✉ 21 rue Maucoudinat, 33000 Bordeaux ☎ 05 56 44 95 86 🕐 Mon–Sat noon–3, 6–1 am

Restaurant de Fromages Baud et Milet €€

This family-run restaurant in Bordeaux is a little temple to the cheese-makers' art. There are more than 200 varieties of cheese on offer, and the patron can enthuse about each one. There's an all-you-can-eat cheese board on the menu, plus a good selection of mouthwatering traditional cheese-based dishes, such as *raclette* (melted cheese with potato, pickles and onions).

✚ 212 A1 ✉ 19 rue Huguerie, 33000 Bordeaux ☎ 05 56 79 05 77 🕐 Mon–Sat 11:30–2, 7–11

Chez Germaine €–€€

Lying beneath the bell tower of the church in the middle of St-Emilion, this appealing stone-built restaurant majors on traditional French dishes, including *foie gras*, scallops, fish soup and *coq au vin*. The macaroons are a local speciality, and remarkably light and tasty.

✚ 212 A1 ✉ 13 place du Clocher, 33330 St-Emilion ☎ 05 57 74 49 34 🕐 Daily 9–7

Les Pyrénées €–€€

There's a different sort of regional cuisine at this family-run restaurant in St-Jean-Pied-de-Port, infused with the flavours of the Pyrenees. Lamb and truffles are two of the local delicacies, but you'll also find anchovies, sardines, cod and tuna. The setting is a luxuriously restored former coaching inn.

✚ 206 A2 ✉ 19 place de Général-de-Gaulle, 64220 St-Jean-Pied-de-Port ☎ 05 59 37 01 01 🕐 Wed–Mon noon–3, 7–midnight; closed 5–28 Jan, mid-Nov to mid-Dec

Marie Colline €€€

If you're visiting Cahors, this vegetarian restaurant is a great place to stop for lunch. There is usually a choice of two daily specials, along with a much wider selection of different dishes and desserts. Look out for *gratin au chèvre* (melted goat's cheese) and *clafoutis aux fruits* (a cake made with red fruits).

✚ 207 F5 ✉ 173 rue Georges Clemenceau, 46000 Cahors ☎ 05 65 35 59 96 🕐 Tue–Fri noon–3; closed Aug

La Corderie Royale €€–€€€

On the banks of the Charente River in Rochefort-sur-Mer, just south of La Rochelle, this stylish restaurant takes its name from the historic rope factory in town. Enjoy the views as you tuck into seafood or perhaps beef in a cream sauce.

✚ 211 F3 ✉ rue Audebert, 17300 Rochefort-sur-Mer ☎ 05 46 99 35 35 🕐 Daily noon–2:30, 7–10, Apr–Nov; Tue–Sun noon–2:30, 7–10, Dec–Jan, Mar; closed Feb

Where to... Shop

There's plenty to shop for in this region, with excellent food markets in the rural towns, fashion in the seaside resorts and cities, and mouthwatering chocolate and pastries everywhere. Bordeaux is at the heart of France's wine growing industry, and Cognac is famous for its eponymous brandy.

FOOD AND DRINK

Bordeaux has several markets, of which the most popular must be **Marché Campagnard** beside the Garonne River, the haunt of local producers and artisans (quai Chartron, open Sun 9–noon). The **Marché St-Michel** is a fun flea-market which competes on Sunday mornings, expanding four times a

year to become a huge bric-a-brac sale (place St-Michel, Sun 9–noon). The **Marché Capucins** on cours de la Marne is the place to go for local delicacies such as cheese, *foie gras* and the creamy little cakes called *canelé* (Tue–Sun 9–1).

The Dordogne region is famous for its *foie gras* and other dishes from geese and ducks (such as *confit* and terrines), its truffles and its walnuts. Seek them out amid the other delicious treats on offer in the **markets of Périgueux** (place du Coderc and place de la Claure, Wed and Sat 9–noon), **Sarlat-la-Canéda** (town centre, Sat 8:30–6 and other days) and **Ribérac** (place du Marché, Fri 9–noon). If you'd rather buy from a delicatessen, try **Rougié Sarlat**, in Sarlat, which has been going strong since 1875 – most products are canned (5 rue des Consuls, tel: 05 53 31 72 00, open Mon–Sat 10–1, 2–6).

Cahors' open-air **Marché Traditionnel** is also worth a detour, with gastronomic delights including

goats' cheese, *foie gras* and local wines (place de la Cathédrale, Wed and Sat 7:30 am–12:30 pm). Toulouse has an excellent **covered market** (place Victor Hugo, Tue–Sun 8–1), and a popular Sunday morning **flea-market** around the Basilique St-Sernin (8–1).

Chocoholics should make their way to renowned **Chocolaterie Letuffe** at Angoulême, where chocolate artistry reaches new heights and the *guinettes* (cherry and cognac) are to die for (10 place Francis-Louvel, tel: 05 45 95 00 54). **L'Artisan Chocolatier** in Albi is also a chocolate favourite, with great cakes and pastries (4 rue du Docteur Camboulives, tel: 05 63 54 18 46, open Tue–Sat 9–12:30, 2:30–7:30, Sun 9–12:30; also Mon 2:30–7, winter only).

GIFTS AND SOUVENIRS

You can find unusual gifts, beautifully presented, at **Violettes & Pastels** in Toulouse, a shop

partly dedicated to the humble violet and its many uses, including as a flavouring for tea, jam and exotic oils (10 rue St-Pantaléon, tel: 05 61 22 14 22, open Mon–Sat 10–7).

The city of Limoges is famous for its porcelain, and a great selection can be found at **La Maison de Limoges** (3 boulevard Victor-Hugo, tel: 05 55 77 31 61, open Mon 2–6, Tue–Sat 9–1, 2–7).

The work of contemporary painters from France and further afield is exhibited and sold at the high-class **Galerie des Remparts** in Bordeaux (63 rue des Remparts, tel: 05 56 52 22 25, open Mon 2:30–7, Tue–Sat 10:30–7, closed Aug). If you're looking for antique furniture, try the **Village Notre-Dame** in Bordeaux, where around 30 dealers and experts gather conveniently under one roof (61–67 rue Notre-Dame, tel: 05 56 52 66 13, open Mon–Sat 10–12:30, 2–7 all year; also Sun 2–7, Oct–Apr).

Where to...
Be Entertained

Inevitably, the main centres for entertainment are the major cities, including Bordeaux and Toulouse, with resorts along the coast from Biarritz in the south to La Rochelle in the north offering a wide variety of summertime options.

MUSIC, DANCE, THEATRE

Traditional **folk dancers** take to the old streets of the wine town of Bergerac, at 9 pm on weekday evenings in summer (usually Tue, Jul–Aug) – look out for them setting off from the square in front of the church of St-Jacques.

Biarritz has its own ballet company, in a venue operated by choreographer Thierry Malandain, with performances year-round

(**Ballet Biarritz**, Gare du Midi, 23 avenue Foch, tel: 05 59 24 67 19, www.balletbiarritz.com).

There are several big venues for concerts, musicals and theatre in Bordeaux, including the architecturally splendid neo-classical **Grand Théâtre** on place de la Comédie (tel: 05 56 00 85 95), and the sleek, modern **Espace Culturel du Pin Galant**, west of the city (34 avenue de Maréchal de Lattre de Tassigny, Mérignac, tel: 05 56 97 82 82).

Toulouse's National Orchestra performs regularly in the **Halle aux Grains** (place Dupuy, tel: 05 61 62 02 70/63 13 13, www.onct.mairie-toulouse.fr). The grandiose **Théâtre du Capitole** is the city's main theatre venue, with opera,

concerts and ballet as well (1 place du Capitole, tel: 05 61 22 31 31/ 63 13 13).

CINEMAS

The ten-screen **UGC Ciné Cité** in Bordeaux, at 15 rue Georges Bonnac shows the latest movies in their original language (tel: 0892 70 00 00).

In Toulouse, the **Cinémathèque** at 69 rue Taur is the place for art-house and foreign-language films (tel: 05 62 30 30 10, www.lacine-mathequedetoulouse.com).

BARS AND CLUBS

Treat yourself to a genteel cocktail amid the crystal chandeliers and book-filled shelves at **Le Shadow Lounge** on the riverbank in Bordeaux (5 rue Cabanac, tel: 05 56 49 36 93). If you prefer, **Herald's Pub** offers a relaxed venue with polished brass at the bar and jazz music in the background (5

rue du Parlément Ste-Catherine, tel: 05 56 81 37 37).

Le Père Louis, a historic wine bar in Toulouse, also serves bistro food from noon (45 rue des Tourneurs, tel: 05 61 21 33 45, open Mon–Sat 9 am–3, 5–10 pm).

In Lourdes, try out the **Mayflower Café**, an inexpensive pub with rock and Celtic music and a varied clientele (6 rue de l'Égalité, tel 05 62 94 01 56, open nightly Apr–Oct, Fri–Sat Nov–Mar).

SPA

For something totally different, treat yourself to a spot of "vinotherapy" at Martillac, just a 15-minute drive south of Bordeaux. It's not about pouring more wine down your throat, but rather a unique spa where wine and wine by-products are the basis of different treatments, from a Sauvignon massage to a Premier Grand Cru facial (**Les Sources de Caudalie**, 4 chemin de Bourran, tel: 05 57 83 83 82).

Practicalities

Websites
- French Tourist Office: www.franceguide.com
- French Government Tourist Office, for US visitors: www.france-tourism.com
- Paris Tourist Office: www.paris-touristoffice.com
- Tourist offices across France: www.tourist-office.org

In the UK
French Tourist Office
178 Piccadilly
London W1V 0AL
☎ 09068 244123

BEFORE YOU GO

WHAT YOU NEED

- ● Required
- ○ Suggested
- ▲ Not required
- △ Not applicable

	UK	Germany	USA	Canada	Australia	Ireland	Netherlands	Spain
Passport (or National Identity Card where applicable)	●	●	●	●	●	●	●	●
Visa (for stays of less than 3 months)	▲	▲	▲	▲	▲	▲	▲	▲
Onward or Return Ticket	▲	▲	▲	▲	▲	▲	▲	▲
Health Inoculations (tetanus and polio)	▲	▲	▲	▲	▲	▲	▲	▲
Health Documentation	●	●	●	●	●	●	●	●
Travel Insurance	○	○	○	○	○	○	○	○
Driving Licence (national)	●	●	●	●	●	●	●	●
Car Insurance Certificate	○	○	n/a	n/a	n/a	○	○	○
Car Registration Document	●	●	n/a	n/a	n/a	●	●	●

WHEN TO GO

Paris

High season | Low season

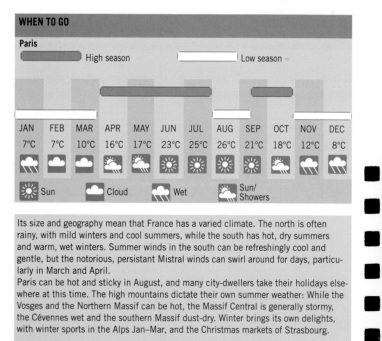

JAN	FEB	MAR	APR	MAY	JUN	JUL	AUG	SEP	OCT	NOV	DEC
7°C	7°C	10°C	16°C	17°C	23°C	25°C	26°C	21°C	18°C	12°C	8°C

☀ Sun   ☁ Cloud   🌧 Wet   ⛅ Sun/Showers

Its size and geography mean that France has a varied climate. The north is often rainy, with mild winters and cool summers, while the south has hot, dry summers and warm, wet winters. Summer winds in the south can be refreshingly cool and gentle, but the notorious, persistant Mistral winds can swirl around for days, particularly in March and April.

Paris can be hot and sticky in August, and many city-dwellers take their holidays elsewhere at this time. The high mountains dictate their own summer weather: While the Vosges and the Northern Massif can be hot, the Massif Central is generally stormy, the Cévennes wet and the southern Massif dust-dry. Winter brings its own delights, with winter sports in the Alps Jan–Mar, and the Christmas markets of Strasbourg.

In the US
French Tourist Office
444 Madison Avenue
16th Floor, New York,
NY10022
☎ 212/838 7800

In Australia
French Tourist Office
Level 20, 25 Bligh Street
Sydney, NSW 2000
☎ (02) 9231 5244

In Canada
French Tourist Office
1981 avenue McGill
College, Suite 490
Montreal H3A 2W9
☎ 514-876 9881

GETTING THERE

By Air France has major international airports at Paris, Marseille, Toulouse, Strasbourg, Lyon and Bordeaux, plus around 170 smaller connecting airports. International flights from within Europe also land at smaller airports such as Montpellier.
From the UK, carriers include France's international airline, Air France (tel: 0845 0845 111 in UK; 0802 802802 in France; www.airfrance.com), British Airways (tel: 0845 7733377; www.ba.com), easyJet (tel: 0871 750 0100; www.easyjet.com), and Ryanair (tel: 0870 156 9569; www.ryanair.com). Flying time varies from about 1 to 2.5 hours.
From the US and Canada, numerous carriers operate direct flights, including American Airlines (tel: 1 800 433 7300 in US; www.aa.com), Delta (tel: 1 800 241 4141 in US; www.delta.com) and Air Canada (tel: 1 888 247 2262 in Canada; www.aircanada.com). Flying time varies from 12 hours (US west coast) to 7.5 hours (Montréal).

By Rail Paris is the main railway hub, with six major railway stations, each handling traffic to different parts of France and Europe. SNCF, the national carrier, operates high-speed trains (TGV) to Paris from main stations throughout France. The Eurostar passenger train service (tel: 08705 186186 in Britain) from London Waterloo via the Channel Tunnel to Paris Gare du Nord takes 3 hours.

By Sea Several ferry companies operate regular services from England and Ireland to north and northwest France. Crossing times from England vary from 35 minutes to 9 hours, and from Ireland around 14 to 18 hours.

TIME

France is on Central European Time, one hour ahead of Greenwich Mean Time (GMT +1). From late March, when clocks are put forward one hour, until late October, French summer time (GMT +2) operates.

CURRENCY AND FOREIGN EXCHANGE

Currency France is one of the 12 European countries to use a single currency, the Euro (€). Euro coins are issued in denominations of 1, 2, 5, 10, 20 and 50 cents and €1 and €2. Notes (bills) are issued in denominations of €5, €10, €20, €50, €100, €200 and €500.

Exchange You can exchange travellers' cheques at some banks and at bureaux de change at airports, main railway stations or in some department stores, and exchange booths. All transactions are subject to a commission charge, so you may prefer to rely on cash and credit cards. Travellers' cheques issued by American Express and VISA may also be changed at many post offices.

Credit cards are widely accepted in shops, restaurants and hotels. VISA (Carte Bleue), MasterCard (Eurocard) and Diners Club cards with four-digit PINs can be used in most ATM cash dispensers. Some smaller shops and hotels may not accept credit cards – always check before you book in.

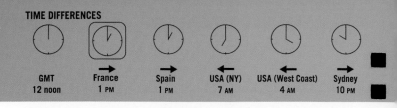

GMT	France	Spain	USA (NY)	USA (West Coast)	Sydney
12 noon	1 PM	1 PM	7 AM	4 AM	10 PM

WHEN YOU ARE THERE

CLOTHING SIZES

UK	France	USA	
36	46	36	
38	48	38	
40	50	40	
42	52	42	Suits
44	54	44	
46	56	46	
7	41	8	
7.5	42	8.5	
8.5	43	9.5	
9.5	44	10.5	Shoes
10.5	45	11.5	
11	46	12	
14.5	37	14.5	
15	38	15	
15.5	39/40	15.5	
16	41	16	Shirts
16.5	42	16.5	
17	43	17	
8	34	6	
10	36	8	
12	38	10	
14	40	12	Dresses
16	42	14	
18	44	16	
4.5	38	6	
5	38	6.5	
5.5	39	7	
6	39	7.5	Shoes
6.5	40	8	
7	41	8.5	

NATIONAL HOLIDAYS

1 Jan	New Year's Day
Mar/Apr	Easter Sunday and Monday
1 May	May Day
May	VE (Victory in Europe) Day
6th Thu after Easter	Ascension Day
May/Jun	Whit Sunday and Monday
14 Jul	Bastille Day
15 Aug	Assumption Day
1 Nov	All Saints' Day
11 Nov	Remembrance Day
25 Dec	Christmas Day

Banks, museums and most shops close on these days.

OPENING HOURS

- ○ Shops
- ● Offices
- ● Banks
- ● Post Offices
- ◐ Museums/Monuments
- ◐ Pharmacies

☐ Day   ▨ Midday   ☐ Evening

Shops In addition to the times shown above, many shops close noon–2 pm, and all day Sunday and Monday. Large department stores open until 9 pm or 10 pm one day a week. Food shops open 7 am–1:30 pm and 4:30–8 pm, and may open Sunday until noon. Tourist-orientated shops and hypermarkets may have longer opening hours and open on Sunday, especially in summer.

Banks Some open extended hours including Saturday morning, but may close on Monday instead. Banks close at noon on the day before a national holiday, as well as on the holiday itself.

Museums Museums usually close on at least one day a week, and this varies across the country.

EMERGENCY NUMBERS

POLICE 17

FIRE 18

AMBULANCE 15

PERSONAL SAFETY

Petty crime, particularly theft of wallets and handbags, is fairly common in the major cities. Be aware of scruffy, innocent-looking children: they may be working the streets in gangs, fleecing unwary tourists. Report any loss or theft to the *Police Municipale* (blue uniforms). To be safe:

• Watch your bag on the Métro, in busy tourist areas and in museum queues.

• Cars should be well secured; do not leave anything valuable in them.

• Keep valuables in your hotel safe (*coffre-fort*).

• Avoid walking alone in dark city streets at night.

Police assistance:
 17 from any phone

TELEPHONES

In addition to coin-operated models, an increasing number of public phones take phonecards (télécarte). These are sold in units of 50 and 120 and can be bought from France Telecom shops, post offices, tobacconists and at railway stations. Cheap call rates generally apply Mon–Fri 7 pm–8 am, Sat–Sun all day.

All telephone numbers in France comprise ten digits. There are no area codes; simply dial the number. Paris numbers all begin with 01.

International Dialling Codes
Dial 00 followed by

UK:	44
USA / Canada:	1
Irish Republic:	353
Australia:	61
New Zealand:	64

POST

Post offices are identified by a yellow or brown "La Poste" or "PTT" sign, and post boxes are usually square and yellow. Most post offices open from 8 am to 7 pm, and they usually have an ATM.

ELECTRICITY

The power supply in France is 220 volts. Sockets accept two-round-pin (or increasingly three-round-pin) plugs, so an adaptor is needed for most non-Continental appliances. A transformer is needed for appliances operating on 110–120 volts.

TIPS/GRATUITIES

Restaurant, café and hotel bills must by law include a service charge so a tip is not expected, although many people do leave a few coins in restaurants.

Taxis	€0.50–€1.50
Tour guides	€0.50–€1.50
Porters	€0.50–€1.50
Usherettes	small change
Hairdressers	€0.50–€1.50
Lavatory attendants	small change

UK
☎ 01 44 51
31 00

US
☎ 01 43 12
22 22

Australia
☎ 01 40 59
33 00

Canada
☎ 01 44 43
29 00

New Zealand
☎ 01 45 01
43 43

HEALTH

Insurance Nationals of EU countries can obtain medical treatment at reduced cost in France with the relevant documentation (on presentation of form E111 for Britons), although medical insurance is still advised, and is essential for all other visitors.

Dental Services As for general medical treatment (see above, Insurance), nationals of EU countries can obtain dental treatment at reduced cost. Around 70 per cent of standard dentists' fees are refunded, but private medical insurance is still advised for all.

Weather July and August are likely to be sunny and hot. When sightseeing, cover up, apply a good sunscreen, wear sunglasses and drink plenty of fluids.

Drugs Pharmacies – recognised by their green cross sign – possess highly qualified staff able to offer medical advice, provide first-aid and prescribe a wide range of drugs, although some are available by prescription (*ordonnance*) only.

Safe Water Tap water is safe to drink, but never drink from a tap marked *eau non potable* (not drinking water). Bottled water is also widely available.

CONCESSIONS

Students/Youths Holders of an International Student Identity Card (ISIC) are entitled to discounted admission to museums and sights, air and ferry tickets and meals in some student cafeterias. Holders of the International Youth Travel Card (or GO 25 Card) qualify for similar discounts as ISIC holders.

Senior Citizens If you are over 60 you can get discounts (up to 50 per cent) in museums, on public transport and in places of entertainment. You will need a Carte Vermeil which can be purchased from the Abonnement office of any main railway station. You may get a discount if you show your passport.

TRAVELLING WITH A DISABILITY

Many older public facilities and attractions lack amenities for people with disabilities, although most hotels with two or more stars have lifts (elevators). Few Métro stations have lifts, but RATP and SNCF run an Accompaniment Service to assist people with reduced mobility (tel: 01 45 19 15 00). The service is not free, however, and you will need to book in advance of your journey.

CHILDREN

Children are welcomed in most hotels and restaurants. Many sights and attractions offer reductions; entrance to museums for under 18s is generally free. Baby-changing facilities are excellent in newer museums and attractions, but limited elsewhere.

TOILETS

Modern unisex, self-cleaning, coin-operated toilets are found on the streets of most major cities. In smaller towns and villages, free public toilets can normally be found by the market square or near tourist offices. Cleanliness varies, and some older or more remote establishments may have a squat toilet. Café toilets are for the use of customers only.

SURVIVAL PHRASES

Yes/no **Oui/non**
Hello **Bonjour/bonsoir**
Goodbye **Au revoir**
How are you? **Comment allez-vous?**
Please **S'il vous plaît**
Thank you **Merci**
Excuse me **Excusez-moi**
I'm sorry **Pardon**
You're welcome **De rien/avec plaisir**
Do you have...? **Avez-vous...?**
How much is this? **C'est combien?**
I'd like... **Je voudrais...**

DIRECTIONS

Is there a phone box around here?
 **Y a-t-il une cabine téléphonique
 dans le coin?**
Where is...? **Où se trouve...?**
...the nearest Métro
 le Métro le plus proche
...the telephone **le téléphone**
...the bank **la banque**
...the toilet **les toilettes**
Turn left/right **tournez à gauche/droite**
Go straight on **allez tout droit**
The first/second (on the right)
 le premier/le deuxième (à droite)
At the crossroads **au carrefour**

IF YOU NEED HELP

Could you help me, please?
 Pouvez-vous m'aider?
Do you speak English?
 Parlez-vous anglais?
I don't understand
 Je ne comprends pas
Could you call a doctor quickly,
 please? **Voulez-vous vite appeler un
 médecin, s'il vous plaît?**

RESTAURANT

I'd like to book a table **Puis-je
 réserver une table?**
A table for two please **Une table pour
 deux personnes, s'il vous plaît**
Do you have a fixed price menu?
 Vous avez un menu prix fixe?
Could we see the menu please?
 Nous pouvons avoir la carte?
Could I have the bill please?
 L'addition, s'il vous plaît
A bottle/glass of... **Une bouteille/un
 verre de...**

MENU READER

apéritifs appetisers
boissons alcoolisées
 alcoholic beverages
boissons chaudes hot beverages
boissons froides cold beverages
carte des vins wine list
coquillages shellfish
fromage cheese
gibier game
hors d'oeuvres starters
légumes vegetables
plats chauds hot dishes
plats froids cold dishes
plat du jour dish of the day
pâtisserie pastry
plat principal main course
potages soups
service compris service included
service non compris
 service not included
spécialités régionales
 regional specialities
viandes meat courses
volaille poultry

NUMBERS

0	**zéro**	12	**douze**	30	**trente**	110	**cent dix**
1	**un**	13	**treize**	31	**trente et un**	120	**cent vingt**
2	**deux**	14	**quatorze**	32	**trente-deux**	200	**deux cents**
3	**trois**	15	**quinze**			300	**trois cents**
4	**quatre**	16	**seize**	40	**quarante**	400	**quatre cents**
5	**cinq**	17	**dix-sept**	50	**cinquante**	500	**cinq cents**
6	**six**	18	**dix-huit**	60	**soixante**	600	**six cents**
7	**sept**	19	**dix-neuf**	70	**soixante-dix**	700	**sept cents**
8	**huit**	20	**vingt**	80	**quatre-vingts**	800	**huit cents**
9	**neuf**			90	**quatre-vingt-dix**	900	**neuf cents**
10	**dix**	21	**vingt et un**	100	**cent**		
11	**onze**	22	**vingt-deux**	101	**cent un**	1,000	**mille**

agneau lamb
ail garlic
ananas pineapple
anguille eel
banane banana
beurre butter
bifteck steak
bière (bière pression) beer (draught beer)
boeuf beef
boudin noir/blanc black/white pudding
brochet pike
cabillaud cod
calmar squid
canard duck
champignons mushrooms
chou cabbage
choucroute sauerkraut
chou-fleur cauliflower
choux de Bruxelles Brussels sprouts
citron lemon
civet de lièvre jugged hare
concombre cucumber
confiture jam
coquilles Saint-Jacques scallops
cornichon gherkin
côte/côtelette chop
côtelettes dans l'échine spare ribs
couvert cutlery
crevettes grises shrimps
crevettes roses prawns
croque monsieur toasted ham and cheese sandwich
cru raw
crustacés seafood
cuisses de grenouilles frogs' legs
cuit (à l'eau) boiled
eau mineral

gazeuse/non gazeuse sparkling/still mineral water
ecrevisse crayfish
entrecôte sirloin steak
entrées first course
épices spices
épinards spinach
épis de maïs corn (on the cob)
escargots snails
farine flour
fenouil fennel
fèves broad beans
figues figs
filet de boeuf fillet
filet mignon fillet steak
filet de porc tenderloin
fines herbes herbs
foie gras goose liver
fraises strawberries
framboises raspberries
frit fried
friture deep-fried
fruit de la passion passion fruit
fruits de la saison seasonal fruits
gaufres waffles
gigot d'agneau leg of lamb
glace ice-cream
glaçons ice cubes
grillé grilled
groseilles redcurrants
hareng herring
haricots blancs haricot beans
haricots verts french beans
homard lobster
huîtres oysters
jambon blanc/cru/fumé ham (cooked/Parma style/smoked)
jus de citron lemon juice
jus de fruits fruit juice

jus d'orange orange juice
lait demi-écrémé/entier milk semi-skimmed/full-cream
langouste crayfish
langoustine scampi
langue tongue
lapin rabbit
lentilles lentils
lotte monkfish
loup de mer sea bass
macaron macaroon
maïs sweetcorn
marron chestnut
menu du jour/à la carte menu of the day/à la carte
morilles morels
moules mussels
mousse au chocolat chocolate mousse
moutarde mustard
myrtilles bilberries
noisette hazelnut
noix walnut
noix de veau fillet of veal
oeuf à la coque/dur/au plat egg soft/hard-boiled/fried
oignon onion
origan oregano
pain au chocolat croissant with chocolate centre
part portion
pêche peach
petite friture fried fish (whitebait or similar)
petits (biscuits) salés savoury biscuits
petit pain roll
petits pois green peas

pintade guinea fowl
poire pear
pois chiches chick peas
poisson fish
poivre pepper
poivron green/red pepper
pomme apple
pommes de terre potatoes
pommes frites chips
poulet (blanc) chicken (breast)
prune plum
pruneaux prunes
queue de boeuf oxtail
ragoût stew
ris de veau sweetbread
riz rice
rôti de boeuf (rosbif) roast beef
rouget red mullet
saignant rare
salade verte lettuce
salé/sucré salted/sweet
saumon salmon
saucisses sausages
sel salt
soupe à l'oignon onion soup
sucre sugar
thon tuna
thym thyme
tripes tripe
truffes truffles
truite trout
truite saumonée salmon trout
vapeur (à la) steamed
venaison venison
viande hachée minced meat/mince
vin blanc white wine
vin rosé rosé wine
vin rouge red wine
vinaigre vinegar
xérès sherry

Atlas

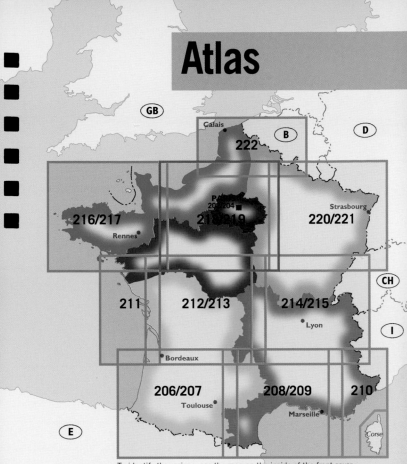

To identify the regions, see the map on the inside of the front cover

Regional Maps

Major route	City / Town
Motorway (Expressway)	Featured place of interest
National road	Place of interest
Regional road	Airport
International boundary	
Regional boundary	
National park	

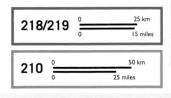

City Plans

Main road / minor road	Métro station
Featured place of interest	
Information	

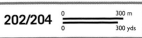

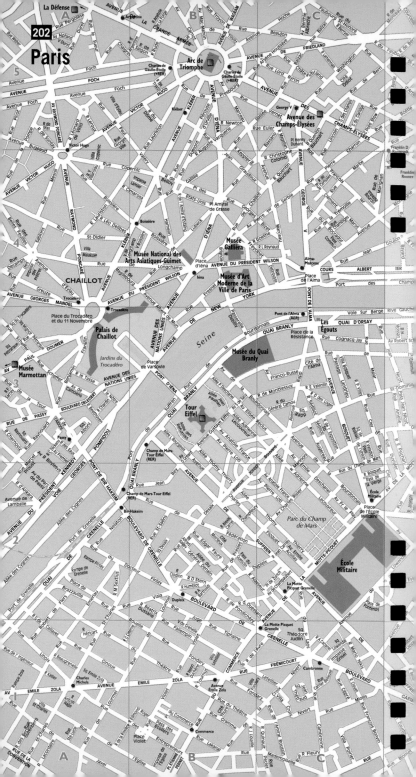

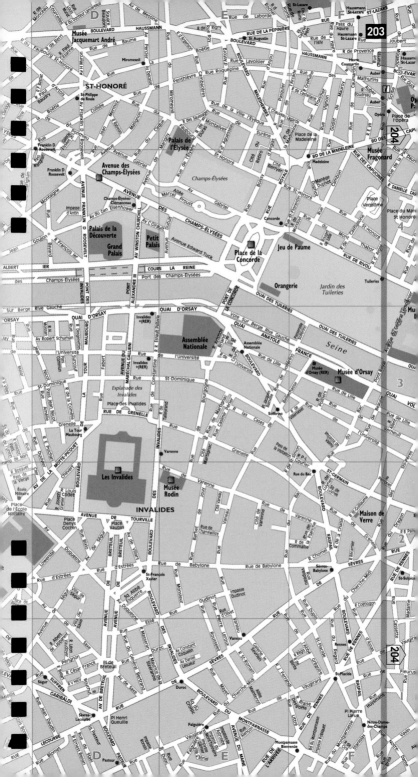

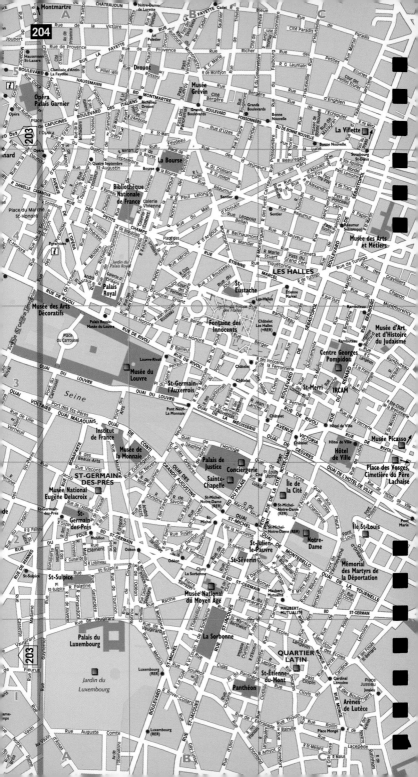

Street Index

l'Abbé Grégoire, Rue de 203 F1
d'Aboukir, Rue 204 B4
Adrienne Lecouvreur, Allée 202 C2
Albert 1er, Cours 202 C4
Alexandre III, Pont 203 D4
l'Alma, Pont de 202 C4
Anatole France, Quai 203 E3
l'Arcade, Rue de 203 F5
Arts, Pont des 204 A3
d'Assas, Rue 204 A1
Auber, Rue 203 F5
Auguste Comte, Rue 204 A1
Babylone, Rue de 203 E2
Bac, Rue du 203 F3
Balzac, Rue 202 C5
Barbet de Jouy, Rue 203 E2
Bassano, Rue de 202 C5
Beaubourg, Rue 204 C3
Bellechasse, Rue de 203 E3
Benjamin Franklin, Rue 202 A3
Berger, Rue 204 B3
Bergère, Rue 204 B5
Berri, Rue de 202 C5
Bir Hakeim, Pont de 202 A2
Boétie, Rue la 203 E5
Boissière, Rue 202 A4
Boissy d'Anglas, Rue 203 E4
Bonaparte, Rue 204 A2
Bonne Nouvelle, Boulevard de 204 C5
Bosquet, Avenue 202 C3
Bourdonnais, Avenue de la 202 C2
Bourgogne, Rue de 203 E3
Bourse, Place de la 204 B4
Branly, Quai 202 B3
Breteuil, Avenue de 203 D2
Cambon, Rue 203 F4
Cambronne, Rue 202 C1
Capucines, Boulevard des 204 A5
Capucines, Rue des 203 F4
Cardinal Lemoine, Rue du 204 C1
Carrousel, Place du 204 A3
Cases, Rue las 203 E3
Caumartin, Rue de 203 F5
Champs-Élysées, Avenue des 203 E4
Champs-Élysées, Port des 203 E4
Châteaudun, Rue de 204 A5
Chaussée d'Antin, Rue de la 204 A5
Cherche-Midi, Rue du 203 F2
Christine, Rue 204 B2
Cité, Rue de la 204 C2
Cléry Rue de 204 C4
Clovis, Rue 204 C1
Colisée, Rue du 203 D5
Commerce, Rue du 202 B1

Concorde, Pont de la 203 E4
Conti, Quai de 204 B3
Copernic, Rue 202 A4
Croix des Petits Champs, Rue 204 B4
Croix Nivert, Rue de la 202 C1
Cygnes, Allée des 202 A2
Danielle Casanova, Rue 204 A4
Danton, Rue 204 B2
Dauphine, Rue 204 B2
Delessert, Boulevard 202 A3
Docteur Finlay, Rue du 202 B2
Drouot, Rue 204 B5
Dupleix, Rue 202 B2
Duquesne, Avenue 203 D2
Duroc, Rue 203 D1
l'Echiquier, Rue de 204 C5
l'École Militaire, Place de 202 C2
Écoles, Rue des 204 C1
Emeriau, Rue 202 A2
Emile Zola, Avenue 202 A1
Entrepreneurs, Rue des 202 B1
d'Estrées, Rue 203 D2
Etats-Unis, Place des 202 B4
Étienne Marcel, Rue 204 B4
d'Eylau, Avenue 202 A4
Fabert, Rue 203 D3
Faubourg Montmartre, Rue du 204 B5
Faubourg Poissonnière, Rue du 204 C5
Faubourg St-Honoré, Rue du 203 D5
Fayette, Rue la 204 A5
Fédération, Rue de la 202 B2
Fleurs Quai aux 204 C2
Foch, Avenue 202 A5
Fondary, Rue 202 B1
Four, Rue du 204 A2
François 1er, Rue 203 D4
Franklin D Roosevelt, Avenue 203 D4
Frémicourt, Rue 202 C1
Friedland, Avenue de 202 C5
Gabriel, Avenue 203 E4
Galande, Rue 204 C2
Galilée, Rue 202 B4
Garibaldi, Boulevard 203 D1
Général Lemonnier, Avenue du 204 A3
George V, Avenue 202 C4
Georges Mandel, Avenue 202 A4
Georges Pompidou, Voie 202 A3
Gesvres, Quai de 204 C3
Godot de Mauroy, Rue 203 F5
Grande Armée, Avenue de la 202 B5
Grands Augustins, Quai des 204 B2
Grands Augustins, Rue des 204 B2
Gravilliers, Rue des 204 C4
Grenelle, Quai de 202 A2

Grenelle, Boulevard de 202 B2
Grenelle, Rue de 203 E3
Guénégaud, Rue 204 B2
Gustave Eiffel, Avenue 202 B3
Guynemer, Rue 204 A1
Harpe, Rue de la 204 B2
Haussmann, Boulevard 203 F5
d'Hauteville, Rue 204 C5
Hoche, Avenue 202 C5
l'Horloge, Quai de 204 B2
l'Hôtel de Ville, Quai de 204 C2
l'Hôtel de Ville, Rue de 204 C2
Huchette, Rue de la 204 B2
d'Iéna, Avenue 202 B4
d'Iéna, Pont 202 B3
Invalides, Boulevard des 203 E1
Invalides, Pont des 203 D4
Italiens, Boulevard des 204 A5
Jade, Rue du 204 A2
Jean-Jacques Rousseau, Rue 204 B4
Jeûneurs, Rue des 204 B4
Joseph Bouvard, Avenue 202 B2
Jour, Rue du 204 B4
Kléber, Avenue 202 B5
Lacepède, Rue 204 C1
Laffitte, Rue 204 B5
Lagrange, Rue 204 C2
Lamennais, Rue 202 C5
Laos, Rue du 202 C1
Lauriston, Rue 202 A4
Lecourbe, Rue 203 D1
Lhomond, Rue 204 B1
Lille, Rue de 203 F3
Longchamp, Rue de 202 B4
Lourmel, Rue de 202 A1
Louvre, Quai du 204 A3
Louvre, Rue du 204 B4
Lowendal, Avenue de 202 C2
Madame, Rue 204 A2
Madeleine, Boulevard de la 203 F4
Madeleine, Place de la 203 F5
Mail, Rue du 204 B4
Maine, Avenue du 203 E1
Malaquai, Quai 204 A2
Malesherbes, Boulevard 203 E5
Marceau, Avenue 202 C4
Maréchal Gallieni, Avenue du 203 D3
Mathurins, Rue des 203 F5
Matignon, Avenue 203 D5
Mazarine, Rue 204 A2
Mégisserie, Quai de la 204 B3
Miromesnil, Rue de 203 E5
Monge, Rue 204 C1
Monnaie, Rue du la 204 B3
Monsieur le Prince, Rue 204 B2
Mont Thabor, Rue du 203 F4

Montaigne, Avenue 203 D4
Montebello, Quai de 204 C2
Montmartre, Boulevard 204 B5
Montmartre, Rue 204 B4
Montmorency, Rue de 204 C4
Montparnasse, Boulevard du 203 E1
Montparnasse, Rue du 203 F1
Montpensier, Rue de 204 A4
Motte-Picquet, Avenue de la 202 C2
Nations Unies, Avenue des 202 B3
Neuf, Pont 204 B3
New York, Avenue de 202 B3
Notre-Dame des Victoires, Rue 204 B4
l'Odéon, Rue de 204 B2
l'Opéra, Avenue de 204 A4
l'Opéra, Place de 204 A5
d'Orsay, Quai 203 D3
Oudinot, Rue 203 E2
Ours, Rue aux 204 C4
Palais, Boulevard du 204 B2
Panthéon, Place du 204 B1
Paradis, Rue de 204 C5
Passy, Rue de 202 A3
Pasteur, Boulevard 203 D1
Paul Doumer, Avenue 202 A3
Pépinière, Rue de la 203 E5
Pérignon, Rue 203 D1
Petites Ecuries, Cour des 204 C5
Petites Ecuries, Rue des 204 C5
Petits Champs, Rue des 204 A4
Pierre 1er de Serbie, Avenue 202 C4
Pierre Charron, Rue 202 C4
Poissonnière, Boulevard 204 B5
Président Kennedy, Avenue du 202 A2
Président Wilson, Avenue du 202 B4
Provence, Rue de 204 A5
Pyramides, Rue des 204 A4
Quatre Septembre, Rue du 204 B5
Rambuteau, Rue 204 C3
Rapp, Avenue 202 C3
Raspail, Boulevard 203 F2
Raymond Poincaré, Avenue 202 A4
Réaumur, Rue 204 B4
Reine, Cours la 203 E4
Renard, Rue du 204 C3
Rennes, Rue de 203 F2
Richelieu, Rue de 204 A4
Richer, Rue 204 B5
Rive Gauche, Voie Sur Berge 203 E3
Rivoli, Rue de 204 A4
Royal, Pont 203 F3

Royale, Rue 203 E4
Saxe, Avenue de 203 D1
Scheffer, Rue 202 A3
Scribe, Rue 203 F5
Sébastopol, Boulevard de 204 C4
Ségur, Avenue de 203 D2
Sèvres, Rue de 203 E1
Solférino, Rue de 203 E3
Sorbonne, Rue de la 204 B1
St-Augustin, Rue 204 A4
St-Charles, Rue 202 A1
St-Denis, Rue 204 C4
St-Didier, Rue 202 A4
St-Dominique, Rue 203 D3
St-Germain, Boulevard 204 A2
St-Honoré, Rue 204 A4
St-Jacques, Rue 204 B1
St-Lazare, Rue 203 F5
St-Louis, Pont 204 C2
St-Martin, Rue 204 C3
St-Michel, Boulevard 204 B1
St-Michel, Quai 204 B2
St-Placide, Rue 203 F1
St-Roch, Rue 204 A4
St-Séverin, Rue 204 B2
Sts-Pères, Rue des 204 A2
St-Sulpice, Place 204 A2
St-Sulpice, Rue 204 A2
Suffren, Avenue de 202 C2
Temple, Rue du 204 C3
Théâtre, Rue du 202 B1
Thomy Thierry, Allée 202 C2
Tour Maubourg, Boulevard de la 203 D3
Tournelle, Quai de la 204 C2
Tournon, Rue de 204 A2
Tourville, Avenue de 203 D2
Trémoille, Rue de la 202 C4
Trévise, Rue du 204 B5
Tronchet, Rue 203 F5
Tuileries, Quai des 203 F3
Turbigo, Rue de 204 C4
l'Université, Rue de 203 D3
Valois, Rue de 204 B4
Vaneau, Rue 203 E2
Varenne, Rue de 203 E2
Vaubin, Place 203 D2
Vaugirard, Rue de 203 F1
Verneuil, Rue de 203 F3
Verrerie, Rue de la 204 C3
Victoire, Rue de la 204 A5
Victor Hugo, Avenue 202 B5
Victoria, Avenue 204 C3
Violet, Rue 202 B1
Vivienne, Rue 204 B4
Voltaire, Quai 204 A3
Wagram, Avenue de 202 B5
Washington, Rue 202 C5
Winston Churchill, Avenue 203 D4
Vendôme, Place 203 F4
Concorde, Place de la 203 E4
Victoires, Place des 204 B4

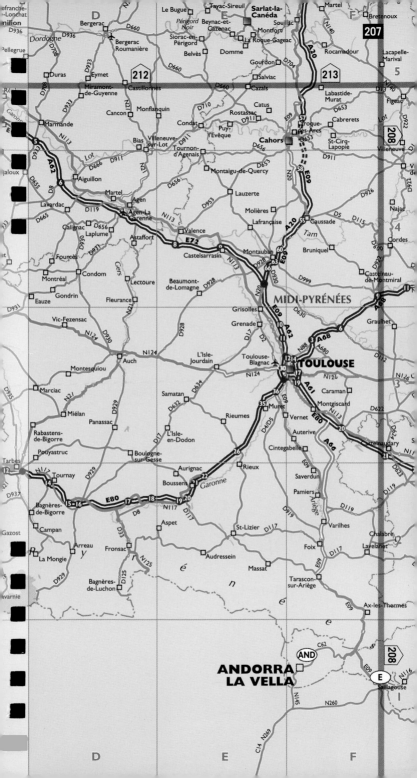

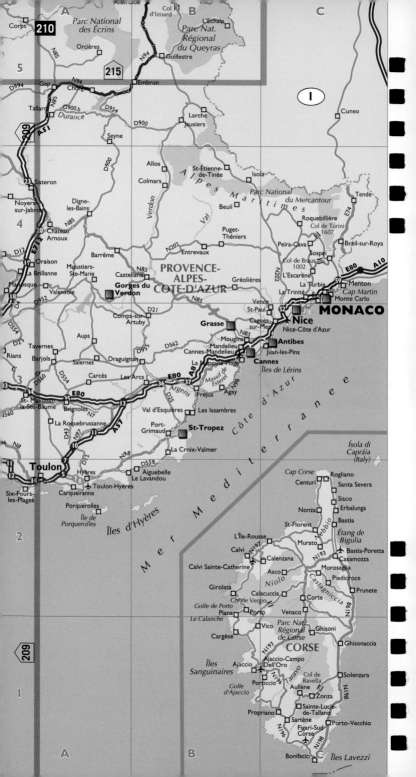

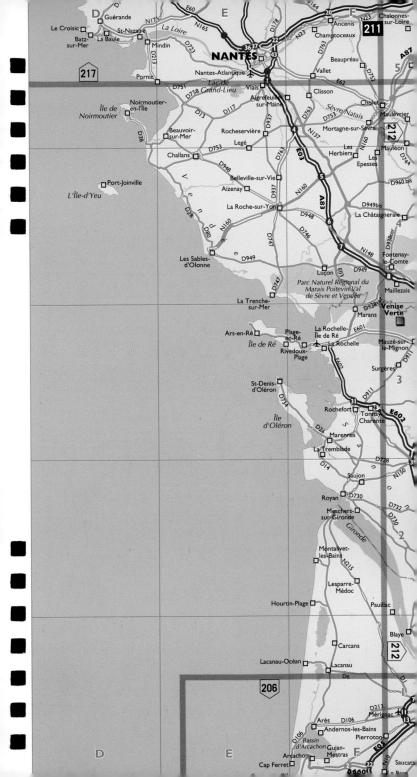

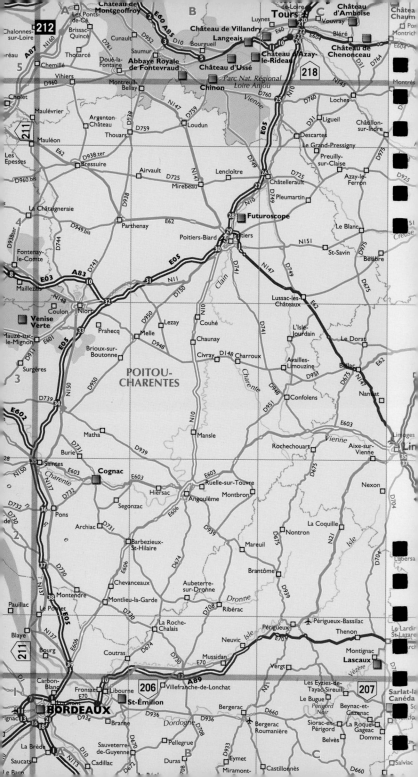

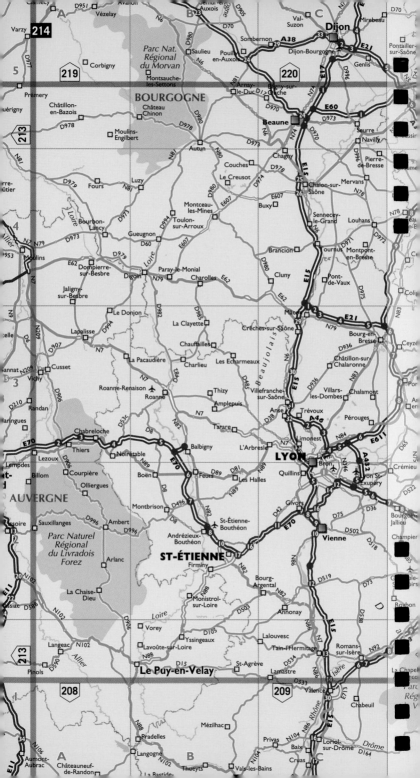

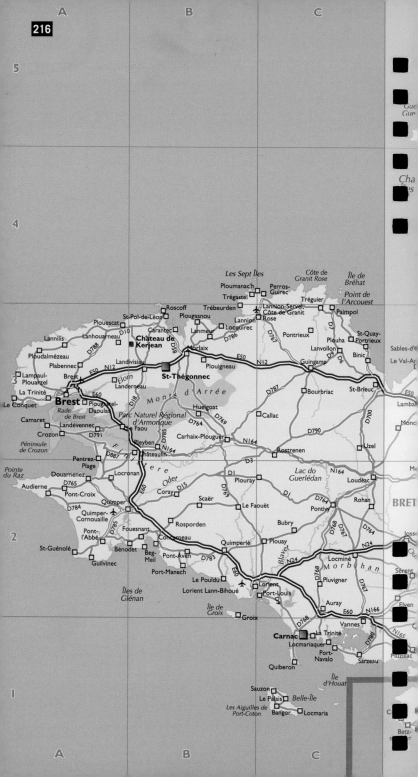

216

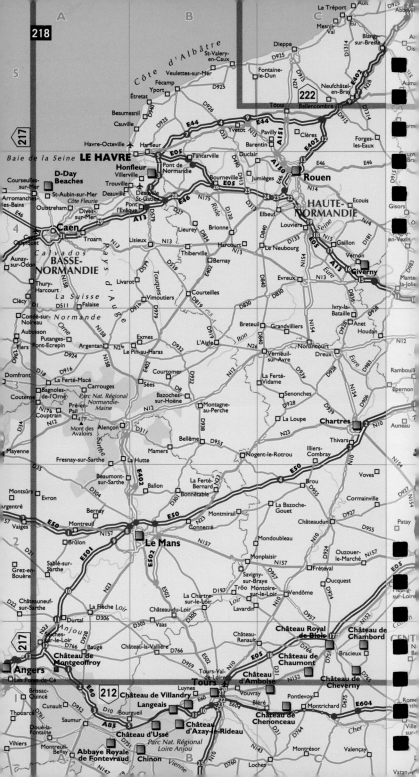

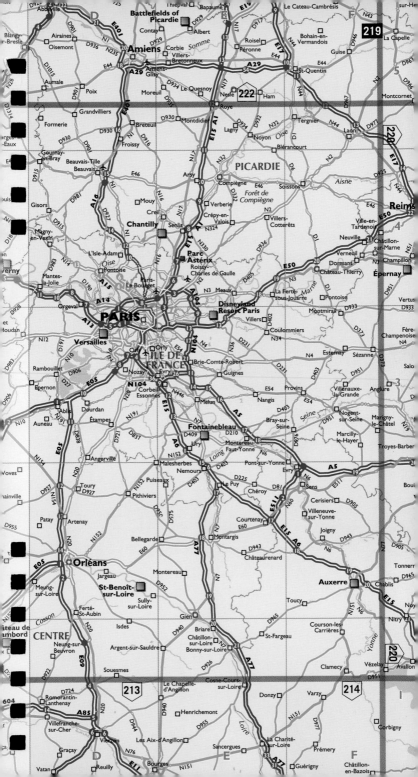

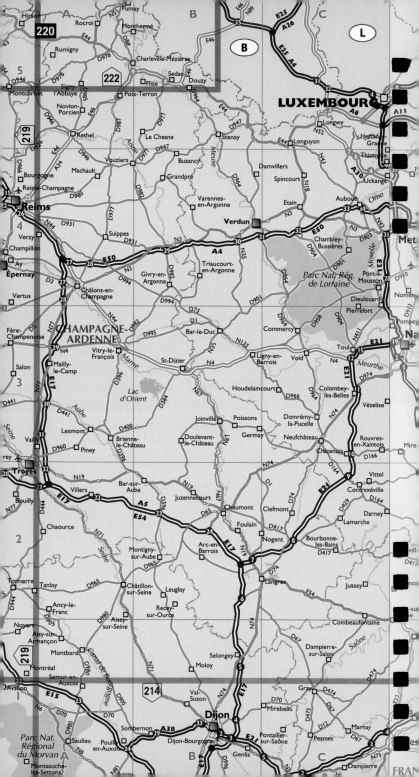

Index of places

Abbaye de Fontfroide 208 K14
Abbeville. 222 B1
Ablis. 219 D3
Abreschviller. 221 E3
Accous. 206 B2
Agay. 210 B3
Agde. 208 C3
Agen. 207 D4
Agon-Coutainville 217 E4
Aiguebelle. 210 B2
Aigues-Mortes 209 D4
Aiguillon 207 E4
Ailefroide 215 E1
Aime 215 F2
Airaines 222 B1
Aire-sur-l'Adour 206 C3
Airvault 212 B4
Aisy-sur-Armançon 220 A1
Aix-en-Provence 209 F3
Aixe-sur-Vienne 212 C3
Aix-les-Bains 215 E2
Aizenay 211 E4
Ajaccio 210 B1
Alban 208 A4
Albert 222 C1
Albertville 215 E2
Albi 208 A4
Alençon 218 A3
Alès 209 D4
Allevard 215 E2
Allos 210 B4
Altkirch 221 E1
Alzon 208 C4
Ambérieu-en-Bugey 215 D3
Ambert 214 A2
Amboise 218 C1
Amiens 222 B1
Amou 206 B3
Amplepuis 214 B3
Ancenis 217 F1
Ancy-le-Franc 220 A2
Andernos-les-Bains 206 B5
Anet 218 C3
Angers 218 A1
Anglet 206 A3
Anglure 219 F3
Angoulême 212 B2
Annecy 215 E3
Annemasse 215 E3
Annonay 214 C2
Anse 214 C3
Antibes 210 C3
Apt 209 F4
Arcachon 206 B5
Arc-en-Barrois 220 B2
Archiac 212 A2
Arès 211 F1
Argelès-Gazost 206 C2
Argelès-sur-Mer 208 B1
Argentan 218 A3
Argentat 213 E1
Argenton-sur-Creuse 213 D4
Argentré 217 F2
Argent-sur-Sauldre 219 E1
Arlanc 214 A2
Arles 209 E3
Armentières 222 C2
Arnay-le-Duc 214 B5
Arracourt 221 D3
Arras 222 C2
Arreau 207 D2
Arrens-Marsous 206 C2
Arromanches-les-Bains 217 F4
Ars-en-Ré 211 E3
Artenay 219 D2

Arudy 206 C2
Asco 210 C2
Aspet 207 E2
Aubagne 209 F3
Aubenas 209 D5
Aubusson 213 E4
Auch 207 D3
Auderville 217 F5
Audierne 216 A2
Audressein 207 E2
Aullène 210 C1
Ault 222 A1
Aumale 219 D5
Aumont-Aubrac 208 B5
Aunay-sur-Odon 218 A4
Auneau 219 D3
Aups 210 A3
Auray 216 C2
Aurignac 207 E2
Aurillac 213 E1
Auterive 207 F3
Autun 214 B5
Auxerre 219 F2
Auxi-le-Château 222 B1
Auzances 213 E3
Avallon 219 F1
Avesnes-sur-Helpe 222 D1
Avignon 209 E4
Avranches 217 E3
Ax-les-Thermes 207 F2
Ay 220 A4
Azay-le-Ferron 212 C4
Azay-le-Rideau 212 B5

Baccarat 221 D3
Badonviller 221 E3
Bagnères-de-Bigorre 207 D2
Bagnères-de-Luchon 207 D2
Bagnoles-de-l'Orne 218 A3
Bagnols-les-Bains 208 C5
Bagnols-sur-Cèze 09 D4
Bailleul 222 C3
Bains-les-Bains 221 D2
Baix 209 E5
Ballon 218 B2
Bapaume 222 C1
Baraqueville 208 A4
Barbezieux-St-Hilaire 212 A2
Barentin 218 C5
Barenton 217 F3
Barfleur 217 F5
Barjols 210 A3
Bar-le-Duc 220 B3
Barr 221 E3
Barrême 210 A4
Bar-sur-Aube 220 B2
Bastia 210 C2
Battlefields of Picardie 222 C1
Batz-sur-Mer 217 D1
Baugé 218 A1
Baume-les-Dames 221 D1
Bayeux 217 F4
Bayonne 206 A3
Bazoches-sur-Hoëne 218 B3
Beaucaire 209 E4
Beaulieu-sur-Dordogne 213 D1
Beaumesnil 218 B5
Beaumont-de-Lomagne 207 E4
Beaumont-sur-Sarthe 218 A2
Beaune 214 C5
Beaupréau 211 F5
Beauvais 219 D4
Beauvoir-sur-Mer 211 E1

Bédée 217 E2
Bélâbre 212 C4
Belfort 221 E1
Bellac 212 C3
Bellegarde 209 D3
Bellegarde 219 E2
Bellegarde-sur-Valserine 215 D3
Bellême 218 B3
Bellencombre 218 C5
Belley 215 D3
Belvès 207 E5
Benfeld 221 F3
Bénodet 216 B2
Berck-Plage 222 A2
Bergerac 212 B1
Bergues 222 B3
Bernay 218 FA2
Besançon 215 E5
Bessines-sur-Gartempe 213 D3
Béthune 222 C2
Beuil 210 B4
Beynac-et-Cazenac 212 C1
Béziers 208 B3
Biarritz 206 A3
Bias 206 B4
Bias 207 D5
Bidart 206 A3
Binic 216 C3
Biscarrosse-Plage 206 A5
Blain 217 E1
Blangy-sur-Bresle 222 A1
Blaye 212 A1
Bléancourt 219 E4
Bléré 212 C5
Bligny-sur-Ouche 214 C5
Blois 218 C1
Boëge 215 E3
Boën 214 B2
Bohain-en-Vermandois 222 D1
Bollène 209 E4
Bonifacio 210 C1
Bonlieu 215 D3
Bonnétable 218 B2
Bonneval-sur-Arc 215 F3
Bonneville 218 B4
Bordeaux 212 A1
Bort-les-Orgues 213 E2
Bouilly 220 A2
Boulogne-sur-Mer 222 A2
Bourbon-Lancy 214 A4
Bourbonne-les-Bains 221 D1
Bourbriac 216 C3
Bourg 212 A1
Bourganeuf 213 D3
Bourg-Argental 214 C2
Bourg-en-Bresse 214 C3
Bourges 213 E5
Bourgogne 220 A4
Bourgoin-Jallieu 215 D2
Bourgueil 212 B5
Bourneville 218 B4
Boussens 207 E2
Bouxwiller 221 E4
Bozel 215 F2
Bracieux 218 C1
Brancion 214 C4
Branne 212 A1
Brantôme 212 C2
Bray-sur-Seine 219 F3
Breil-sur-Roya 210 C4
Bressuire 212 A4
Brest 216 A3
Bretenoux 213 D1
Breteuil 218 C3
Breteuil 219 D5
Briançon 215 F1
Briare 219 E1

Brie-Comte-Robert 219 E3
Brienne-le-Château 220 A3
Brignoles 210 A3
Brionne 218 B4
Brissac-Quincé 218 A1
Brive-la-Gaillarde 213 D1
Broons 217 D3
Brou 218 C2
Brûlon 218 A2
Bruniquel 207 F4
Bucquoy 222 C1
Burie 212 A3
Bussang 221 E2
Buxy 214 C4
Buzancy 220 B4

Cabrerets 207 F5
Cadillac 206 C5
Caen 218 A4
Cagnes-sur-Mer 210 C3
Cahors 207 F5
Calacuccia 210 C2
Calais 222 B3
Calenzana 210 C2
Calignac 207 D4
Callac 216 C3
Calvi 210 B2
Camarès 208 B3
Camaret 216 A3
Cambo-les-Bains 206 A3
Cambrai 222 C1
Campan 207 D2
Cancale 217 E3
Cancon 207 D5
Canet-Plage 208 B2
Cannes 210 B3
Cap Corse 210 C2
Cap Ferret 206 A5
Capbreton 206 A3
Capestang 208 B3
Caraman 207 F3
Carantec 216 B3
Carbère 208 B1
Carcans 211 F1
Carcassonne 208 A2
Carcès 210 A3
Cargèse 210 B1
Carhaix-Plouguer 216 B3
Carnac 216 C1
Carpentras 209 E4
Carqueiranne 210 A2
Carrouges 218 A3
Carteret 217 E4
Casamozza 210 C2
Cassel 222 B3
Cassis 209 F3
Casteljaloux 206 C4
Castellane 210 B4
Castelnaudary 207 F3
Castelsarrasin 207 E4
Castets 206 B4
Castillonnès 207 D5
Castres 208 A3
Castries 209 D3
Catus 207 E5
Caudry 222 C1
Caussade 207 F4
Cauterets 206 C2
Cavaillon 209 E4
Cazals 207 E5
Centuri 210 C2
Céret 208 B1
Cernay 221 E2
Ceyzériat 215 D3
Chabeuil 214 C1
Chablis 219 F2
Chabreloche 214 A3
Chagny 214 C4
Chalabre 207 F2
Challans 211 E4
Châlons-en-Champagne 220 A4

Chalon-sur-Saône 214 C4
Chambéry 215 E2
Chambord 218 C1
Chamonix-Mont-Blanc 215 F3
Champagnole 215 D4
Champier 215 D2
Champillon 219 F4
Champtoceaux 217 E1
Chantelle 213 F3
Chantilly 219 E4
Chaource 220 A2
Charavines 215 D2
Charleville-Mézières 220 A5
Charlieu 214 B3
Charolles 214 B4
Charroux 212 B3
Chartres 218 C3
Château Chinon 214 B5
Château de Kerjean 216 B3
Château de Montgeoffroy 218 A1
Château du Fleckenstein 221 F4
Château Ussé 212 B5
Château-Arnoux 210 A4
Châteaubriant 217 E2
Château-du-Loir 218 B2
Châteaudun 218 C2
Châteaugiron 217 E2
Château-la-Vallière 218 B1
Châteaulin 216 B3
Châteaumeillant 213 E4
Châteauneuf-de-Randon 208 C5
Châteauneuf-du-Pape 209 E4
Châteauneuf-sur-Sarthe 217 F1
Châteaurenard 219 E2
Château-Renault 218 C2
Châteauroux 213 D4
Château-Salins 221 D4
Château-Thierry 219 F4
Châtel 215 F3
Châtelguyon 213 F3
Châtellerault 212 C4
Châtenois 220 C3
Châtillon-en-Bazois 214 A5
Châtillon-sur-Chalaronne 214 C3
Châtillon-sur-Indre 213 C5
Châtillon-sur-Loire 219 E1
Châtillon-sur-Marne 219 F4
Châtillon-sur-Seine 220 A2
Chauffailles 214 B3
Chaumergy 215 D4
Chaumont 220 B2
Chaumont-sur-Loire 218 C1
Chaussin 215 D5
Chemillé 212 A5
Chénérailles 213 E3
Chenonceaux 218 C1
Cherbourg 217 E5
Chinon 212 B5
Cholet 211 F5
Chorges 210 A5
Ciboure 206 A3
Civray 212 B3
Clairvaux-les-Lacs 215 D4
Clamecy 219 F1
Clécy 218 A4
Clefmont 220 C2

Clermont-Ferrand
213 F2
Clermont-l'Hérault
208 C3
Clisson 211 F5
Cluny 214 C4
Cluses 215 E3
Cognac 212 A2
Coligny 215 D4
Collioure 208 B1
Colmars 210 B4
Colombey-les-Belles
220 C3
Combeaufontaine
220 C2
Combourg 217 E3
Combronde 213 F3
Commercy 220 C3
Compiègne 219 E4
Comps-sur-Artuby
210 B3
Concarneau 216 B2
Condat 207 E5
Condé-sur-Noireau
218 A3
Condom 207 D4
Confolens 212 C3
Connerré 218 B2
Contay 222 B1
Contrexéville 220 C2
Coray 216 B2
Corbeil-Essonnes
219 E3
Corbie 222 B1
Cordes 207 F4
Cormery 212 C5
Corps 215 E1
Corte 210 D2
Cosne-Cours-sur-Loire
219 E1
Côte d'Opale 222 B3
Couches 214 B4
Couhé 212 B3
Coulommiers 219 E3
Couptrain 218 A3
Courchevel 215 F2
Cour-Cheverny 218 C1
Courpière 214 A2
Courseulles-sur-Mer
218 A4
Courteilles 218 B4
Courtenay 219 E2
Courtomer 218 B3
Coutances 217 E4
Couterne 218 A3
Coutras 212 A1
Craon 217 F2
Crécy-en-Ponthieu
222 B1
Creil 219 E4
Crémieu 215 D2
Crépy-en-Valois 219 E4
Cressensac 213 D1
Creutzwald 221 D4
Crocq 213 E3
Crozon 216 A3
Cruas 209 E5
Cuiseaux 215 D4
Culan 213 E4
Cunault 218 A1
Cusset 214 A3

Dabo 221 E3
Dampierre 215 D5
Damvillers 220 B4
Darney 220 C2
Dax 206 B3
Deauville 218 A4
Decazeville 208 A5
Delle 221 E1
Denain 222 C2
Descartes 212 C5
Die 209 F5
Dieppe 222 A1
Dieulouard 220 C4
Digne-les-Bains 210 A4
Digoin 214 B4

Dijon 220 B1
Dinan 217 D3
Dinard 217 D3
Disneyland Resort Paris
219 E3
Dives-sur-Mer 218 A4
Dol-de-Bretagne 217 E3
Dole 215 D5
Domfront 218 A3
Domme 207 E5
Dompierre-sur-Besbre
214 A4
Domrémy-la-Pucelle
220 C3
Donzenac 213 D2
Donzy 219 E1
Dormans 219 F4
Dortan 215 D4
Douai 222 C2
Douarnenez 216 A2
Doucier 215 D4
Doué-la-Fontaine
212 A5
Doullens 222 B1
Dourdan 219 D3
Douzy 220 B5
Draguignan 210 B3
Dreux 218 C3
Drusenheim 221 F4
Duclair 218 C4
Duingt 215 E3
Dunkerque 222 B3
Dun-sur-Auron 213 E4
Duras 207 D5
Durtal 218 A2

Eauze 207 D4
Elbeuf 218 C4
Elven 217 D2
Embrun 210 B5
Ensisheim 221 E2
Entrevaux 210 B4
Épernay 219 F4
Epernon 219 D3
Épinal 221 D2
Erbalunga 210 C2
Ernée 217 F3
Erquy 217 D3
Erstein 221 F3
Espalion 208 B5
Esternay 219 F3
Etain 220 C4
Étamples 219 D3
Etaples 222 A1
Etretat 218 B5
Eu 222 A1
Evaux-les-Bains 213 E3
Evian-les-Bains 215 E4
Evreux 218 C4
Evron 218 A2
Exmes 218 B3
Eygurande 213 E2
Eymet 207 D5
Eymoutiers 213 D2
Eze 210 C4

Falaise 218 A4
Faverges 215 E3
Fécamp 218 B5
Felletin 213 E3
Fère-Champenoise
220 A3
Ferrette 221 E1
Ferté-St-Aubin 219 D2
Feurs 214 B2
Figeac 207 F5
Firminy 214 B2
Flers 218 A3
Fleurance 207 D4
Fleury 208 B2
Flize 220 B5
Florac 208 C4
Foix 207 F2
Fontainebleau 219 E3
Fontaine-de-Vaucluse
209 E4

Fontaine-le-Dun
218 B5
Fontenay-le-Comte
211 F4
Fontevraud-l'Abbaye
212 B5
Forbach 221 E4
Forcalquier 209 F4
Forges-les-Eaux 218 C5
Fouesnant 216 B2
Fougères 217 F3
Fourcès 207 D4
Fournels 213 F1
Fours 214 A4
Frangy 215 D3
Fréjus 210 B3
Fresnay-sur-Sarthe
218 A3
Fresnes 218 C1
Fréteval 218 C2
Frévent 222 B1
Froissy 219 D5
Fronsac 207 D2
Fronsac 212 A1
Fruges 222 B2
Fumay 222 E1
Futuroscope 212 B4

Gabarret 206 C4
Gaël 217 D2
Gaillon 218 C4
Gannat 213 F3
Gap 210 A5
Gavarnie 206 C2
Genêts 217 E3
Genlis 214 C5
Génolhac 208 C4
Gérardmer 221 E2
Germay 220 B3
Gex 215 E4
Ghisonaccia 210 C1
Ghisoni 210 C1
Gien 219 E2
Gignac 208 C3
Girolata 210 B2
Giromagny 221 E2
Gisors 219 D4
Giverny 218 C4
Givet 222 E1
Givors 214 C2
Givry-en-Argonne
220 B4
Gorges de l'Ardèche
209 D4
Gorges du Verdon
210 A4
Gorron 217 F3
Gourdon 207 E5
Gournay-en-Bray
219 D4
Gouzon 213 E3
Graçay 213 D5
Grandcamp-Maisy
217 F4
Grandvilliers 219 D5
Granville 217 E4
Grasse 210 B3
Graulhet 207 F3
Gray 220 M7
Grenade 207 E3
Grenoble 215 D2
Gréolières 210 B4
Grignols 206 C4
Groix 216 B2
Gruissan 208 B2
Guémené-Penfao
217 E1
Guer 217 D2
Guérande 217 D1
Guéret 213 D3
Guérigny 213 F5
Gueugnon 214 B4
Guignes 219 E3
Guillestre 210 B5
Guilvinec 216 A2
Guînes 222 B3
Guingamp 216 C3

Guise 222 D1
Gujan-Mestras 206 B5

Hagetmau 206 B3
Haguenau 221 F4
Ham 219 E5
Ham 222 B1
Harcourt 218 B4
Harfleur 218 B4
Hasparren 206 A3
Haut Kœnigsbourg
221 E3
Hazebrouck 222 B2
Hédé 217 E3
Henrichemont 213 E5
Héricourt 221 E1
Herment 213 F2
Hesdin 222 B2
Hiersac 212 B2
Hirson 222 D1
Honfleur 218 B4
Hordain 222 C2
Hossegor 206 A3
Houdain 222 B2
Houdan 218 C3
Houdelaincourt 220 C3
Hourtin-Plage 211 F2
Huelgoat 216 B3
Hunspach 221 F4
Hyères 210 A2

Illiers-Combray 218 C3
Ingwiller 221 E4
Isigny-sur-Mer 217 F4
Isola 210 B4
Issoire 213 F2
Issoudun 213 E5
Istres 209 E3
Ivry-la-Bataille 218 C3

Janzé 217 E2
Jargeau 219 D2
Jarnages 213 E3
Jausiers 210 B5
Joigny 219 F2
Joinville 220 B3
Josselin 217 D2
Jougne 215 E4
Joyeuse 209 D5
Juan-les-Pins 210 C3
Jullouville 217 E3
Jumièges 218 B4
Jussey 220 C2
Juzennecourt 220 B2

L'Aigle 218 B3
L'Arbresle 214 C3
L'Echalp 215 F1
L'Escarène 210 C4
L'Île-Rousse 210 C2
L'Isle-Adam 219 D4
L'Isle-en-Dodon 207 E3
L'Isle-Jourdain 207 E3
L'Isle-Jourdain 212 C3
L'Isle-sur-la-Sorgue
209 E4
L'Isle-sur-le-Doubs
221 D1
La Bassée 222 C2
La Baule 217 D1
La Bazoche-Gouet
218 C2
La Brède 206 C5
La Brillanne 209 F4
La Capelle 222 D1
La Cavalerie 208 B4
La Chaise-Dieu 214 A2
La Charité-sur-Loire
213 F5
La Châtaigneraie
212 A4
La Châtre 213 E4
La Ciotat 209 F2
La Clayette 214 B3
La Cluse 215 D3
La Coquille 212 C2
La Courtine 213 E2

La Croix-Valmer 210 B3
La Cure 215 E4
La Ferté-Bernard
218 B2
La Ferté-Macé 218 A3
La Ferté-sous-Jouarre
219 E4
La Ferté-Vidame
218 C3
La Flèche 218 A2
La Gacilly 217 D2
La Grand-Combe
209 D4
La Grave 206 C5
La Grave 215 E1
La Guerche-de-Bretagne
217 F2
La Malène 208 C4
La Mongie 207 D2
La Motte-Chalancon
209 F5
La Pacaudière 214 A3
La Petite-Pierre 221 E4
La Réole 206 C5
La Roche-Bernard
217 D1
La Roche-Chalais
212 B1
La Rochelle 211 F3
La Roche-sur-Foron
215 E3
La Roche-sur-Yon
211 E4
La Rochette 215 E2
La Roquebrussanne
210 A3
La Salvetat-sur-Agout
208 B3
La Souterraine 213 D3
La Tremblade 211 F3
La Trenche-sur-Mer
211 E4
La Trinité 210 C4
La Turbie 210 C4
Labastide-Murat 207 F5
Labouheyre 206 B4
Lacanau 211 F1
Lacapelle-Marival
207 F5
Lacq 206 B3
Lafrançaise 207 E4
Lagrasse 208 A2
Laguiole 208 B5
Laissac 208 B4
Lalouvesc 214 C1
Lamarche 220 C2
Lamastre 214 C1
Lamballe 217 D3
Lambesc 209 F3
Landerneau 216 A3
Landévennec 216 A3
Landivisiau 216 B3
Landivy 217 F3
Langeac 214 A1
Langeais 212 B5
Langogne 208 C5
Langon 206 C5
Langon 217 E2
Langres 220 C2
Lanmeur 216 C5
Lannilis 216 B5
Lannion 216 C5
Lanslebourg-Mont-Cenis
215 F2
Lanvollon C3
Laon 219 F5
Lapalisse 214 A3
Laqueuille 213 F2
Larche 210 B5
Larche 213 D1
Largentière 209 D5
Laroque-des-Arcs
207 F5
Larrau 206 EB2
Lascaux 212 C1
LaTour-du-Pin 215 D2
Laubrières 217 F2

Lauterbourg 221 F4
Lauzerte 207 E4
Laval 217 F2
Lavardac 207 D4
Lavardin 218 B2
Lavelanet 207 F2
Le Barp 206 B5
Le Blanc 212 C4
Le Bugue 212 C1
Le Cateau-Cambrésis 222 D1
Le Caylar 208 C4
Le Chapelle-d'Angillon 219 E1
Le Chesne 220 B5
Le Conquet 216 A3
Le Creusot 214 B4
Le Croisic 217 D1
Le Crotoy 222 A1
Le Donjon 214 A3
Le Dorat 212 C3
Le Faouët 216 B2
Le Grand-Bourg 213 D3
Le Havre 218 B4
Le Hohwald 221 E3
Le Lardin-St-Lazare 213 D1
Le Lavandou 210 A2
Le Mans 218 B2
Le Markstein 221 E2
Le Mont-Dore 213 F2
Le Mont-St-Michel 217 E3
Le Muret 206 B5
Le Neubourg 218 C4
Le Palais 216 C1
Le Pontet 212 A2
Le Pouldu 216 B2
Le Puy 219 E2
Le Puy 221 D1
Le Puy-en-Velay 214 B1
Le Quesnoy 219 E5
Le Quesnoy 222 C1
Le Rozier 208 B4
Le Thillot 221 E2
Le Touquet-Paris-Plage 222 A2
Le Tréport 222 A1
Le Val-André 217 D3
Le Vigan 208 C4
Lectoure 207 D4
Legé 211 E5
Lembach 221 F4
Lempdes 214 A2
Lencloître 212 B4
Lens 222 C2
Léon 206 A4
Les Abrets 215 D2
Les Aix-d'Angillon 213 E5
Les Arcs 210 B3
Les Arcs 215 F2
Les Baux-de-Provence 209 E3
Les Contamines-Montjoie 215 F3
Les Echarmeaux 214 B3
Les Eyzies-de-Tayac-Sireuil 212 C1
Les Halles 214 B2
Les Herbiers 211 F4
Les Issambres 210 B3
Les Lecques 209 F2
Les Pieux 217 E5
Les Ponts-de-Cé 218 A1
Les Sables-d'Olonne 211 E4
Les Trois-Epis 221 E2
Les Vans 209 D5
Lesmont 220 A3
Lesparre-Médoc 211 F2
Leuglay 220 B2
Levier 215 E5
Lezay 212 B3
Lezoux 214 A3
Libourne 212 A1
Lieurey 218 B4

Lignières 213 E4
Ligny-en-Barrois 220 B3
Liguel 212 C5
Lille 222 C2
Lillers 222 B2
Limoges 213 D3
Limoux 208 A2
Lisieux 218 B4
Livarot 218 B4
Loches 212 C5
Locmariaquer 216 C1
Locminé 216 C2
Locquirec 216 B3
Locronan 216 A2
Lodève 208 C3
Lohéac 217 E2
Lomme 222 C2
Longuyon 220 C5
Longwy 220 C5
Lons-le-Saunier 215 D4
Lorient 216 C2
Loriol-sur-Drôme 209 E5
Lormont 212 A1
Loudéac 216 C2
Loudun 212 B3
Louhans 214 C4
Lourdes 206 C2
Louviers 218 C4
Lubersac 213 D2
Luçon 211 F4
Lumbres 222 B2
Lunel 209 D3
Lunéville 221 D3
Lure 221 D2
Lus-la-Croix-Haute 209 F5
Lussac-les-Châteaux 212 C4
Lussan 209 D4
Luxeuil 215 D5
Luynes 218 B1
Luzy 214 B4
Lyon 214 C3

Machault 220 A4
Mâcon 214 C3
Magescq 206 A3
Magny-en-Vexin 219 D4
Maillezais 212 A4
Mailly-le-Camp 220 A3
Malaucène 209 E4
Malesherbes 219 D3
Malestroit 217 D2
Malicorne 212 C5
Malicorne 217 E3
Mamers 218 B3
Mandelieu 210 B3
Manosque 209 F4
Mansle 212 B3
Mantes-la-Jolie 219 D4
Marans 211 F3
Marchaux 221 D1
Marciac 207 D3
Marennes 211 F3
Mareuil 212 B2
Maringny-le-Châtel 219 F3
Maringues 214 A3
Marlenheim 221 E3
Marmande 207 D5
Marnay 220 C1
Marquise 222 B3
Marseillan-Plage 208 C3
Marseille 209 F3
Martel 207 D4
Martel 213 D1
Martigues 209 E3
Marvejols 208 B5
Massat 207 E3
Massiac 213 F2
Matha 212 A3
Mathay 221 E5
Maubeuge 222 D2
Mauléon 212 A5
Mauléon-Licharre 206 B3

Maulévrier 212 A5
Mauron 217 D2
Maury 208 A2
Mauzé-sur-le-Mignon 212 A3
Mayenne 217 F3
Mazamet 208 A3
Meaux 219 E4
Megève 215 F3
Mélisey 220 C2
Melle 212 B3
Melun 219 E3
Menat 213 F3
Mende 208 C3
Menton 210 C4
Merdrignac 217 D2
Méribel 215 F3
Mervans 214 C4
Mesnil-Val 222 A1
Metz 221 D4
Metzervisse 221 D4
Meung-sur-Loire 219 D2
Meymac 213 E2
Meyrueis 208 C4
Meyssac 213 D1
Mèze 208 C3
Mézilhac 214 B1
Miélan 207 D3
Mijoux 215 E4
Millau 208 B4
Mimizan 206 A4
Mindin 211 D5
Miramas 209 E3
Mirebeau 212 B4
Mirebeau 220 C1
Mirecourt 221 D3
Modane 215 F2
Molières 207 E4
Moloy 220 B1
Moncontour 217 D3
Mondoubleau 218 B2
Monflanquin 207 E5
Monistrol-sur-Loire 214 B2
Montagnac 208 C3
Montagne-au-Perche 218 B3
Montalivet-les-Bains 211 F2
Montargis 219 E2
Montauban 207 E4
Montbard 220 A1
Montbazens 208 A5
Montbéliard 221 E1
Montbenoît 215 E5
Montbrison 214 B2
Montbron 212 B2
Montceau-les-Mines 214 B4
Montcornet 219 F5
Mont-de-Marsan 206 C4
Montdidier 219 E5
Montélimar 209 E5
Montendre 212 A2
Montereau 219 E2
Montereau-Faut-Yonne 219 E3
Montesquiou 207 D3
Montfort 206 B3
Montfort 213 D1
Montgiscard 207 F3
Monthermé 222 E1
Montignac 212 C1
Montigny-sur-Aube 220 B2
Montlieu-la-Garde 212 A2
Mont-Louis 208 A1
Montluçon 213 F3
Montmaraült 213 F3
Montmélian 215 E2
Montmirail 218 B2
Montmirail 219 F3
Montoire-sur-le-Loir 218 B2
Montpellier 208 C3
Montréal 207 G12

Montréal 208 A2
Montréal 220 A1
Montreuil 218 A2
Montreuil 222 B2
Montreuil-Bellay 212 B5
Montrichard 218 C1
Montsauche-les-Settons 214 B5
Montsûrs 218 A2
Mordelles 217 E2
Moreuil 219 E5
Morez 215 E4
Morlaàs 206 C3
Morlaix 216 B3
Morosaglia 210 C2
Mortagne-sur-Sèvre 211 F5
Morteau 215 E5
Morzine 215 F3
Mouchard 215 D5
Mougins 210 B3
Moulins 214 A4
Moustiers-Ste-Marie 210 A4
Moûtiers 215 E2
Mouy 219 D4
Mulhouse 221 E2
Murat 213 F1
Mur-de-Barrez 213 F1
Muret 207 E3
Mussidan 212 B1
Muzillac 217 D1

Najac 207 F4
Nancy 221 D3
Nangis 219 E3
Nant 208 C4
Nantes 211 E5
Nantiat 212 C3
Nantua 215 D3
Narbonne 208 B2
Narbonne 215 D2
Navilly 214 C5
Nemours 219 E2
Néris-les-Bains 213 F3
Nérondes 213 F5
Nesle 219 E5
Neuf-Brisach 221 F2
Neufchâteau 220 C3
Neufchâtel-en-Bray 218 C5
Neung-sur-Beuvron 219 D1
Neuvic 212 B1
Neuvic 213 E2
Nevers 213 F5
Nexon 212 C2
Nice 210 B3
Nîmes 209 D4
Niort 212 A3
Nitry 219 F2
Nogent 220 C2
Nogent-le-Rotrou 218 B3
Nogent-sur-Seine 219 F3
Noirétable 214 A3
Noirmoutier-en-l'Île 211 D5
Nonancourt 218 C3
Nontron 212 C2
Nonza 210 C2
Nordausques 222 B3
Nort-sur-Erdie 217 E1
Nouvion 222 B1
Noyers 220 A1
Noyon 219 E5
Nozay 217 E1
Nyons 209 E4

Oisemont 222 B1
Olargues 208 B3
Olette 208 A1
Olliergues 214 A2
Oloron-Ste-Marie 206 B2

Oraison 210 A4
Orange 209 E4
Orbey 221 E2
Orcières 210 A5
Orgeval 219 D4
Orléans 219 D2
Orthez 206 B3
Oucquest 218 C2
Ouistreham 218 A4
Ouzouer-la-Marché 218 C2
Oyonnax 215 D3

Paimpol 216 C3
Palavas-les-Flots 208 C3
Pamiers 207 F2
Panassac 207 D3
Paray-le-Monial 214 B4
Parc Astérix 219 E4
Parentis-en-Born 206 B4
Paris 219 D3
Parthenay 212 A4
Pau 206 C3
Pauillac 211 F2
Pavilly 218 C5
Péaule 217 D1
Pellegrue 206 C5
Pentrez-Plage 216 A3
Percy 217 F4
Périgueux 212 C1
Péronne 222 C1
Pérouges 214 C3
Perpignan 208 B2
Perros-Guirec 216 C4
Pertuis 209 F3
Pesmes 215 D5
Pézenas 208 C3
Piana 210 B2
Piedicroce 210 C2
Pierrefort 213 F1
Pierroton 206 B5
Pinols 214 A1
Pipriac 217 E2
Pirou-Plage 217 E4
Pithiviers 219 D2
Plabennec 216 A3
Plage-en-Ré 211 E3
Plancoët 217 D2
Pleumartin 212 C4
Pleyben 216 B3
Ploërmel 217 D2
Plouay 216 C2
Ploudalmézeau 216 A3
Plouescat 216 A3
Plougasnou 216 B3
Plougastel-Daoulas 216 A3
Plouha 216 C3
Plouigneau 216 B3
Pluvigner 216 C2
Poissons 220 B3
Poitiers 212 B4
Poix 219 D5
Poix-Terron 220 A5
Pompey 221 D3
Pons 212 A2
Pont du Gard 209 D4
Pont l'Évêque 218 B4
Pontailler-sur-Saône 220 C1
Pont-à-Mousson 220 C4
Pontarlier 215 E5
Pontaubault 217 E3
Pont-Aven 216 B2
Pontcharra 215 E2
Pontchâteau 217 D1
Pont-Croix 216 A2
Pont-d'Ain 215 D3
Pont-de-Roide 221 E1
Pont-de-Vaux 214 C4
Pontgibaud 213 F3
Pontivy 216 C2
Pont-l'Abbé 216 A2
Pontlevoy 218 C1
Pontoise 219 D4

Pontoise 219 F4
Pontorson 217 E3
Pont-sur-Yonne 219 F3
Pornic 211 E5
Porquerolles 210 A2
Portbail 217 E4
Port-de-Bouc 209 E3
Port Grimaud 210 B3
Porticcio 210 C1
Port-Joinville 211 D4
Port-Louis 216 C2
Port-Manech 216 B2
Port-Navalo 216 C1
Porto 210 B2
Porto-Vecchio 210 C1
Port-sur-Saône 221 D2
Pouancé 217 F2
Pouilly-en-Auxois
    214 B5
Pouyastruc 207 D3
Pradelles 208 C5
Prahecq 207 F1
Prats-de-Mollo-la-Preste
    208 A1
Préchac 206 C5
Pré-en-Pail 218 A3
Prémery 214 A5
Preuilly-sur-Claise
    212 C4
Privas 209 D5
Propriano 210 C1
Provins 219 F3
Prunete 210 C2
Puiseaux 219 E2
Puy-l'Evêque 207 E5

Questembert 217 D1
Quiberon 216 C1
Quillan 208 A2
Quillins 214 C2
Quimper 216 A2
Quimperlé 216 B2
Quineville 217 F5
Quissac 209 D4

Rambervillers 221 D3
Rambouillet 219 D3
Randan 214 A3
Raon-l'Etape 221 E3
Réalmont 208 A3
Redon 217 D1
Reignier 215 E3
Reims 220 A4
Remiremont 221 D2
Rennes 217 E2

Rethel 220 A5
Retiers 217 E2
Reuilly 213 E5
Rhinau 221 F3
Rians 209 F3
Ribérac 212 B2
Rieumes 207 E3
Rieux 207 E2
Rignac 208 A5
Riom 213 F3
Riquewihr 221 E2
Riscle 206 C3
Rivedoux-Plage 211 F3
Rivesaltes 208 B2
Roanne 214 B3
Rocamadour 207 F5
Rochechouart 212 C3
Rochefort 211 F3
Rocheservière 211 E5
Rocroi 222 E1
Rodez 208 A4
Rogliano 210 C2
Roisel 222 C2
Romans-sur-Isère
    214 C1
Romorantin-Lanthenay
    219 D1
Ronchamp 221 D2
Roquebillière 210 C4
Roquefort 206 C4

Rosans 209 F5
Roscoff 216 B3
Rosporden 216 B2
Rostassac 207 E5
Rostrenen 216 C3
Roubaix 222 C2
Rouen 218 C4
Rougemont 221 D1
Roussillon 209 F4
Royan 211 F2
Roybon 215 D2
Roye 219 E5
Rue 222 B2
Ruffieux 215 D3
Rumigny 220 A5

Sablé-sur-Sarthe
    218 A2
Sabres 206 B4
Saillagouse 207 F1
St-Amand-Montrond
    213 E4
St-Avold 221 D4
St-Benoît-sur-Loire
    219 D2
St-Brieuc 216 C3
St-Cast-le-Guildo
    217 D3
St-Claude 215 D4
St-Dié 221 E3
St-Dizier 220 B3
Ste-Mère-Église 217 F4
St-Emilion 212 F11
Ste-Enimie 208 C4
Saintes 212 A2
Stes-Maries-de-la-Mer
    209 D3
St-Étienne 214 B2
St-Étienne-de-Tinée
    210 B4
St-Fargeau 219 E1
St-Florent 210 C2
St-Florent 213 E5
St-Flour 213 F1
St-Hilaire-du-Harcouët
    217 F4
St-Jean-de-Luz 206 A3
St-Jean-Pied-de-Port
    206 A2
St-Laurent 217 F4
St-Lizier 207 E2
St-Lô 217 F4
St-Lunaire 217 D3
St-Malo 217 E3
St-Maximin-la-Ste-
    Baume 210 A3
St-Méen 217 D2
St-Nazaire 217 D1
St-Omer 222 B3
St-Palais 206 B3
St-Paul 210 C3
St-Pierre-le-Moûtier
    213 F4
St-Pierre-sur-Mer 208 B2
St-Pol-de-Léon 216 B3
St-Pol-sur-Ternoise
    222 B2
St-Quay-Portrieux
    216 C3
St-Quentin 219 F5
St-Rémy-de-Provence
    209 E4
St-Riquier 222 B1
St-Savin 212 C4
St-Symphorien 206 C5
St-Thégonnec 216 B3
St-Tropez 210 B3
St-Vaast-la-Hougue
    217 F5
St-Valery-en-Caux
    218 B5
St-Valery-sur-Somme
    222 A1
Saissac 208 A3
Salernes 210 A3
Salies-de-Béarn 206 B3
Sallanches 215 F3

Salles 206 B5
Salon-de-Provence
    209 E3
Salviac 207 E5
Samatan 207 E3
Samoëns 215 F3
Sancergues 213 F5
Sancoins 213 F4
Santa Severa 210 C2
Sarlat-la-Canéda
    213 D1
Sarralbe 221 E4
Sarrebourg 221 E3
Sarreguemines 221 E4
Sarron 206 C3
Sartène 210 C1
Sarzeau 216 C1
Saucats 206 B5
Saujon 211 F2
Saulieu 214 B5
Sault 209 F4
Saumur 212 B5
Sauternes 206 C5
Sauveterre-de-Béarn
    206 B3
Sauveterre-de-Guyenne
    206 C5
Sauxillanges 214 A2
Sauzon 216 C1
Saverdun 207 F2
Saverne 221 E3
Savigny-sur-Braye
    218 B2
Scaër 216 B2
Seclin 222 C2
Sedan 220 B5
Séderon 209 F4
Sées 218 B3
Segonzac 212 A2
Segré 217 F1
Seiches-sur-le-Loir
    218 A1
Sélestat 221 E3
Selongey 220 B1
Semur-en-Auxois
    220 A1
Senlis 219 E4
Sennecey-le-Grand
    214 C4
Senonches 218 C3
Senones 221 E3
Sens 219 F2
Sérent 217 D2
Serres 209 F5
Sète 208 C3
Seurre 214 C5
Seyne 210 A5
Sézanne 219 F3
Sigean 208 B2
Signy-l'Abbaye 220 A5
Siorac-en-Périgord
    212 C1
Sisteron 210 A4
Six-Fours-les-Plages
    210 A2
Soissons 219 F4
Solenzara 210 C1
Sombernon 220 B1
Sommières 209 D3
Sospel 210 C4
Souesmes 219 E1
Souillac 213 D1
Soumoulou 206 C3
Steenvoorde 222 C3
Stenay 220 B5
Strasbourg 221 F3
Suippes 220 A4
Sully-sur-Loire 219 D2
Surgères 212 A3

Tain-l'Hermitage
    214 C1
Tallard 210 A5
Tanlay 220 A2
Tarare 214 B3
Tarascon-sur-Ariège
    207 F2

Tarbes 206 C2
Tarnos 206 A3
Tauves 213 F2
Tavernes 210 A3
Tende 210 C4
Tergnier 219 F5
Thann 221 E2
Thenon 212 C1
Thérouanne 222 B2
Thiepval 222 C1
Thiers 214 A3
Thionville 220 C4
Thivars 218 C3
Thizy 214 B3
Thonon-les-Bains
    215 E4
Thouarcé 212 F7
Thouars 212 A5
Thueyts 209 D5
Thury-Harcourt 218 A4
Tignes 215 F2
Tinchebray 217 F3
Tonnay-Charente
    212 E9
Tonnerre 220 A2
Tôtes 218 C5
Toucy 219 F2
Toul 220 C3
Toulon 210 A2
Toulouse 207 F3
Tourcoing 222 C2
Tournay 207 D2
Tournon-d'Agenais
    207 F4
Tournus 214 C4
Tours 218 B1
Toury 219 D2
Trébeurden 216 B3
Trégastel 216 B4
Tréguier 216 C3
Treignac 213 D2
Trets 209 F3
Trévoux 214 C3
Troarn 218 A4
Trôo 218 B2
Trouville 218 B4
Troyes 220 A2
Truchtersheim 221 F3
Tuchan 208 B2
Tulle 213 D2
Tullins 215 D2

Uckange 220 C4
Ury 219 E3
Ussel 213 E2
Uzel 216 C3
Uzès 209 D4

Vaas 218 B2
Vaiges 218 A2
Vailly 220 A3
Vaison-la-Romaine
    209 E4
Val d'Isère 215 F2
Valbonnais 215 E1
Valençay 213 D5
Valence 207 E4
Valence 214 C1
Valenciennes 222 D2
Valensole 210 A4
Vallet 211 F5
Valloires 222 B2
Vallon-Pont-d'Arc
    209 D5
Vallorcine 215 F3
Valmorel 215 E2
Valognes 217 E5
Valras-Plage 208 C2
Vals-les-Bains 209 D5
Val-Suzon 220 B1
Vannes 217 C1
Varennes-en-Argonne
    220 B4
Varilhes 207 F2
Varzy 219 F1
Vatan 213 D5
Vauvert 209 D3

Vauvillers 221 D2
Venaco 210 C2
Vence 210 C3
Vendôme 218 C2
Verdun 220 B4
Vergt 212 C1
Verneuil 219 F4
Verneuil-sur-Avre 218 C3
Vernon 218 C4
Versailles 219 D3
Vertus 220 A4
Verzy 220 A4
Vesoul 221 D1
Veulettes-sur-Mer
    218 B5
Vézelay 219 F1
Vézelise 220 C3
Viais 211 E5
Vias 208 C3
Vic 213 E4
Vic-Fezensac 207 D3
Vichy 214 A3
Vic-sur-Cère 213 F1
Vienne 214 C2
Vierzon 213 E5
Vieux-Boucau-les-Bains
    206 A4
Vihiers 212 A5
Villandraut 206 C5
Villandry 218 B1
Villard-de-Lans
    215 D1
Villars-les-Dombes
    214 C3
Villedieu-les-Poêles
    217 F3
Ville-en-Tardenois
    219 F4
Villefort 208 C5
Villefranche-sur-Cher
    213 D5
Villefranche-sur-Saône
    214 C3
Villenauxe-la-Grande
    219 F3
Villeneuve 207 F5
Villeneuve-sur-Lot
    207 D5
Villeneuve-sur-Yonne
    219 F2
Villers-Bretonneux
    222 B1
Villers-Cotterêts 219 E4
Villersexel 221 D1
Villers-le-Lac 215 E5
Vimoutiers 218 B4
Vinça 208 A1
Vire 217 F3
Virieu 215 D2
Vitré 217 F2
Vitry-le-François
    220 A3
Vittel 220 C2
Viviers 209 E5
Vizille 215 D1
Void 220 C3
Voiron 215 D2
Volvic 213 F3
Vorey 214 B1
Vouvray 218 B1
Vouziers 220 A4
Voves 218 C2
Vron 222 B2

Wasselonne 221 E3
Wimereux 222 A3
Wissembourg 221 F4
Wormhout 222 B3

Yenne 215 D2
Yport 218 B5
Yssingeaux 214 B1
Yvetot 218 B5
Yvoire 215 E4

Zonza 210 C1

Abbaye Royale de Fontevraud **135**
Aboard Rafting 164
accommodation 31–32; *see also* individual areas
admission charges 30
airports and air services 26–27, 28, 195
Aix-en-Provence 7, 9, 14, 161
Albert 86
Albi 181
Amboise 126, 133
Angers 135
Antibes 163
Aquaboulevard 61
Arc du Triomphe 52–53
architecture 19
Arènes, les 146
Arles 148–149
Arromanches 87
art galleries
  Asian Arts Museum 156
  Carée d'Art 146
  Centre Georges Pompidou 56–57
  Espace Montmartre Salvador Dalí 64
  Fondation Angladon Dubrujeaud 151
  Fondation Vincent Van Gogh 149
  Musée d'Art Contemporain, Bordeaux 179
  Musée d'Art et d'Histoire, Nice 156
  Musée d'Art Moderne et Contemporain, Strasbourg 104
  Musée d'Art Moderne et d'Art Contemporain, Nice 156
  Musée d'Orsay 47–49
  Musée d'Unterlinden 112
  Musée des Beaux-Arts, Blois 128
  Musée des Beaux-Arts, Bordeaux 179
  Musée des Beaux-Arts, Dijon 107
  Musée des Beaux-Arts, Lyon 157
  Musée des Beaux-Arts, Nice 156
  Musée des Beaux-Arts, Rennes 85
  Musée des Beaux-

Arts, Rouen 79
  Musée des Beaux-Arts, Tours 133
  Musée du Louvre 54–55
  Musée du Message Biblique 156
  Musée Henri Matisse 156
  Musée Marc Chagall 156
  Musée Marmottan 59
  Musée National d'Art Moderne 57
  Musée National du Moyen-Age–Thermes de Cluny 45–46
  Musée Picasso, Paris 60–61
  Musée Picasso, Antibes 163
  Musée Rodin 58
  Musée Toulouse-Lautrec 181
  Palais des Beaux-Arts, Lille 101
Auxerre 113
Avignon 150–151
Azay-le-Rideau 131

Baker, Josephine 20, 57, 69
Bartholdi, Frédéric Auguste 112
Basilique St-Cernin 180
Basilique St-Rémi 102
Battlefields of Picardie 86
Bayeux 81
Beaubourg *see* Centre Georges Pompidou
Beaune 24, 108–109
Berthelot, Gilles 131
Besançon 113
Béziers 6, 145
Biarritz 185
Blériot, Louis 86
Bois de Boulogne 23
Bois de Vincennes 23
Bordeaux 178–179
Boudin, Eugène 87
Buggy Cross 164
bus services 26–27, 28
Buttes Chaumont 23

Cahors 186
Calais, arriving in 27
Camargue, the 148–149
camping 32
Canal de Bourgogne 113
Canal du Midi 24,

144, 145, 159, 180
Canal du Nivernais 113
Cannes 163
Cap Fréhel 89
Cap Griz-Nez 86
Capdenac 186
car rental 30
Carcassonne 14–145
Carée d'Art 146
Carnac 88
Carnac-Plage 88
cartoons 11, 81
Cathédral de Notre-Dame de Strasbourg 103–4
Cathédral Notre-Dame, Reims 102
Cathédrale St-Vincent 84
Catherine de' Médicis 60, 129, 132
Centre Euralille 100, 101
Centre Georges Pompidou 19, 56–57
Centre National d'Art Contemporain 158
Cézanne, Paul 61, 151, 161
Chagall, Marc 57, 110, 156
champagne 17, 102, 114
Champs Élysées 52–53
Chantilly 65
Charles VIII 132, 134
Charleville-Mezières 15
Chartres 66, 179
Château d'Amboise 132–133
Château d'Angers 135
Château d'Azay-le-Rideau 130–131
Château d'If 162
Château d'Ussé 24, 134
Château de Bienassis 91
Château de Bourbensais 88
Château de Chambord 126–127
Château de Champ de Bataille 22
Château de Chaumont 132
Château de Chenonceau 129, 132
Château de Cheverney 132
Château de Haute Koenigsbourg 112

Château de la Hunaudaye 89
Château de Villandry 133
Château Royale de Blois 128
children 61, 88, 114, 135, 164, 186, 198
Chinon 134
Chopin, Frédéric 15, 61
Chrétien de Troyes 114
Cimetière du Père-Lachaise 61
Citadelle Souterraine 110
Cité de l'Espace 180
Cité de Sciences et de l'Industrie 60
Clement V, Pope 150
clothing sizes 196
Cluny museum *see* Musée National du Moyen-Age
Cocteau, Jean 51, 165
Cognac 183
Colmar 112–113
comic strips 11
Conciergerie, the 43
Corniche Sublime 152, 154
Côte d'Émeraud 89–90
Côte d'Opale 86
Côtes d'Armor 89–90
Coulon 183
Council of Europe 103
currency 195

D-Day Beaches 87
da Vinci, Leonardo 55, 126–127, 133
de Gaulle, Charles 21, 53, 100
de Maupassant, Guy 51
denim 147
dental services 198
Diane de Poitiers 129, 132
Dijon 106–107
Dinan 88
disabled travellers 198
Disneyland Resort Paris 65
drives 89–90, 115–116, 165–167
driving 29–30
Dumas, Alexandre 162

Église du Dome 59
Église St-Symphorien 131

Eiffel Tower see Tour Eiffel
Eleanor of Aquitaine 135, 178
electricity 197
embassies 198
emergency numbers 197
entertainment 36; see also individual areas
Epernay 114
Erquy 90
Étang de Vaccares 149
Étretat 24
European Court 103
European Parliament 105

faïance 80, 154
fashion 12–13, 58; see also shopping in regions
Ferme Equestre du Bosc Clar 186
ferry services 27, 195
festivals 14–15
  Angoulême International Comics Festival 11
  Avignon International Festival 14
  Ban des Vendages 184
  Cannes film festival 163
  Flaneries d'Eté 15 gardens, Chaumont 132
  gypsy fair 148, 149
  International Celtic Festival, Lorient 36
  Jazz Sous les Pommiers 14
  Joan of Arc 80 marionnettes 15
  Perigord Noir 14
  Pierre Boulez Festival 14
  surf, Biarritz 185
  water jousting 159
Flaubert, Gustave 79–80
Fleury 110
Fontainebleau 66–67
food and drink 33–34; see also individual areas
Forêt de Gérardmer 115
Fort la Latte 89–90
François I 54, 65, 126, 127, 128, 130, 133
François II 133
Futuroscope 183

gardens 22–23
  Giverny 23, 86–87
  Jardin d'Acclim-atation 61
  Jardin d'Altitude du Haut-Chitelet 116
  Jardin d'Angelique 23
  Jardin des Tuileries 60
  Jardin Sauvage 64
  Parc Citroën 23
  Promenade Plantée 23
  Shakespearean garden 23
Gaugin, Paul 148
Gérardmer 115, 116
Giverny 23, 86–87
Gorges du Tarn 24, 158–159
Gorges du Verdon 152–154
Grand Bé 84
grand prix racing 36
Grande Arche see La Défence
Grasse 164
Grenoble 158
Grimaldis of Monaco 9, 21, 163, 164
Grünewald, Matthias 112
gypsy fair 148, 149

health 198
Henri II 127, 128, 129, 132
Henry II of England 134, 135, 178
Honfleur 87
Hotel Negresco 155
Hôtel-Dieu 108–109
Hugo, Victor 43, 61, 113

Île de la Cité 42–44
Île St-Louis 58
Im@ginarium 145
in-line skating 186
insurance 198
international dialling codes 197

Joan of Arc 20, 78, 79, 134
jousting 145

Kermario 88

La Capelière 149
La Défense 19, 59–60
La Turbie 167
La Villette 60
Lac de Ste-Croix 152, 154
Langeais 134–135

language guide 199–200
Lascaux 182
Latin Quarter see Quartier Latin
Le Mans 35, 135
le Nôtre, André 22, 53, 60, 66, 135
Le Touquet 86
Les Baux-de-Provence 160
Les Invalides 59
Leszczynski, Stanislas 110–111
Levens 167
Lille 7, 100–101
Loire, The 121–138
  Abbaye Royale de Fontevraud 135
  accommodation 136
  Angers 135
  Château d'Amboise 132–133
  Château d'Azay-le-Rideau 130–131
  Château d'Ussé 134
  Château de Chambord 126–127
  Château de Chaumont 132
  Château de Chenonceau 129
  Château de Cheverney 132
  Château de Villandry 133
  Château Royale de Blois 128
  Chinon 134
  eating out 137
  entertainment 138
  Langeais 134–135
  Le Mans 135
  map 122–123
  shopping 138
  St-Benoit-sur-Loire 132
  three-day itinerary 124–125
  Tours 133
Louis XIV 9, 10, 21, 53, 59, 66
Louis XVI 8, 10, 60, 66
Lourdes 186
Louvre see Musée du Louvre
Lucéram 166
Lyon 7, 157, 158
  arriving in 27

Maison Carée 146
Marais 58, 60, 61
Marais Poitevin 183
Marie-Antoinette 8, 20, 43, 66
Marseille 9, 162

arriving in 26–27
Martel, Édouard-Alfred 152
Matisse, Henri 47, 57, 58, 61, 156
Menton 165
Metz 110
Monaco 164
Monet, Claude 23, 47, 59, 86–87, 92, 101
money 195
Mont St-Michel 24, 82–83
Montaigne, Michel Eyquem de 178
Monte Carlo 35, 164
Montignac 182
Montmartre 18, 47, 62–64, 181
Montpellier 160
Moustiers-Ste-Marie 152, 154
Moutarderie Fallot, la 114
Mur Je t'Aime 24
Musée Alsacien 104
Musée Arlatan 148
Musée Automobile de la Sarthe 135
Musée d'Orsay 47–49
Musée d'Unterlinden 112
Musée de l'Armée 59
Musée de l'Ordre de la Libération 59
Musée de la Céramique 80
Musée de la Civilisation Gallo-Romaine 157
Musée de la Contrafaçon 24
Musée de la Mer 185
Musée de la Préhistoire des Gorges du Verdon 19, 154
Musée de la Tapisserie Con-temporaine 135
Musée du Chocolat 185
Musée du Louvre 54–55
Musée du Temps 113
Musée du Vin 108
Musée de St-Romain-en-Gaul 158
Musée Fabre 160
Musée Flaubert 80
Musée Granet 161
Musée Mémorial 81
Musée National d'Art Moderne 57
Musée National du Moyen-Age–

Thermes de Cluny
45–46
Musée Picasso, Paris
60–61
Musée Rodin 58
Musée Vivant du
Cheval 65
mustard 107

Nancy 110–111
Napoléon Bonaparte
8, 21, 52, 53, 54,
59, 164
Napoléon III 9, 43
Narbonne 159
national holidays
196
National Music Day
14
national stud 89
Nausicaa 24
Nice 7, 14, 155–156
Nîmes 146–147
Nohant 15
Northeast France
95–118
accommodation
117
Auxerre 113
Beaune 108–109
Besançon 113
Château de Haute
Koenigsbourg 112
Colmar 112–113
Dijon 106–107
drive 115–116
eating out 118
entertainment 120
Epernay 114
four-day itinerary
98–99
Lille 100–101
map 96–97
Metz 110
Nancy 110–111
Reims 102
Riquewihhr 111
shopping 119
Strasbourg
103–105
Troyes 114
Verdun 110
Northwest France
73–94
accommodation
91
Battlefields of
Picardie 86
Bayeux 81
Carnac 88
Côte d'Opale 86
D-Day Beaches 87
Dinan 88
drive 89–90
eating out 92–93
entertainment 94
Giverny 86–87
Honfleur 87
map 74–75

Mont St-Michel
82–83
Rennes 85
Rouen 78–80
shopping 93
Somme 86
St-Malo 84
St-Thégonnec 88
three-day itinerary
76–77
Notre-Dame-de-Paris
42–43, 44, 58

**opening hours 35,
196**

**Palais de Tau
museum 102**
Palais des Papes 150
Palais Rohan 104
Paradis des Enfants,
le 135
Parc Astérix 88
Parc Citroën 23
Parc National du
Mercantour
165–167
Parc Naturel
Régional Loire
Anjou 134
Paris 9, 23, 38–64
arriving in 26
driving in 28
getting around 30
Paris and the Île de
France 37–72
accommodation
68
Arc du Triomphe
52–53
Centre Georges
Pompidou 56–57
Champs Élysées
52–53
Chantilly 65
Chartres 66
Cimetière du Père-
Lachaise 61
Disneyland Resort
Paris 65
eating out 69–70
entertainment 72
Fontainebleau
66–67
Île de la Cité
42–44
Île St-Louis 58
Jardin des Tuileries
60
La Défense 59–60
La Villette 60
Les Invalides 59
map 38–39
Musée d'Orsay
47–49
Musée du Louvre
54–55
Musée Marmottan
59

Musée Picasso
60–61
Musée Rodin 58
Place de la
Concorde 60
Place des Vosges
61
Quartier Latin
45–46
hopping 70–71
St-Germain-des-
Prés 58
three-day itinerary
40–41
Tour Eiffel 50–51
Versailles 67
walk 62–64
Pau 185
Perrault, Charles 134
pharmacies 198
Piaf, Edith 20, 61
Picasso, Pablo 57,
60–61, 151, 163
Place de la Concorde
60
Place des Vosges 61
Planète Sauvage 135
police 197
Pompidou Centre see
Centre Georges
Pompidou
Pont d'Avignon 150,
151
Pont du Gard 24,
146–147
Pont St-Benezet 150,
151
Pont Valentré 186
post 197
Poulenc, Francis 187

**Quartier Latin
45–46**
Quercyrail 186

rail services see
train services
Reims 102
Rennes 85
Renoir, Pierre
Auguste 59, 61,
63, 101
Revolution (1793) 8,
9, 23, 43, 54, 58,
60, 61, 66, 126,
135
Riquewihhr 111
Rodin, Auguste 24,
49, 58, 114
Rouen 78–80
Route des Crêtes,
Verdon 152
Route des Crêtes,
Vosges 115–116
Route du Vin
d'Alsace 111, 112

Sacré-Cœur 64
Sainte-Chapelle

43, 44
Saintes-Maries-de-la-
Mer 149
St Bernadette 186
St-Benoit-sur-Loire
132
St-Émilion 184
St-Étienne 14, 19
St-Germain-des-Prés
11, 58
St-Jean-Pied-de-Port
185
St-Malo 7, 84
St-Rémy-de-
Provence 160–161
St-Thégonnec 88
St-Tropez 162
Sand, George 15, 20
Sarlat-la-Canéda 184
Satie, Erik 87
senior concessions
198
Sète 145, 159
shopping 35; see also
individual areas
Sleeping Beauty 134
Somme 86
son-et-lumière perfor
mances 15, 131
Sospel 165
Southeast France
139–172
accommodation
168–169
Aix-en-Provence
161
Antibes 163
Arles 148–149
Avignon 150–151
Camargue, the
148–149
Cannes 163
Carcassonne
14–145
drive 165–167
eating out
169–170
entertainment 172
four-day itinerary
142–143
Gorges du Tarn
158–159
Gorges du Verdon
152–154
Grasse 164
Grenoble 158
Les Baux-de-
Provence 160
Lyon 157
map 140–141
Marseille 162
Monaco 164
Montpellier 160
Narbonne 159
Nice 155–156
Nîmes 146–147
Pont du Gard
146–147
Sète 159

shopping 171
St-Rémy-de-
Provence 160–161
St-Tropez 162
Vienne 158
Southwest France
173–192
accommodation
189
Albi 181
Biarritz 185
Bordeaux 178–179
Cahors 186
Cognac 183
eating out 190
entertainment 192
four-day itinerary
176–177
Futuroscope 183
Lascaux 182
Lourdes 186
map 175
Pau 185
Sarlat-la-Canéda
184

shopping 191
St-Émilion 184
St-Jean-Pied-de-
Port 185
Toulouse 180
Venise Verte 183
walk 187–188
Strasbourg 7, 103–105
arriving in 27
surf festival 185

taxis 29
telephones 197
Thau lagoon 24, 159
time differences 195,
196
tipping 197
toilets 198
Toulouse 145, 180
arriving in 27
Toulouse-Lautrec,
Henri de 49, 181
Tour de France 36,
53
Tour Eiffel 50–51

tourist offices, inter-
national 194–195
tourist offices, local
see individual
entries
Tours 133
train services 26–27,
28, 195
Troyes 114

urban transport 30
Uzès 147

**Van Gogh, Vincent
47, 148–149,
160–161**
Vauban, Sebastien le
Prestre de 101,
113, 163, 185
Venise Verte 183
Verdun 110
Versailles 22, 67, 127
Vienne 158
Vosges 111, 115–116
Vulcania 24

**walks 62–64,
187–188**
water jousting 159
weather 194, 198
websites 194
where to stay 31–32;
see also individual
areas
Willhelm II, Kaiser
112
wine 16–18, 108,
109, 111, 161,
178, 179, 184
words and phrases
199–200
World War I 53, 66,
86, 110, 112, 116
World War II 53, 78,
79, 81, 84, 86, 87,
102, 113, 151,
162, 165

Picture Credits

Abbreviations for terms appearing below: (t) top; (b) bottom; (l) left; (r) right; (c) centre.

The Automobile Association would like to thank the following libraries for their assistance in the preparation of this book.

Bridgeman Art Library Portrait of Emperor Louis Napoleon III, after the original painting by Francois Xavier Winterhalter (1806-73) 1853 (oil on canvas) by Auguste Boulard (1825-97) Chateau de Versailles, France; **Corbis** 15t, 15b; **Disney Corporation** 65; **Ronald Grant Archive** 11t, 11c, 11b, 20b; **Photononstop** 13,19 (© ADAGP, Paris and Dacs, London 2004); **Rex Features** 20/21, 21c; **World Pictures** 97c, 98c, 99t,102t, 102b, 103t, 104c, 104b, 105, 140, 177t, 178c, 181, 184t.

The Following photographs are held in the Automobile Association's own photo library (AA World Travel Library) and were taken by the following photographers:
Adrian Baker 3(ii), 121, 141b, 142t, 143t, 149t, 150, 154t, 154c, 161b, 164t, 164b; Ian Dawson 13, 74b, 75b, 82t, 82/83, 197cr; Roger Day 97t, 98b, 100t, 100c, 101; Steve Day 3(v), 6t, 77c, 84t, 84c, 84b, 85, 88, 90, 193; Jerry Edmanson 124, 125t, 125b, 126, 128t, 129t, 130/131t,130/131b, 134t, 197cl; Philip Enticknap 41t, 48, 54c, 55; Max Jourdan 2(i), 5, 12, 40b, 46t, 46c, 46b, 49t, 54b, 57/57, 58, 60r, 62, 63l 63r, 67, 20l; Paul Kenward 14t, 15c, 39, 50, 52b, 60l, 178t, 184c, 187; Alex Kouprianoff 2(iv), 73; Rob Moore 6/7. 7t, 14b, 17t, 75t, 78, 79t, 79b, 80, 123, 122t, 126/127, 127, 128b, 129b, 130/131, 132, 132/133, 133, 134b, 134/135, 135, 143b; David Noble 22, 41b, 66t, 66c; Tony Oliver 96, 111b, 114, 166; I Powys 115r; Ken Paterson 2(iii), 37, 45c, 52t, 6; Douglas Robertson 86b, 116; Bertrand Reiger 59c; Clive Sawyer 3(iii), 22/23, 23, 24, 40t, 41c, 42c, 42b, 42/43, 44, 45b, 47c, 56t, 64, 77t, 82c, 83, 86c, 87, 139, 141t, 148b, 151t, 151c, 152, 153t, 153b, 155t, 155c, 161t, 162/163t, 163, 165l; Neil Setchfield 2(ii), 3(iv), 25, 144, 145t, 145b, 158/159, 159, 160, 173, 174t, 174c, 176t, 176b, 178b, 179. 180t, 180c, 180b, 183b, 185, 186tr, 188; Michael Short 17b, 99b, 106bl, 106br,107t, 108t, 109t, 112/113, 113, 197t; Barry Smith 7c, 99c, 110/111, 165r, 174b, 175, 177b, 182b, 186t; Tony Souter 38, 43, 47b, 56b; Rick Strange 6b, 16t, 16b, 142b, 146, 147, 148t, 148c, 150/151, 156, 160, 162/163b, 167; James Timms 45t, 49b, 5l, 53, 59t; Roy Victor 7b, 74t; Jon Wyand 3(i),18b, 95, 106t, 107c, 108b, 109c, 157.

Cover Acknowledgements

Front & back covers: (t) AA/M Jourdan; (ct) AA/R Strange; (cb) AA/D Noble; (b) AA/C Sawyer; Spine AA/R Strange.

S
P
I
R
A
L
G
U
I
D
E

Questionnaire

Dear Traveller
Your comments, opinions and recommendations
are very important to us. So please help us to improve
our travel guides by taking a few minutes to complete
this simple questionnaire.

You do not need a stamp (unless posted outside the UK). If you do not
want to remove this page from your guide, then photocopy it or write your
answers on a plain sheet of paper.

Send to: The Editor, Spiral Guides, AA World Travel Guides,
FREEPOST SCE 4598, Basingstoke RG21 4GY.

Your recommendations...
We always encourage readers' recommendations for restaurants, night-life or shopping
– if your recommendation is used in the next edition of the guide, we will send you a
FREE AA Spiral Guide of your choice. Please state below the establishment name,
location and your reasons for recommending it.

_____

_____

_____

_____

_____

Please send me AA Spiral _____
(see list of titles inside the back cover)

About this guide...
Which title did you buy?

_____ **AA Spiral**

Where did you buy it? _____

When? m m/ y y

Why did you choose an AA Spiral Guide? _____

_____

_____

_____

Did this guide meet your expectations?

Exceeded ☐   Met all ☐   Met most ☐   Fell below ☐

Please give your reasons _____

_____

_____

_____

_____

continued on next page...

Were there any aspects of this guide that you particularly liked?

_____

_____

_____

_____

_____

Is there anything we could have done better?

_____

_____

_____

_____

About you...

Name (Mr/Mrs/Ms) _____

Address _____

_____

_____ **Postcode** _____

Daytime tel no _____ **email** _____

Please _only_ give us your email address and mobile phone number if you wish to hear from us about other products and services from the AA and partners by email or text or mms.

Which age group are you in?

Under 25 ☐   25–34 ☐   35–44 ☐   45–54 ☐   55–64 ☐   65+ ☐

How many trips do you make a year?

Less than one ☐   One ☐   Two ☐   Three or more ☐

Are you an AA member? Yes ☐   **No** ☐

About your trip...

When did you book? mm/ y y   **When did you travel?** mm/ y y

How long did you stay? _____

Was it for business or leisure? _____

Did you buy any other travel guides for your trip? ☐ Yes   ☐ No

If yes, which ones? _____

_____

Thank you for taking the time to complete this questionnaire. Please send it to us as soon as possible, and remember, you do not need a stamp (unless posted outside the UK).